ST. JOSEPH'S INSTITUTION, EMMETTSBURG, MD.

5 Orphan asylum. 3 Infirmary building. 2 Cloister buildings. 1 Academy buildings. 7 Chapel in the boarders [grounds
6 Chapel of St. Joseph, in community grounds.
4 Chapel, fronting the road.

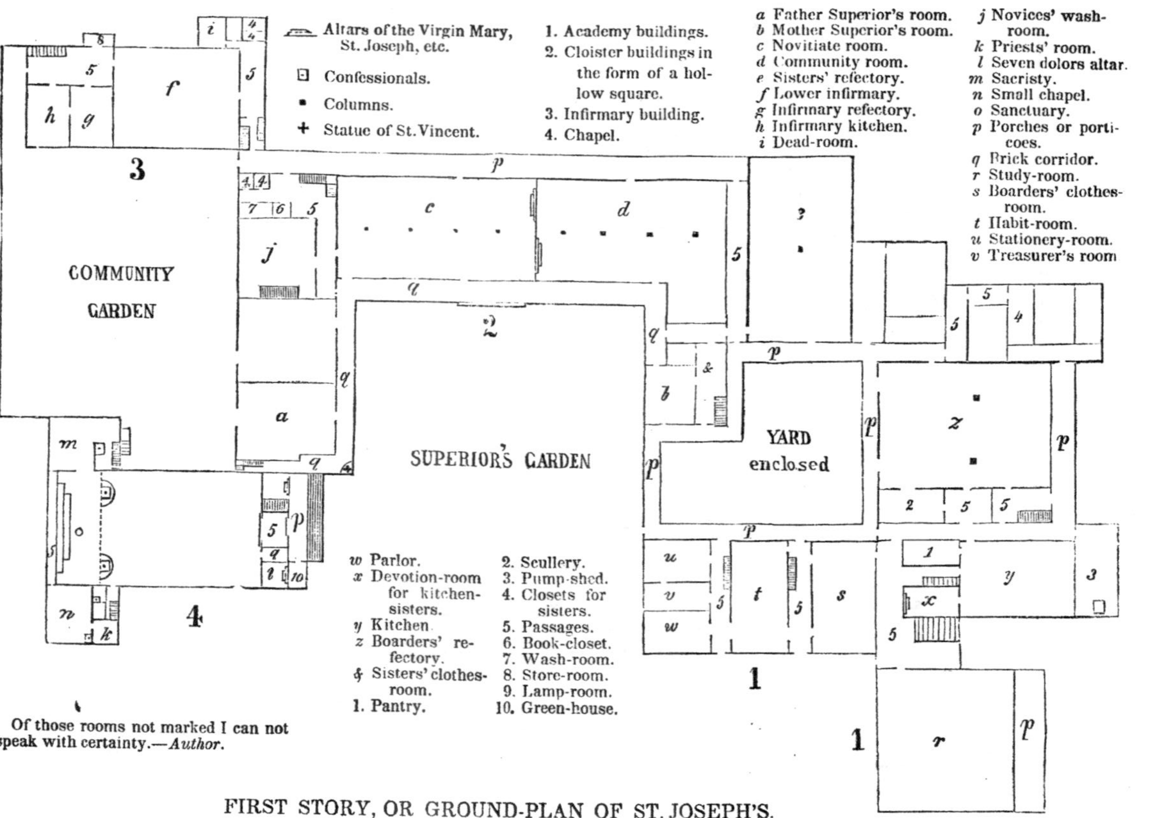

FIRST STORY, OR GROUND-PLAN OF ST. JOSEPH'S.

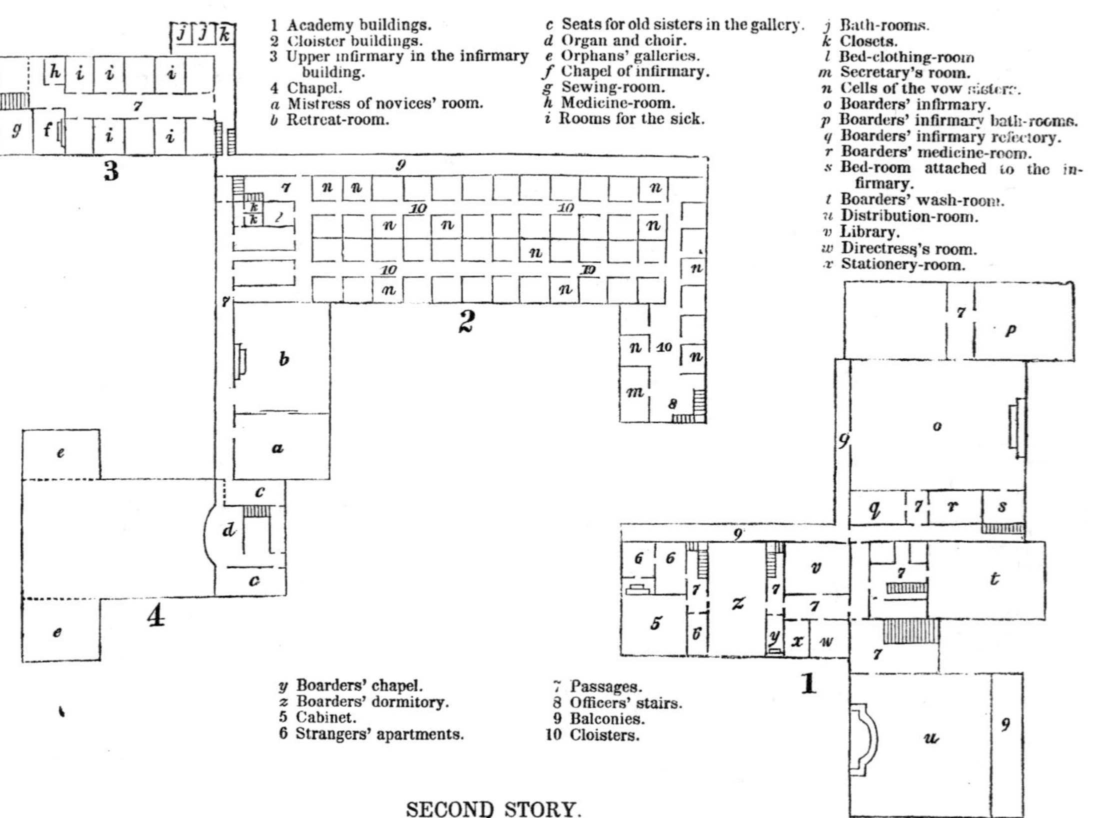

SECOND STORY.

Screens around beds, which are placed in rows along the cloisters. All these *cells* are formed with curtains only.
1
2
a
b
c
d
e
f
g
h
i
j
l
m
n
1 Academy buildings.
2 Cloister buildings.
a Rooms for the old and infirm.
b Sister J. P.'s room.
c Wood-room.
d Wash-room.
e Cells for novices.
f Cloisters.
g Tapestry and drawing room.
h Music-room.
i Class-rooms.
j Boarders' dormitories.
k Circular stairs to cupola.
l Balcony.
m Passages.
n Piano, harp, and guitar rooms.

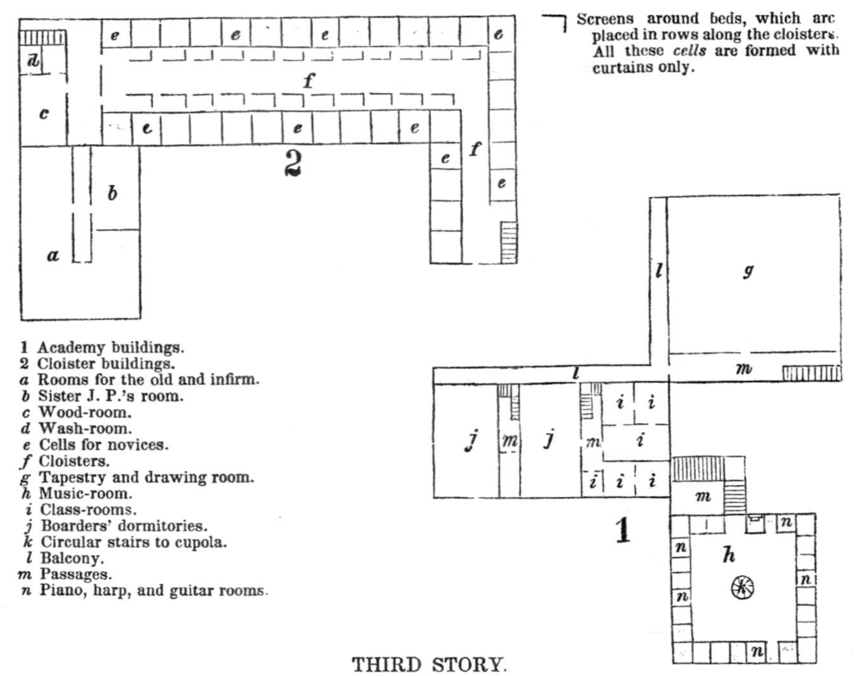

THIRD STORY.

THE ENGRAVINGS.

THE *view* of St. Joseph's, at or near Emmettsburg, is taken from an engraving given in one of the circulars of that institution, designed to show the academy buildings; of course, those buildings are made the most conspicuous and prominent in the picture, but, by close observation, the cloister-buildings are seen *forming a large hollow square* beyond the chapel and the large building occupied by the boarders.

The *interior plans* of the Institution were made by Miss Bunkley, entirely from recollection, some months before the engraving was obtained, and, of course, may be in many respects imperfect, particularly as to the relative proportions of the rooms. The ground-plan was found remarkably correct in the outline as compared with the engraving, and in reducing it to the proper size for the book, in accordance with the engraving, its relative proportions have been but little altered.

The cells are doubtless *too few* in number. They are drawn too large for the scale, in order to make them more distinct. In the main, it is believed that the interior will prove a correct delineation, and will show an admirable arrangement for non-intercourse between the community and the boarding-scholars.

The infirmary building stands distant from the cloister building by the width of the balcony or porch in its rear, but we have joined them, in order to bring the cuts within the page.

At the conclusion of this volume will be found a Note, giving a full description of St. Joseph's Institution, extracted from the "Life of Mrs. Seton," its founder; published by Dunigan and Brother in 1853. This description came to the knowledge of the editor only as the present work was going to press. The reader may, for himself, compare it with Miss Bunkley's delineations; they will be found to correspond with remarkable precision, though prepared by her in June last, and without the aid of any official statements.

MISS BUNKLEY'S BOOK.

THE TESTIMONY

OF

AN ESCAPED NOVICE

FROM THE

SISTERHOOD OF ST. JOSEPH,

EMMETTSBURG, MARYLAND,

THE MOTHER-HOUSE OF THE SISTERS OF CHARITY
IN THE UNITED STATES.

BY

JOSEPHINE M. BUNKLEY.

NEW YORK:
HARPER & BROTHERS, PUBLISHERS,
FRANKLIN SQUARE.
1855.

ADVERTISEMENT.

THE history of this book is almost as remarkable as that of its subject. Shortly after Miss Bunkley had escaped from St. Joseph's in the manner she has stated in her narrative, the Superior of that convent published a defamatory letter against her. This decided Miss Bunkley not only to defend herself, but also to give an exhibition of convent life, as it had come under her observation, for the information and warning of her American countrymen; and, in coming to this determination, she did not act on her own judgment only, but availed herself of the advice of judicious friends, who believed that it was a sacred duty to the American community and the best interests of society to do so.

In accordance with this resolution, she wrote a narrative of what she had seen and heard while in the institution of St. Joseph, and committed the same for revision, with other papers bearing on the subject, to a gentleman in Norfolk, Virginia, the city of her father's residence.

This gentleman, without consulting her, made an arrangement with a publishing house in the city of

New York for the publication of the work, and sent away a large portion of the manuscript, without permitting her to read it after he had revised it. This fact came to the knowledge of a friend in New Jersey, a gentleman of position and great courage and perseverance, who has taken a deep interest in this whole affair, and has enabled her to conduct the matter to a successful issue. Without delay, she demanded, through legal counsel, her narrative and other papers; but this demand was refused. She was compelled, in these circumstances, to give an order to her counsel to file a bill for injunction to prevent the publication. After several weeks fruitlessly spent by them in endeavoring to obtain possession of her manuscript for examination, a bill of injunction was at length filed in the United States Court to suppress the publication of the work, which had in the mean time been printed, but not yet issued.

A great deal was said in the newspapers, political and religious, Protestant and Roman Catholic, about this affair, which induced Miss Bunkley to set forth, in a card to the public, that neither the publishers referred to nor any one else had been authorized by her to publish her book, and stating that, in view of these circumstances—not being able to recover her manuscript—she should be under the necessity of rewriting her narrative, which would, of course, occasion some delay in its publication. That she and her friends had good reason to pursue the course which she did, a very slight perusal of the work—a copy of which the publishers brought into court—abundantly proved. Another injunction was also obtained on her likeness and autograph, which it was discovered had been prepared for circulation with the book.

Foiled in their attempt to bring before the public the work just mentioned, the parties in question shortly after issued an anonymous and fictitious work, under the title of THE ESCAPED NUN, against which Miss Bunkley felt it to be her duty to warn the public, inasmuch as it was spoken of in the papers in some quarters as her own.

Neither discouraged by these vexatious disappointments, nor intimidated by the threats of the hierarchy of Rome and their abettors, Miss Bunkley, with the advice of reliable friends, went forward, and, having re-written her narrative, engaged the services of a gentleman, every way competent to the task, to revise it and superintend the printing of her book. This task he has executed with ability and fidelity, and to her entire satisfaction.

Not a fact has been distorted; not a sentiment has been modified; he has contented himself with performing the office of an editor, so far as Miss Bunkley's narrative is concerned. He has, however, subjoined many notes, that contain facts and statements, derived from authentic sources, which confirm the truth and enhance the value of the narrative. He also added some chapters on the whole question of conventual establishments, which will command, as they deserve, profound consideration; and extracts from a long and most important letter from the Rev. Dr. De Sanctis, who, from his former official position in the Romish Church, and at Rome itself, is well qualified to speak on this subject. The whole book will be read, we are confident, with great interest by our American citizens. It sets before the world, in a clear and authentic manner, the true nature of convent life, even in the most popular and the most *worthy* (if we may be allowed the application of the epithet to any such establishment) of all the female "communities" of the Roman Catholic organization. The appearance of the work, though much delayed by the circumstances of which we have spoken, will still be opportune, and (with God's blessing) do much good.

MISS BUNKLEY'S BOOK.

CHAPTER I.

IMPRESSIONS OF CHILDHOOD.

THE church bell chimed the hour of prayer; sweetly and solemnly the sound floated upon the evening wind, as a little child lingered to listen near an old church-yard in the city of Norfolk. Heated and tired with play, she stood in the cool breeze, curiously watching the crowds of people who passed rapidly by and flocked into the sanctuary. The composed and devout expression of their countenances, as they eagerly pressed forward to reach the place in season, attracted the attention of the child, who besought her nurse to follow the throng and enter the sacred precincts. Her attendant—one of those faithful domestics of the South who are intrusted with the charge of young children, and who delight in obeying almost implicitly the commands of their infantile masters and mistresses — readily consented; and, crossing the church-yard, they passed into the vestibule of the edifice. Pausing with childish surprise to gaze at those who performed the ceremony of sprinkling and crossing themselves with holy water at the door, the little girl seated herself near the entrance. While yet absorbed with the novelty of her position, and admiringly alive to the wonders that presented themselves to her view, the deep tones of the organ swelled forth in a melody of such surpassing sweetness that she clasped her hands in an ecstasy of delight; and turning to her nurse, her innocent face radiant with pleasure, she whispered, "How sweet! how beautiful!" The music ceased, but left that young susceptible heart entranced, bewildered, captivated. With wondering delight she continued to gaze upon the scene before her: the altar with its rich decorations, the burning tapers, the ascending cloud of incense, the paintings, the gorgeous vestments of the priests, the successive acts and postures that contribute to the dramatic effect of the Roman Catholic ritual—all this she beheld for the first time in rapt and mute astonishment. It was as if some heavenly vision were opened to her inspection, and emotions newly awakened and indefinable fluttered in her bosom. The pleasing variety of sounds, the sweet perfume of aromatic exhalations, the unwonted, the imposing solemnities before her, the sentiment of reverential awe that breathed in all around—all contributed to enhance the impression of the senses, and caused her heart to throb with pleasurable excitement; and when, the service over, she rose and took the hand of her nurse to return homeward, the child sighed deeply, even as one aroused from happy dreams to the dull realities of common life.

But far different were the impressions made by this incident from those of a passing dream. They were deep and abiding, and were destined to control—oh! how much and how powerfully!—the after life of that child, upon whose sensitive being the seductive allurements of a sensual system had thus, at the early age of six years, produced marked and permanent effects. Results of momentous importance flowed from these simple causes, which, operating so easily and so naturally upon the delicate organism of childhood, were yet no random or accidental influences, but directed with the nicest calculation, in accordance with the most consummate knowledge of the intricacies of the human heart, in every stage of its development from the cradle to the grave—a knowledge ever applied with unscrupulous skill and inflexible purpose to the advancement of the interests of the Church and the subservience of her designs.

Reader, the little child of this slight episode, as the subject of these artful machinations, and in after years the witness of their cruel success, narrates in the following pages her unvarnished story. How similar allurements, one by one, like the threads of a strong net, were cast around her; how other and more overt influences were woven in, till mind and body were alike enthralled; what schemes, what arts, what arrogance and tyranny she beheld and suffered while under the restraints and within the toils of Romanism—these will constitute the burden of her narrative.

CHAPTER II.

EARLY IMPRESSIONS DEEPENED.

THE imaginative and impressible disposition thus early indicated was developed in childhood, not altogether without the control and guidance of a religious education. I can not recall the time when my heart was not imbued with a natural reverence for sacred things, or when they had not already awakened in my mind a strong and unaffected interest. But these inclinations, common to most of those who have been trained up under Christian nurture and admonition, did not then lead me to that simple and humble apprehension of the saving truths of the Gospel, which would have satisfied the longings of a restless heart, and obtained for it that peace which it vainly sought in a system of ceremonial forms. Lofty aspirations that reached toward some ideal good, unseen and uncomprehended by all around me, drew me away from that lowly position where, at the foot of the Cross of Calvary, I might have realized the ardent desires of a soul seeking communion with its Maker. These very aspirations were bringing me toward that religion which offered them their full consummation, without apparently requiring all the sacrifice of ambition and pride which the sterner doctrines of the Bible demand.

The recollections of those brilliant and attractive rites which had been witnessed with delight and wonder in early childhood, served as a continual contrast with the severe simplicity of the Protestant worship, and the rigid requirements of the Protestant faith. Often were these alluring ceremonies resorted to, and with increasing pleasure, as my disrelish for the religion of my childhood grew stronger. The fanciful but plausible and poetic explanation of the services I beheld interested me. I saw beauty in the symbolic ritual of Romanism, and began to inquire into the doctrinal basis of this edifice so stately and fair, upon whose threshold already I stood.

My parents were worshipers in the Protestant Episcopal Church, and from childhood I was educated in the doctrines of that Church, attending its public ministrations, and receiving instruction in the Sabbath-school. At the age of fourteen I was solicited to present myself for Confirmation, but I steadily refused to do so, my attachment having been estranged already, if not entirely diverted to another system of worship. It was then that I came to the definite conclusion of investigating the tenets of the Roman Catholic Church. I commenced the reading of books explanatory of those tenets. These works were willingly furnished me by Roman Catholic acquaintances, who had learned my sentiments, and who, without directly and openly interfering to bias my convictions, urged me, with seeming candor and liberality, to acquaint myself with "both sides" of the controversy, and to distinguish between the good and the evil of a system so commonly misrepresented. Thus the very disposition to rise superior to vulgar prejudices, and exercise an independent and responsible judgment in matters of belief, was made a snare to me, as it has been to multitudes of youthful minds. Let me caution such against this hidden danger. There is but one infallible guide to all spiritual truth. Without his direction, no research of intellect is lawful, or can be fruitful of good. The indications of his presence and assistance are felt and manifested only in that honest, humble, teachable, and self-distrustful temper, which becomes and invariably distinguishes the searcher after truth. One who has most painfully felt the possibility of self-deception, in the blind following out of hastily-formed opinions, and concession to the impulsive promptings of a misguided enthusiasm, would fain warn others to heed the counsels of the wise and virtuous, the mature and experienced around them, before they commit their spiritual welfare and their temporal happiness to the guidance of men presumptuously arrogating to themselves the prerogative of Deity. The pure ray of heavenly light will attract and illuminate those only who steadily turn aside their gaze from the glare of delusive phantasms, which amuse, but bewilder and lead astray. God's word alone can furnish that safe and unerring guidance; God's spirit only can teach infallibly the soul.

CHAPTER III.

DOUBTS AND HESITATIONS.

It were needless to recount the various phases of mind through which I passed during the two years preceding my entrance upon a membership of the Roman Catholic Church. It was, as I imagined, a deliberate course of mature reflection that led me thither. Fascinated by the tinsel glitter and pompous parade that conceal the internal hollowness and corruption of popery, I was ill prepared, however, at the age of sixteen, to weigh arguments and discriminate between conflicting statements. Charmed by the consonance of those doctrines of penance and supererogation which I now learned, with my previously conceived notions of self-exertion and merit, I fondly hoped that, in becoming a Roman Catholic, I might discover objects to attract the intellect and engage the heart, exalted sanctity and spiritual repose.

It is not to be supposed that this growing tendency was unobserved and unopposed by my Protestant friends, nor that their remonstrances failed entirely to infuse doubt and hesitation. Often I seemed to stand upon the brink of a fathomless abyss, looking off from the precipice for some ray of light that might show me a deliverance from the difficulties that encompassed me. Sometimes, indeed, the fear would rise lest, under the pressure of perplexity and distress, my mind would utterly give way. All other thoughts were excluded while this one question of duty was incessantly revolved. As my purpose of entering the Church of Rome became confirmed, my friends sought to divert my thoughts from the subject. They urged me to abandon the seclusion to which I had devoted myself, and endeavored to revive my spirits in scenes of amusement and gayety. Finding this ineffectual, my parents sent me to spend some time in the family of a friend, a Protestant clergyman at Baltimore, during which time I was not allowed an opportunity of attending the Roman Catholic service; but, at the expiration of my visit, I returned to Norfolk unaltered in my desire to seek that peace of mind for which I was longing, where so many assured me that I would find it. The impressions fastened by early associations, and by many concurrent influences later, were not of a nature to be dispelled by the frivolities of fashionable society. In these I found not even a transient satisfaction. I had no wish to become a votary of the world; no disposition to look for happiness in its trifling pursuits. The sole alternative that seemed to present itself to a complete absorption in the follies and vanities of earth, was that refuge which, as I was ever reminded by sympathetic and attentive counselors, the true Church offered within her encircling arms to all that were harassed with doubt, and wearied with the cares of this evil world.

CHAPTER IV.

FIRST VISIT TO THE SISTERS.

It was a lovely June evening, shortly after my return from the visit just referred to, when I wended my way toward the house occupied by the Sisters of Charity at Norfolk. I had reached the decision of making known my spiritual state to them, and seeking advice and direction, but without the knowledge or consent of my parents, whose opposition to my change of religious connection continued as strong as ever. I ascended the steps and rang the bell; a little orphan child obeyed the summons; and, having asked for the Superior Sister, I was ushered into the parlor. It was a plainly-furnished apartment, with darkened windows admitting barely light enough to distinguish the various objects. After a short interval I heard a light step; the door opened, and Sister Aloysia, then the Superior Sister there, advanced to receive me. She was dressed in a black habit, with a white linen collar neatly turned over the cape; her face, which was very pale, nearly concealed by a black cambric cap drawn closely around her head. Her beads were suspended from her waist, and she kept her hands clasped before her breast. I introduced myself, and informed her of the purpose of my visit. Smiling pleasantly, she led me to a window overlooking the grounds of the institution, and, partly opening the shutters, she bade me seat myself near her, and begged me to open my heart to her without reserve. I did so. I told her of my wants, my aspirations, my uneasiness as to my eternal safety, and my hope that in the bosom of the Catholic Church I might find peace and rest. I told her that, having had little opportunity of informing myself thoroughly on the subject, I had embraced the resolution of coming to her for counsel and instruction. When I ceased, she clasped my hands in hers, and with cordial tones assured me how willingly she would endeavor to assist me in my inquiries, and satisfy my scruples and doubts. After a long and friendly conversation, she invited me to see the chapel, which was in the second story of the building, and at that time was in quite an unfinished state. As we entered, she knelt reverently before the altar, and said a short prayer, and then, taking thence a crucifix, she devoutly kissed it, remarking, "How can Protestants be so blind as to reject the cross on the ground that it savors of popery, when they know that all their own hopes of salvation must hang upon it?"

I left the house, promising to return after a few days. My second visit was not less pleasing and encouraging: the sister urged me to persevere, assuring me that I would overcome all obstacles, and that in due time my family would cease to oppose my entering the Church. At my third visit, she counseled me to make known the state of my mind to a priest. Meanwhile, however, my friends, having discovered my determination to embrace Romanism, again sent me into the country. Having returned after an absence of a few weeks, I resumed my visits to the Sisters of Charity. A considerable change in the appearance of the house had taken place since my last visit; the parlors were newly furnished, the chapel beautifully adorned, and the grounds of the institution tastefully laid out. The Superior Sister whose acquaintance I had formerly made was no longer there; she had been ordered to another station, and in her place I found one who, by her shrewdness and plausibility, was well fitted to fill the station to which she had been appointed. With five others she conducted a small day-school, composed of orphan children as well as of some whose parents were well able to remunerate them for their services as teachers.

The priest was now informed that I desired an interview. A time was appointed for the purpose, and as such a visit to me could not be agreeable to my family, it was arranged that I should call at his residence. I was accompanied by a young lady, a Roman Catholic friend, who was educated at St. Joseph's, and made a convert there, she being appointed by the priest to accompany me, and was received very kindly by the priest, who undertook to inform me fully as to the doctrines and practices of the Church. A few weeks elapsed, during the course of which I repeated my visit to my spiritual adviser, and at length a day was fixed for my formal admission into the Church of Rome.

CHAPTER V.

THE "BAR OF CONSCIENCE."

PREPARATORY to that formal reception into the Church which I now sought, the candidate is required to make, in the sacrament of penance, a full and general confession of all the sins of past life, in order that the priest, by this secret and solemn communication, may be acquainted with all the experiences of the mind he desires to guide. This office is conducted tenderly and adroitly with the young convert, who naturally shrinks at first from the disclosure of her inmost thoughts and feelings. The kind demeanor, the parental solicitude exhibited by him whom she is now taught to address by the endearing name of father, together with the impression of reverence due to his presumed sanctity and purity, combine most artfully and efficaciously to overcome her timid reluctance. For myself, in the fresh zeal and anxiety of a young proselyte, I was not disposed to evade any means prescribed for attaining the peace of mind for which I was longing. Convinced of the divine claims and authority of the Church, and feeling safe only in following out the advice of my constituted teachers, I thought myself but too happy if permitted to hope that in the path they pointed out I could find the promised reward. I approached the "bar of conscience" as the requisite medium of preparation for worthily receiving the Holy Communion—the great channel for the conveyance of spiritual grace to the soul.

Auricular confession is the chief and most potent appliance by which the Church of Rome gains ascendency, and retains supreme control over individual minds and bodies. Without it, she were a powerless mechanism, a huge, inert mass, deprived of its motive power and ruling energy. Take away this key-stone of the arch that supports the gorgeous structure, and the whole edifice, with all its architectural strength and magnificence, will crumble into ruins. It is the grand secret of her success; the mystery of that tenacious fortitude with which she has endured the countless attacks that have threatened her stability; the sovereign remedy that heals the wounds inflicted by her assailants, counteracts the effects of inward disease, and repairs the ravages of successive reforms and vast numerical losses. Superficial observers ascribe the influence she exerts to the charm of her ostentatious ceremonies and her imposing ritual; to the theatrical display and sensual appeal of her worship. These are indeed the agencies that at first *attract*, but it is the revealments of the confessional that *retain*. These are the bands of flowers thrown around the youthful victim to draw her to the altar; but the ordinance of confession is the sharp hook of steel that grapples her till the sacrifice be accomplished. The robes, the crucifix, the pictures, the incense, the mass, the invocation of saints, the thousand and one enchanting and gorgeous rites, make up, indeed, an attractive image, apparently possessed of vitality and vigor; but confession, as it were, completes the galvanic circle that keeps the form erect and active. Detach this, and the figure falls, a pale, corrupting corpse, to the ground.

Well is this vast potency of the confessional known to the priesthood of the Church of Rome, and hence the solicitude and the zeal with which it has been upheld and defended. So fully conscious are they of its importance, of its indispensable value, that sooner would they part with any other cherished doctrine or institution than with this, the most useful of all. Its capabilities, indeed, can hardly be measured by calculation. Through its agency the hidden thoughts and tendencies of the mind, the disposition, the temper, the temptations, the weaknesses of every penitent, are laid bare to the inspection of the priest, who may then direct and mould them at his will. By this channel he becomes familiar with the thoughts and feelings, not only of those under his immediate charge, but also of all with whom these individual penitents may come in contact; and thus the wide circles of society are opened to his intrigues and contrivances, to make proselytes, to confound the enemies of the Church, or to accomplish other and fouler purposes. Is there a Catholic in the cabinet: what state secret remains unknown to the confessor? Has a Catholic been initiated into the mysteries of Freemasonry or Odd Fellowship: does any one suppose that these will remain unrevealed to the priests? Happy, it may be, are those who, in their ignorance, are unconscious of this far-reaching influence; for communities and nations would tremble could they but realize the dangers to which they are exposed through the power of the Romish confessional.

CHAPTER VI.

MY FIRST CONFESSION AND BAPTISM.

At the appointed hour of the day fixed for my first confession, I was anxiously awaiting in the parlor of the house of the Sisters of Charity the summons that should call me to the little chapel where I was to meet my spiritual instructor. It was already dusk when the message came; and following the sister who had brought it, I entered the door, drew aside the curtain that screened it, and knelt on a hassock before a small table, at which was seated the confessor. The chapel was dark, illumined only by the flickering light of a small lamp that burned before the altar, which was decorated with vases of beautiful flowers, while from the wall above it were suspended several exquisite paintings.

With bowed head, and in trembling tones, from the depths of my soul I poured, without reserve, the feelings and thoughts of my whole life into the ear of one whom I considered my earthly guide; whose duty it was to reprove, instruct, console the subjects of his care with unremitting diligence, until he should deliver up his trust to that God who had commissioned him for the solemn task. My confession made, he breathed over my head a prayer so touching and sublime that my faith seemed strengthened and my spirit calmed by its holy influence. Relief from all those anxieties and perplexities which had long wearied me seemed at length within my reach; I felt myself raised above the atmosphere of earth, and entering upon a sanctuary of repose whence I had no desire to retrace my steps into the world.

I was directed to return within a few days for a second confession, and upon that occasion I received absolution. Arrangements were now to be made for my public reception into the Church; and, accordingly, it was decided that upon "Holy Saturday," or the day after Good Friday, I should be "conditionally" baptized.

Individuals entering the Roman Catholic Church, if they have been baptized in infancy by Protestant Episcopal clergymen, are not absolutely required to receive the ordinance a second time; but, lest there may have been some omission in its performance, which would render the rite invalid according to the Romish conception of it, the sacrament of baptism is then administered by the priest in a hypothetical or conditional manner.

On the morning of "Holy Saturday," without the knowledge of my parents, I left my house for the purpose of visiting a Roman Catholic family who resided near the church, and at whose house I was to prepare for the sacred ordinance. A simple white dress had been provided for the occasion, with a long white veil of muslin, falling over the shoulders and reaching to the floor. No ornament was to be worn save a gold cross suspended from the neck.

The ceremony had been widely made known, and the church was filled to overflowing with curious spectators long before the service began. The moment having arrived, I passed through the sacristy into the church, and took my seat in a pew in front of the altar. The priest soon entered, and we proceeded down the aisle to the door of the church, where stood the marble font filled with water, which he now consecrated for use in the sacred ordinance. The usual ceremonies were performed: a lighted candle was put into my hand; I was anointed with oil; salt was placed upon my tongue; I responded to the questions asked of me, and returned to my pew a baptized member of that Church whose fellowship I had so earnestly craved. The following morning was Easter, the festival of the Resurrection, and upon that holy day I made my first communion.

Did these formalities of profession realize my long-indulged dreams of comfort and peace? Did I enjoy that complete tranquillity promised by the Church to all who, in the proper reception of those sacraments which are the channels of Divine grace to the souls of her children, repose upon her bosom, forsaking all other trust? I was, indeed, most happy. A deep sense of security in the possession of the only true and effectual system of salvation filled my spirit with calm and joy. Morning after morning found me low bending in prayer before the altar of the chapel attached to the church where I had taken my solemn vows. Evening after evening was spent in pious conversation with the Sisters of Charity, and in rapt meditation at that shrine where I had made my first confession. My only happiness was now centred in these blissful moments, and again and again did I bless that Church who had thus conquered my affections and taken captive my will.

But how far removed this security, this mystical repose, these absorbed contemplations, from the spirit and the practice of the Gospel of the Lord Jesus Christ, I can now at length perceive as I could not then. That prayerful dependence upon a crucified and risen Savior, which is the Bible Christian's only hope and support; that conscious assurance of pardon and reconciliation through his blood; those delightful views of his holiness, his condescension, his love, in the work of redemption; that filial obedience which springs from the strong emotion of gratitude and the desire of self-consecration to his service—instead of these blessed enjoyments of the Gospel believer, I was drawing all my strength from a human and earthly source. My Christ, the object of my devotion, the support of my hope, the confidant of all my deepest interior wants, desires, and resolutions, was the Church. I accepted and trusted, not God's word, but the creed of the Church. I relied upon and rejoiced in, not God's promises, but those of the Church; my performance of required duties arose, not from the thankful and grateful consideration of the past mercies and present favors of a reconciled God, but from the hope of acquiring future defense and safety promised to those who blindly follow the commands and precepts of the Church. It was not from a serious and adequate perception of the sinfulness of my own heart; of the holiness and justice of God; of my danger as a guilty and sentenced transgressor, that my religious convictions proceeded, but rather from a poetic sensibility; from a weak desire of passive quiet and spiritual inaction; from a purpose to work out my own righteousness by deeds of meritorious value, in preference to an humble reliance upon the righteousness of Christ which is by faith. That such sentiments and views should have led me to a temporary delusion in the bosom of the Church of Rome is not to be wondered at; that they should have given me no permanent and well-founded repose is still less a matter of surprise.

CHAPTER VII.

ATTRACTIONS OF THE CLOISTER.

It is not in the power of a religion of forms and will-worship to render pleasant and promotive of spiritual comfort those cares and duties which belong to an ordinary course of life. The intelligent Christian, indeed, may find in these employments an opportunity of continual obedience, and a channel of communication with his Savior, who enables him, in whatever he is doing, to glorify God. But the priest-taught and governed subject of Rome learns to regard all the concerns of earth as contradictory to his spiritual frame of life—as conflicting with that ascetic estrangement from all the engagements of mortality; that mystical elevation above human affection and emotion, which is the highest grade of meritorious attainment. Thus, either in the first ardor of conversion, or when the false comforts of her system have been tried and found wanting, the Church of Rome whispers to her disciple longings for the perfect holiness and absolute repose of the secluded convent. To be truly "*religious*," signifies, in her distorted language, not to illustrate the principles of the Gospel in all those humble but sanctified employments that belong to the lot where God has placed us, but to fly from the scene of trial, and to abandon the relations of our providential position, and to waste, in a condition of passivity and mental vacuity, the precious moments of probation.

My religious advisers were not slow to suggest such longings to my mind, and I was well prepared to entertain them. Home and society had already lost their charms, and the details of domestic life had become a painful burden. I found delight only in the contemplative retirement of the sanctuary to which I daily resorted, and in the performance of religious practices which had not yet lost their novelty. I was now led to dwell much upon the happiness of those favored ones who are enabled to abstract themselves entirely from the temptations and anxieties of the world, and dedicate their time without reserve to the service of God. The cloister, I was assured, affords a safe retreat to all who would soar above the atmosphere of earthly love, and gaze upon the pure light of holiness and heaven. There I might find, in the perfect love of God, a depth of peace, a complete repose, such as the blessed on high are enjoying. There are natures, I was told—and to these I felt that mine belonged—so exalted in their aspirations, that human affections can never supply the void of their hearts. Often did I hear described in glowing words the condition of holy men and women who had turned all their thoughts away from earth, consecrated all their powers to God, and spent their lives in ceaseless contemplation and adoring love. I aspired to this perfection. At the church, in the chapel, in my daily private devotions, I earnestly besought Almighty God to make known his will concerning me. I desired to devote my life to his service; yet reason could not but revolt from the monstrous supposition that God, who had given me affections and talents capable of use, would be more honored by crushing them within the walls of a cloister, by wasting strength in inaction, by burying the heart in a living sepulchre. If such were his designs, then he had created but to blight the energies of his creatures; and every object of beauty that his hand had formed on earth was made without profit for man, thus to be shut out from the enjoyment of the natural world.

I indulged not unfrequently in these reflections, and, as usual, opened my heart freely to those whom I had taken for my religious guides. But all such ideas I was told to regard as the suggestions of evil; as temptations of the adversary, who would fain cheat me of my blessed calling to a perfect and entire devotion to the religious life. I was brought to feel that in the service of God the sacrifice of all these earthly considerations was but lightly to be esteemed. Yes, thought I, if this be God's will, I will renounce the world; I will break off every natural tie, and yield myself up a willing offering upon the altar of self-consecration.*

* Thus it is that the inexperience and simplicity of the young are taken advantage of, commonly and systematically, by the priesthood of Rome for the accomplishment of their own ambitious ends. "At an age when the heart is especially open to those impressions which may be called romantic or sentimental, the young person is beset with continual commendations of the heavenly state of a nun; she is told of the innumerable dangers and difficulties that surround those who live in this world, and of the ease with which she can serve God in a cloister."—*Nuns and Nunneries:* Sketches compiled entirely from Romish Authorities. London, 1852.

Two or three instances of the lessons and instructions I thus received will illustrate what I desire to communicate on this subject.

"Whoever," says St. Alphonsus Liguori, "consecrates her virginity to Jesus Christ, is devoted entirely to God, in body as well as in mind. Married persons, being of the world, can think of nothing but of the things of the world. Thus poor worldlings meet with insurmountable difficulties in the way of virtue; and the more exalted their rank, the greater the obstacles to their sanctification. To become a saint in the world, it is necessary for a married woman to adopt the means of sanctification, to frequent the sacraments, to make long and frequent mental prayer, to practice many interior and exterior mortifications, to love contempt, humiliation, and poverty, and, in a word, to make every effort in her power to please God. But how can a married person find the time, the opportunities, and helps necessary for reflection, and continual application to the things of God? The married woman must provide for her family, educate her children, please her husband. [Is this a sin?] The husband must be attended to; if his directions be neglected, or his commands be not immediately executed, he breaks out into complaints and reproaches. The servants disturb the house; at one time by their clamor or their quarrels, at another by their importunate demands. The children, if small, are a perpetual source of annoyance, either by their cries and screams, or by the endless variety of their wants. If grown up, they are an occasion of still greater inquietude, fear, and bitterness, by associating with bad companions, by the dangers to which they are exposed, or the infirmities with which they are afflicted. How, in the midst of so many difficulties and embarrassments, is it possible for the married woman to attend to prayer or to preserve recollection? But would to God," continues this Romish advocate of the monastic life, "that seculars were exposed to no other evils than these obstacles to their devotions, to constant prayer, and the frequent use of the sacraments. Their greatest misfortune is to be in continual danger of losing the grace of God and their immortal souls. At home they must hold constant intercourse with their own families, and with their relations, and with the friends of their husbands. Oh! how great, on such occasions, is the danger of losing God! This is not understood by young persons, but it is well known to those who are settled in the world, and who are daily exposed to such dangers. Oh! how unhappy is the life of the generality

While I was in Richmond, Virginia, an unmarried Protestant clergyman accompanied me to the Roman Catholic church. The next time I saw my confessor, he said he had learned I intended marrying that gentleman. I replied I had never thought of doing so. Then he told me I must never be seen with him again, because it brought scandal on the holy Church. He said he had noticed me from the altar, and then, in a threatening attitude, he farther said, "Just let me see you with him again." He continued for some time in this angry manner to scold and threaten me. I was much alarmed; his violence terrified me; I burst into tears, and assured him again and again that I did not intend marrying, and I should never think of a union with one out of the Church. I promised to obey im-

of married persons! I have known the circumstances, the feelings, and dispositions of numberless married persons, from the highest to the lowest classes of society, and how few of them were contented! The bad treatment of husbands, the disaffection of children, the wants of the family, the control of relatives, the pains of childbirth, which are always accompanied with danger of death; the scruples and anxiety of conscience regarding the flight of opportunities, and the education of children, plunge poor seculars into endless troubles and agitations, and fill their souls with continual regret for not having been called to a happier and more holy state. God grant that in the midst of such troubles and agitations many of them may not lose their immortal souls; and that along with passing through a hell in this life, they may not be condemned to an eternity of torments in the next.

"The state, then," concludes this holy man, "of virgins consecrated to Jesus Christ, and who are entirely devoted to his divine love, is of all states the most happy and sublime. They are free from the danger to which married persons are necessarily exposed. Their affections are not fixed on their families, nor on men of the world, nor on goods of the earth, nor on the dress and vanities of women. They are unshackled by worldly ties, by subjection to friends or relatives, and are far-removed from the noise and tumult of the world."

plicitly his commands, and implored him to overlook and forgive this offense which I had unconsciously committed. After a while he became calm, and permitted me to depart, saying, in the usual manner, "Go in peace, my child." When I returned to my residence, my eyes were so much swollen with weeping that my sister asked the cause. This I durst not communicate to any one, because it occurred in the confessional. This priest was a *vicar-general.*

Another priest once asked me if I were married, to which I answered in the negative. Then he asked me if I thought of marrying, which I also answered in the negative. "Well, my child," said he, "it is infinitely better to live a life of celibacy, and escape all those ills," etc., and proceeded to enumerate in detail what he called the ills of married life.

Such are the representations and arguments which are set forth for the inducement of the young and ignorant to commit themselves to those "priests' prisons for women," where the security of home and domestic defense is exchanged for the oppression of heartless "superiors," where the gentle discipline of care and trial, which God himself has appointed to our lot for progressive culture and sanctification, is bartered for the cruel barbarities of the whip and the sackcloth, exposure to cold and hunger, privation of all comforts, and destitution of all friendly regard; where the active duties of a benevolent Christian life are forsaken for the foolish, senseless absurdities of idol-worship and works of self-righteous zeal.

CHAPTER VIII.

VISITS TO THE CONVENTS.

INFLUENCED by these counsels and suggestions, I inclined strongly, before many weeks had elapsed after my entrance into the Church of Rome, toward the vocation of a recluse. But in order fully to convince myself of the attractions of that calling, I determined, with the approval of my spiritual advisers, to visit some of those institutions of which I had heard such praise. In the summer of 1852 I left Norfolk to visit the Carmelite Nunnery, the Visitation Convent, and the "Mother House" of St. Joseph's, that fountain-head of female Jesuitism in this country.

On arriving at Baltimore, I received a permit from a priest to visit the Carmelite Nunnery on Aisquith Street, occupied by sisters of the order of St. Theresa. I was at once admitted, doubtless in consequence of the fact that my inclination toward the convent life had been made known, since visitors are but rarely permitted to enter the walls of this institution. I did not, however, obtain the desired opportunity of inspecting the internal and domestic arrangements of the place, for the Superior was ill and could not receive me. This message was brought to me at the grating of the parlor by a nun closely veiled, and while conversing with me she suddenly drew aside her veil, and cast upon me an earnest and searching look, expressive of the deepest interest and sympathy. I shall never forget the expression of that countenance, the death-like pallor of which showed traces of long mental and bodily suffering—indications corroborated by the mournful gentleness of her voice. I did not then connect these symptoms with any idea of the cruelties suffered by the inmates of these institutions—cruelties so well calculated to produce them—for I had then no glimpse of the dark side of the picture; but I left the convent with emotion as of one who had looked upon a visitant from another sphere. Poor nun! I have never seen her since. Perhaps she is still pining in her cage, vainly longing for the perfume of flowers, and the health-laden breath of the south wind on her pallid cheek. More likely she has passed away, and her only memorial is the mound in the convent garden that indicates the place where her poor shattered frame is resting in the grave, dug by her own hands while living.

Although at that time aware that the discipline of the Carmelite order of nuns is peculiarly severe, it was not until my residence at St. Joseph's, where I had opportunities of obtaining such information, that I learned the nature of the barbarities practiced by the followers of St. Theresa, under pretext of rendering themselves acceptable to God. A brief statement of these rules may interest those unacquainted with the system, and afford some warning to inexperienced girls against the wiles that might entice them into such a tomb of horrors.

The Carmelite nuns are required to fast during eight months of the year. This fasting, which is often excessive, contributes to their pale and emaciated look. They wear constantly a garment of hair-cloth next to the skin, which keeps up an incessant feverish excitement of the system. During the heat of summer they sleep between woolen blankets, and in the severities of winter they are furnished with scarcely clothing enough to keep them from the effects of the frost. As a penance for the slightest infraction of the regulations, and often as a prescribed religious exercise, the "*discipline*" is used, that is, the application of a whip composed of several leather thongs to the naked back, with all the strength of the person wielding it. The screams of sufferers under this infliction are the only sounds that relieve the dreary silence of these walls, and have been heard at times by passers-by at the lonely hour of midnight. This "discipline" is often continued till the blood flows at every stroke of the whip. For minor faults the nuns are sometimes required to describe a cross on the floor with their tongues, which may leave the mark in blood, in token of deep humility; and, finally, their own graves are dug by themselves during life, as a reminder of the hour of dissolution, the approach of which, by all these enormous barbarities, equaled only in the records of savage or Inquisitorial torture, is so effectually and rapidly hastened.

In this convent it was that Olivia Neal was confined, and from it she made her escape, only to be imprisoned the second time by the use of main force. I shall have occasion hereafter to refer to the case of this unfortunate victim of priestly violence; but, as inquiries have frequently been made as to her present abode, I will here state that she is now an inmate of the asylum at Mount Hope, Baltimore, a hopeless maniac, driven to desperation by her tormentors.

Shortly after my visit to the Carmelite nunnery I called at the Convent of the Visitation, situated upon the corner of Park and Centre Streets, in the same city. This is a large building, with grounds attached, and surrounded by an elevated wall. A nun soon appeared at the grating, when I handed her a note for the Superior. She directed me to walk to the left door. I heard the withdrawal of several bolts, and the door was opened by some invisible hand, then closed behind me, and the bolts were pushed over the door from an adjoining apartment, separated from that where I now stood by iron bars extending from the floor to the ceiling. This was the convent parlor, and through this iron grating persons are sometimes allowed to converse with the nuns. Soon a nun approached the bars, which formed a partition across the entire width of the apartment, and told me that she would open the door to admit me into the rooms beyond. The bolts were withdrawn as before. I returned into the vestibule, and stood at the door where the nun had first appeared. After the removal of several bars and bolts again, this door opened and closed violently behind me; it was fastened as before, and I could just discern, through the almost total darkness, two nuns, one of whom bade me follow her. I was taken through several passages to the library, or large room, well supplied with books, where several nuns were seated and engaged in reading, while others, also with books before them, kept their eyes fixed immovably upon the floor, not even turning to notice the stranger who had entered. I was next taken to the chapel, a circular apartment, with a richly-decorated altar. On one side of the room was a grating in the wall, through which I could distinguish the pale faces of several nuns who were kneeling in prayer. After visiting the dormitory, the music-room, and other apartments occupied by the pupils of the academy attached to the convent—for I was not allowed to visit the cloisters—I left, promising to return soon for the purpose of an interview with the Superior, who, at the time of this first visit, was engaged, and could not conveniently receive me.

CHAPTER IX.

THE SUNNY SIDE OF CONVENT LIFE.

I HAD received from the Superior of the institution of St. Joseph's, at Emmettsburg, an invitation to visit that establishment, of which I had heard frequent eulogy, and which I had long desired to see. I accordingly proceeded thither from Baltimore, and reached the gate of the institution at about nine o'clock in the evening. I left the stage at the gate, and proceeded up the walk. A portress opened the door, and conducted me to the strangers' apartment; as the hour was late, I could not see the Lady Superior till the next morning, and after taking some refreshment I retired.

At an early hour I was awakened by the sound of a sweet strain of music; it proceeded from the chapel near by. The deep tones of an organ swelled forth, accompanying the rich voices of singers in a hymn of solemn and inspiring melody. I listened in a trance of delight to the exquisite combination of parts and the melodious alternations; now subdued and tender, sinking almost to a whisper, and now bursting forth into a full chorus of perfect harmony, while the anthem would be caught up by some single voice, whose thrilling tones, higher and higher ascending, seemed at last, like the matin song of the lark, to come from heaven's gate, pleading for admission there. It were impossible to describe the impressions made by these heavenly sounds, thus rising upon the stillness of the early morning, as heard by one already prepossessed in favor of the religious life whose utterance was heard in such delicious strains. It seemed the outbreathing of a joy and tranquillity such as I had so long thirsted to experience, the source and motive of which were the holy life and the blessed employments in which those singers were engaged.

The few days now spent in this establishment were appropriated, at the recommendation of the Superior, to a "religious retreat," as it is termed—that is, a course of spiritual practices, consisting of prayer, meditation, and devotional reading. During this space of time every attention was paid to me, and every effort made to influence me in favor of the convent life. The condition of a "religious"* was painted in bright and

* The misapplication of this term, and of other words in the Romish dialect, is ably criticised by a popular writer. "Where a perversion of the moral sense has found place," says he, "words preserve oftentimes a record of this perversion. We have a signal example of this—even as it is a notable evidence of the manner in which moral contagion, spreading from heart and manners, invades the popular language — in the use, or, rather, misuse of the word '*religion*,' during all the age of papal domination in Europe. Probably many of you are aware that in those times a '*religious person*' did not mean any one who felt and allowed the bonds that bound him to God and his fellow-men, but one who had taken peculiar vows upon him, a member of one of the monastic orders. A '*religious house*' did not mean, nor does it now mean in the Church of Rome, a Christian household, ordered in the fear of God, but a house in which these persons were gathered together according to the rule of some man—Benedict, or Dominic, or some other. A 'religion' meant, not a service of God, but an order of

glowing colors, and every attraction calculated to please and charm the taste was presented to my view. The very atmosphere of the place seemed redolent with piety, and the inmates encircled, as it were, with a celestial halo. I was surrounded by comforts and luxuries such as I had not supposed were granted to the members of a conventual establishment; the table, furnished with silver, was always well provided with choice viands and fruits; the furniture was neat, and even luxurious.*

In my interview with the Father Superior of the institution, who was a priest from Spain, I explained to him without reserve my reasons for visiting these establishments, and asked his advice respecting my

monkery; and taking the monastic vows was termed going into a 'religion.' Now what an awful light does this one word, so used, throw on the entire state of mind and habit of thought in those ages! That then was religion, and nothing else was deserving of the name. And 'religious' was not a title which might be given to parents and children, husbands and wives, men and women fulfilling faithfully and holily in the world the several duties of their stations, but only to those who had devised self-chosen service for themselves."—TRENCH on the Study of Words, Lecture I. To vindicate this statement against the charge of being grounded on a mere popular use of the word in question, the author quotes a decree of the great Fourth Lateran Council (1215) forbidding the farther multiplication of monastic orders. The passage runs thus: "Ne nimia *religionum* diversitas gravem in Ecclesia Dei confusionem inducat, firmiter prohibemus, ne quis de cetero novam *religionem* inveniat, sed quicunque voluerit ad *religionem* converti, unam de approbatis assumat."

* The community of St. Joseph's at Emmettsburg, which was founded by Mother Seton in 1809, is in the main modeled after the society of St. Vincent de Paul, in Paris, and is the Mother House of the community in the United States. Besides having, like all sisterhoods, a female or Mother Superior, it possesses also a male or Father Superior, who is a priest

embracing a religious life. He encouraged me, and, in order to form a judgment of my religious qualification, desired me to make a full confession, commencing with the time of my entering the Church. I did so, and was told that I had a true call from God—a vocation.

But it had not formed part of my intention to enter at once upon this vocation, and accordingly I left, after a short and delightful stay, the institution of St. Joseph's, to return to my home. At that time it was my purpose to revisit the place, and enter upon my novitiate within the period of six months; but circumstances of the most painful nature prolonged that interval. When I left home upon this visit my mother was in excellent health. How great was my distress at receiving, before I left St. Joseph's, a telegraphic dispatch announcing that my dear mother had been attacked by the yellow fever, and was already at the point of death. I hastened home, but too late to receive her blessing, or even to take a last look at her remains, the message having been delayed at Baltimore. My feelings on reaching my desolate home I shall not attempt to describe; those only who have experienced such a loss can represent its anguish to themselves. My mother left a babe of twelve months, who has ever since been inexpressibly dear to me. I have but once approached her grave, and then was conveyed away in an unconscious state. But this is a theme upon which I can not dwell.

When six months had expired after my return, I received a letter from the Superior, inquiring whether I had relinquished the idea of consecrating myself to the service of God. That letter I left unanswered. A year elapsed, during the latter part of which I frequently visited the Sisters of Charity at their mission-house near my home. They, as well as my spiritual advisers, encouraged me to go forward in the path marked out for me by Providence, assuring me that even on earth I should arrive at a nobler and worthier life than the world could afford.

Had I but heeded one voice, however, which warned me to beware, I should have been spared many days of misery and wretchedness.

CHAPTER X.

ENTRANCE AT ST. JOSEPH'S.

It was in the month of December, 1853, that, notwithstanding the continued opposition of my Protestant friends and family, and entirely without their knowledge, I left Norfolk for Baltimore, with the secret purpose of embracing the life of a "Sister of Charity."

While in Baltimore I was invited to witness the imposing ceremony of the "taking of the black veil" by a novice of the Visitation Convent. This rite has been so often described that it were needless to repeat here the well-known relation. It is a solemn and impressive pageantry, and the mystical character given to the poor victim, the temporary importance to which she is elevated in her own eyes and in the sight of beholders, and the loud hallelujahs sung over this living burial of a soul intended by the Creator for light and happiness, rob the scene of much of its intrinsic horror, and excite in the breast of many an enthusiastic girl the romantic wish to figure in so brilliant a spectacle.*

* While the ceremony here alluded to is familiar to many in its external and dramatic features, there are probably but few who have had the opportunity of examining the nature of the vows and prayers used on these occasions, as they are prescribed in the *Pontificale Romanum* —a work little known outside of the ranks of the Romish clergy. The

I arrived at St. Joseph's at about half past eight on an evening in the early part of January, 1854. Rain

following statements on this subject are from the pen of a friend, and deserve particular notice, as illustrating the wicked and pernicious influences which are brought to the aid of a system based upon falsehood and characterized throughout by gross delusion and shameless deceit.

The most marked peculiarity of this ceremony, writes my friend, is its mystical character, and the complete confusion of material with pseudo-spiritual ideas which pervades the service.

After various chantings and genuflections, the officiating pontiff (bishop) consecrates the vestments of the virgins, and blesses their veils. Then he hallows the rings—the *marriage-rings*—saying,

"Creator Lord, send thy benediction upon these rings, that those who shall wear the same, being fortified with celestial virtue, may maintain entire faith and unbroken fidelity, and as the spouses of Jesus Christ, may guard the vow of their virginity, and persevere in perpetual chastity. Through Christ," etc.

Then he consecrates the *torques*, or necklaces, etc. These actions completed, the virgins, arrayed in the consecrated garments, their veils excepted, return, two by two, to the pontiff, chanting as follows:

"The kingdom of this world, and all secular adorning, I have despised for the love of our Lord Jesus Christ.

"*R.* Whom I have seen, whom I have loved, in whom I have believed, in whom I have delighted.

"My heart hath uttered a good word. I speak of my works to the king."

Then the pontiff, with his hands stretched out before him, repeats sundry prayers, from which we select a few passages:

"Look down, O Lord! on these thy handmaids, who, placing in thy hands the vow of their continence, make an offering of their devotion unto thee, from whom they themselves have received the desire to make this vow. For how otherwise could their mind, compassed with mortal flesh, get the victory over the law of nature, the freedom of license, the force of custom, and the stimulants of youthful age (legem naturæ, libertatem licentiæ, vim consuetudinis, et stimulos ætatis), unless thou, O God, didst mercifully kindle in them, of thy free pleasure, the love of virginity—didst graciously nourish the longing for it in their hearts—didst minister unto their fortitude?"

The following passage can not be given in English:

". . . . De largitatis tuæ fonte defluxit ut cum honorem nuptiarum

was pouring in torrents when the stage stopped at the gate of the yard through which "*postulants*," or can-

nulla interdicta minuissent ac super sanctum conjugium nuptialis benedictio permaneret, existerent tamen sublimiores animæ quæ in viri ac muliebris copula fastidirent connubium, concupiscerent sacramentum, nec imitarentur quod nuptiis agitur, sed diligerent quod nuptiis præ notatur. Amen."

One more passage from this extraordinary prayer:

"Blessed Virginity confesses Him who is her author, and, rivaling the integrity of angels, has devoted herself to the bridal chamber and the bed of Him (illius thalamo, illius cubiculo) who is the spouse of perpetual virginity, like as he is the Son of perpetual virginity."

In putting the consecrated veil upon the head of each successively, the pontiff says,

"Receive thou the sacred veil, whereby thou mayest be known to have contemned the world, as truly and humbly with the whole endeavor of thy heart to have subjected thyself as a wife to Jesus Christ forever, who defend thee from all evil, and bring thee to life eternal. Amen."

The virgins, being veiled, sing, "Posuit signum in faciem meam, ut nullum præter eum *amatorem admittam.*"

Then the virgins are again presented to the pontiff, two and two as before, by the bridemaids; then taking the ring in his right hand, and the virgin's right hand in his left, and putting the ring on the ring-finger of her right hand, he espouses the same to Jesus Christ (desponsat illas J. C.), saying to each severally,

"I espouse thee to Jesus Christ, the son of the Supreme Father, who keep thee undefiled (illæsam). Therefore receive the ring of faith, the seal of the Holy Ghost, so that thou be called the spouse of God, and if thou serve him faithfully, be crowned everlastingly. In nomine Patris," etc.

Then the pontiff, rising, says,

"God the Father Almighty, Creator of heaven and earth, who hath vouchsafed to choose you to an *espousalship* like that of the blessed Mary, mother of our Lord Jesus Christ (ad beatæ Mariæ matris Domini nostri J. C. *consortium*), hallow you, that in the presence of God and of his angels, you may persevere, untouched and undefiled, in the integrity you have professed, and hold on your purpose, love chastity, and keep patience, that you may merit to receive the crown of virginity. Through the same Christ our Lord, Amen."

didates for admission into the establishment, enter. This yard is inclosed on three sides by the chapel,

---

We shall only add some passages from the benedictions, and the anathema with which this ceremony closes.

"O God . . . . . prepare them, under the governance of wisdom, for all the work of virtue and glory, that, overcoming the enticements of the flesh, and rejecting forbidden concubinage, they may inherit the indissoluble *copula* of thy Son Jesus Christ our Lord. These, O Lord! we beseech thee supply with arms not carnal, but mighty through the power of the Spirit, that thou fortifying their feelings and members, sin be not able to lord it in their bodies and souls."

Again: "Let the shower also of thy heavenly grace extinguish in them all hurtful heat (omnem nocivum calorem), and kindle up in them the light of abiding chastity; let not the modest face be exposed to scandals, nor negligence afford to the incautious occasions of falling."

Again: "God make you strong when frail, strengthen you when weak, relieve and govern your minds with piety, direct your ways, etc., etc., that when about to enter the bed-chamber of your spouse (intraturæ sponsi thalamum), he may discover in you nothing noisome, nothing filthy, nothing hidden, nothing corrupt, nothing disgraceful; that when the tremendous day of the repayment of the just and retribution of the bad shall come, avenging fire may find in you nothing to burn, but divine goodness what to crown; as *being those whom a religious life hath already cleansed in this world;* so that when about to ascend to the tribunal of the eternal king and the palaces on high, you may merit to have protection with those who follow the Lamb, and sing the new song without ceasing, there to receive the reward after labor, and remain forever in the region of the living."

The benedictions ended, the pontiff sits down, and publicly pronounces anathema on any who may draw away from divine service those who are under the banner of chastity, and on any one who may purloin their goods, or hinder them from possessing their goods in quiet.

The Curse.—"By the authority of the Omnipotent God, and of St. Peter and St. Paul, his apostles, we firmly, and under the threat of anathema, enjoin that no one carry off these virgins or religious persons here present from divine service, to which, under the standard of chastity, they have been dedicated; that no one plunder their property, but that they enjoy it in quiet. If any one shall have presumed to attempt this, may he be cursed in his home and out of his home; may

the infirmary, and the convent proper. I waited at the entrance for one of the sisters, who admitted me, and led me through a porch, and along a dark corridor, into the "*novitiate*," a room occupied by the novices,

he be cursed in the state (or city) and in the field, cursed in watching and cursed in sleeping, cursed in eating and drinking, cursed in walking and sitting; MAY HIS FLESH AND HIS BONES BE CURSED, AND FROM THE SOLE OF HIS FOOT TO THE CROWN OF HIS HEAD MAY HE ENJOY NO HEALTH. May there light upon him the curse which the Lord sent in the law by Moses on the sons of iniquity; may his name be erased from the book of the living, and not be recorded with the righteous; may his portion and his heritage be with Cain the fratricide, with Dathan and Abiram, with Ananias and Sapphira, with Simon Magus and with Judas the traitor, and with those who said to God, 'Depart from us, we will not follow thy ways.' MAY ETERNAL FIRE DEVOUR HIM WITH THE DEVIL AND HIS ANGELS, unless he make restitution, and come to amendment. So be it. So be it."—*Pontificale Romanum.*

Such, American fathers and mothers, are the disgusting dreams of sensuality, the loathsome caricatures of spiritual truth, the horrible mockery of the holiest relations, which Rome would furnish to your daughters instead of God's own blessing upon a virtuous and useful life! Such are the heathenish and blasphemous representations with which she would fill their minds respecting that adorable Redeemer whose truth she mutilates, and whose character she insults. "Filthy dreamers, ungodly men, turning the grace of our God into lasciviousness, and denying the only Lord God and our Lord Jesus Christ."—Jude, iv., 8. "Having eyes full of adultery, beguiling unstable hearts, they speak great swelling words of vanity; they allure through the lusts of the flesh; . . . . while they promise them liberty, they themselves are the servants of corruption."—2 Peter, ii., 10, 14, 18, 19. Such, too, are the awful imprecations she pronounces upon any—upon *you*—who would presume to attempt to withdraw your child from the barbarous treatment, the close confinement, the unmitigated misery of a forced imprisonment in the nunnery! Say, then, is there no urgent call for such legal provision in this our free and happy country as will secure to these poor victims of fantastic delusions and actual cruelties the permission and the opportunity to leave these "priests' prisons for women," and return to the guardianship of your love and the protection of their homes? Answer in the name of God and of your own obligations as parents, as citizens, as reasonable beings.

or "seminary sisters," as they are indifferently styled. At the door of this room I was asked in a harsh tone for the key of my trunk. On presenting it to the sister appointed to receive it, I was told, in a firm and decided manner, "*With this key you renounce your own will forever.*" The words fell like a doom on my heart, and I could not but contrast the severity of this language with my treatment upon my former visit. I was then conducted to the refectory, where a small piece of bread, and some coffee in a tin cup, were given me. I scarcely tasted this food, and soon left the refectory with a sister who conducted me to my sleeping apartment. We crossed a passage leading near the Superior's room, walked down the corridor to a passage beyond, and ascended a flight of stairs which communicated with a number of cloisters, on each side of which was a row of cells. We entered a room at the end of the passage, containing seven or eight small curtained bedsteads. The sister who accompanied me pointed to one of these, which was numbered, and, placing a dim lamp in a recess near the door, left the room. It was with mingled emotions of surprise and fear that I gazed upon this novel and unexpected scene, scarcely lighted by the faint rays of the lamp.

CHAPTER XI.

THE CONTRAST.

I NOW presumed that the introductory ordeal was finished, and began to make preparations to retire and obtain the rest so much needed after the fatigue and excitement of the day. But my trials for the night were not yet ended. Hearing a slight noise at the upper end of the room, where there was another door, nearly opposite the one through which I had entered, I looked anxiously in that direction. Presently an aged sister, dressed in the "holy habit"—a costume which will be described hereafter—came in, and approached me, holding in her hand a large cup filled with a dark mixture, which she commanded me to drink. I attempted compliance, but, finding the taste intensely bitter and nauseous, after swallowing about half the quantity, begged to be excused from taking the remainder. Placing it again to my lips, she sternly ordered me to drink the whole. I obeyed in silence. The sister then informed me that she was the "mistress of novices," and had charge over their conduct and employment, adding, that I must not rise from my bed until called. She then withdrew.

A strange sensation of bewilderment and stupor succeeded this incident, and I had scarcely strength to draw the curtain around my bed, when I fell into a deep slumber. I was awakened about four o'clock by the deep toll of the morning bell calling to prayers in the chapel.

The details here given show the art and skill employed to impress on the mind of the novice the absolute subjection to which she must submit, and of which these are, as it were, the preliminary tests. They go to prove that, from her first entrance within the walls of the institution as a candidate for admission into the community, she must learn to obey, without hesitation or demur, whatever may be commanded her, as the first step of her initiation. This, if rightly managed, is an important point gained; for here, as in all other matters, the impression made at the outset is the most lasting and profound. Besides, the manner in which these preparatory injunctions are submitted to, whether cheerfully and instantly, or with expostulation and sullenness, must afford an insight into the character and disposition of the postulant, of which advantage is taken in future proceedings, in order to render her docile and obedient. In a word, these first requirements are designed to teach the subject of them that *henceforth she has no will of her own, but the will of the Superior is her law, which must be obeyed even to the slightest particular.*

It was some time after the first bell had sounded that a sister entered the room, approached my bed, and in a low tone said that I might now rise and go to mass, as the bell would ring in a few minutes. I rose and dressed in haste, and then waited for the sister, who conducted me to the chapel, where the community had already assembled. I was directed to a seat among the "postulants," near the sanctuary. The altar of this chapel is of white marble; above it is a large statue of the Virgin Mary, bearing in her arms the infant Jesus. At the foot of this statue there is usually placed a vase of beautiful flowers. On one side of the sanctuary is a small chapel with a confessional-box; on the other is the sacristy. A narrow corridor behind the altar leads from the sacristy to this chapel; this is the passage for the priests, and those who resort to the confessional. There are two confessionals in the chapel where the community assemble, another in a small chapel on one side of the sanctuary, and another below, in a chapel on the ground floor, besides a chapel in the infirmary in which confessions are made. Those who are too ill to leave their beds are attended by a priest, who seats himself beside them. At the time of a jubilee, or a religious or annual retreat—which lasts from eight to ten days—all these confessionals are supplied with priests.

I shall, in continuing this statement, be compelled to recount facts and incidents as they recall themselves to my mind, begging of the reader indulgence for whatever repetition or want of order may consequently be observable in my narrative.

CHAPTER XII.

THE INSTITUTION AT EMMETTSBURG.

The institution of St. Joseph is situated in a beautiful vale about a quarter of a mile from the town of Emmettsburg. The church or chapel fronts upon the avenue leading to the main road. It forms one side of a square inclosing a large yard, on the other side of which stands the infirmary. In the rear of this yard is the building occupied by the community, and beyond it another quadrangle, which is the academy—a separate edifice, connected with the "Mother House," as it is sometimes called, by porticoes and by a balcony, over which the sisters pass when going to their duties in the academy. Those inmates who are not employed in the latter institution are not permitted to speak to or even look at one of the boarders, either when crossing the porticoes attached to their house, or while at work in their dormitories or in their refectory. This I was told on the first day after my arrival, during my interview with the Lady Superior. I was also directed to consider myself as henceforth entering upon a new life, so that I must not recognize nor address as an acquaintance any individual in the academy whom I had previously known "in the world."

After an interview with the Father Superior of the

institution, I was shown over a part of the house occupied by the community. On one side of a corridor paved with brick, upon the first floor, are the community-room, the novitiate, the Lady Superior's room, and the priest's room. On the second floor are the cells, the retreat-room, an apartment occupied by the mistress of novices, and a number of other apartments, two or three of which were often kept entirely closed, though I had reason to think they were inhabited at the time. The walls of the cells occupied by the sisters do not reach to the ceiling. An open space of several feet above them not only affords ventilation, but permits every sound to communicate from cell to cell and to the cloisters.

The *community-room* is used by those sisters who have been for eight or ten years members of the sisterhood; prior to that time they occupy the *novitiate.* There are, however, members sent forth upon missions, who, as will be explained hereafter, have never occupied the community-room, having always been in the novitiate. The Superior seldom leaves her own apartment. Should she desire to see a sister, the individual is sent for by one who has charge of her room, and who attends at her door. No sister enters the room of the Superior without permission. Should a priest enter while she is there, it would be her duty to withdraw at once, unless told to remain. The male and female Superiors always see each other alone, except *in council*—that is, in a secret meeting of the Superiors and their officers. When a sister commits an offense, she is brought before the council, and all affairs of importance are settled by these inquisitors at such meetings. I was frequently threatened with arraignment before this tribunal, but fortunately was not brought up for trial.

A few weeks after my admission, I observed that on every Wednesday, between the hours of two and three in the afternoon, the windows of the novitiate and community-room were closed, and the doors carefully locked. All the "postulants" were then sent to the kitchen, myself among the number, there to remain at work until the sound of the three o'clock bell. This I shall explain hereafter. This period of the day is designated as the "silence hour;" it is a season of *strict silence;* not one word may be uttered; the eyes are kept fixed on the work or on the floor. It was some time before I learned the object of this rule, as indeed of many others—not until I had made my "*retreat,*" which, as I have elsewhere stated, is an interval of several days spent in prayer, meditation, and spiritual reading. During this retreat, the rules and regulations are for the first time made known or read to the "postulants" by the mistress of novices.

Those who have recently entered the community, and are called novices or seminary sisters, and not vowed or professed sisters, are nevertheless bound and compelled to keep the vows with even greater strictness than those who are professed. The vows of poverty, chastity, and obedience are to be observed by those young sisters; but a priest* may violate his vows with impunity, and the sisters will be constrain-

* I speak here of the priests of the Order of "Lazarists," or Congregation of Missions, which has the same founder with the Order of St. Joseph—the priests being called the sons, and the sisters the daughters.

ed to obey, being under the vow of obedience, which is of superior force to the other obligations taken. He may err, but she will do right in *obeying*.

A *religieuse* can not hold property of her own; from the moment that she enters the community, it belongs to the Superior. She can not, if at any time visited by her family or friends, see them without permission; she can not receive or send a letter; neither can she give or receive any object, even from a member of the community, without obtaining permission. Should one sister desire to give another a small picture from her prayer-book, she must first go to the mistress of novices, kneel, and ask to be allowed to make the gift. Sometimes the request will be granted, at others the article will be taken from her. Should the Superior or the officers suppose that a sister prefers a particular duty, she is assigned one that she is known to dislike. Often is a sister required to part with some sacred ornament even, as a set of beads, or a crucifix, on the ground that there may be a special attachment for the object. The rule requires that particular friendships should be guarded against. One sister is not suffered to converse with another respecting her own private feelings, nor to ask or answer a question, unless in the performance of a task, and that only when absolutely necessary. In such a case it must be done in a very few words, and in a very low tone of voice, almost in a whisper. A sister is not allowed to speak with or recognize another in the corridor, or in any part of the house; but should an officer—one having authority under the Superior—meet a sister, the latter must answer in a low tone of voice, in as few words as possible, and with downcast eyes. No one is permitted to look through a window, or to gaze around her; she must walk with a measured step, her hands clasped on her breast, and her eyes fixed upon the ground. Sisters are forbidden to look each other in the face; to do so is a breach of the rules. They may not ask for any object whatever, and must receive every duty imposed without murmuring.

When a sister is sent for by the Father Superior, she is generally called by the sister who keeps the door. She pauses at the threshold until told to enter, closes the door, advances, and, kneeling, kisses the floor, at the same time saying, "Father, your blessing." This given, she seats herself and listens to his instructions. When told to depart, she again kneels and kisses the floor, and asks his blessing. This degrading act is performed by every sister when entering or leaving the novitiate, saying at the same time an *Ave Maria*—that is, repeating once the angel's salutation to the Virgin, "Hail Mary," etc. Those who wear the cornet, a head-dress hereafter to be described, kiss the crucifix which hangs at the side attached to their beads, and say the Hail Mary.

This prayer is generally said kneeling in front of an altar dedicated to the patron of the institution, St. Joseph. It may be repeated, however, in any part of the novitiate, except near the door. After this short petition, those who leave the room, if more devout than the rest, sometimes turn toward the statue of the saint and make a bow. A sister, in passing the statue of St. Vincent, founder of the order, always bows and says a prayer invoking his intercession. Upon the altar in the community-room is a very large statue of the Virgin Mary; every one bows toward it when entering or leaving the room.

Members of the community are sometimes allowed to have a small statue of a saint in their rooms, or a picture of some devotional subject hanging upon the wall; but they can not keep either *without permission*, and must resign the object if commanded to give it up. This is occasionally done, doubtless as a test of obedience. Not a word is to be spoken after the "silence bell," which rings about eight in the evening. No sister is permitted to take a drink of water after that time; it is a breach of the rule, and will be reported by those who watch, who are placed around the house as spies, to notice every movement and make known all infractions of order to the authorities of the institution.

When suffering from thirst, it is deemed acceptable to God, and the suffering is offered to the Virgin Mary as an atonement for some past sin.

CHAPTER XIII.

ROUTINE OF A DAY—MORNING.

THE daily occupations of the inmates of a "religious house" consist wholly of devotional exercises and domestic tasks. A brief relation of the manner in which a single day is passed will give a correct idea of the ordinary routine of novitiate life at St. Joseph's, and may be of interest to the reader.

At the first stroke of the bell, which rings at four o'clock in the morning, every novice or seminary sister rises hastily from her bed, falls prostrate, and kisses the floor. At the same time, one who has been appointed utters this aspiration in a loud, shrill tone of voice, that echoes through the dormitory, "In the name of God, my sisters, let us rise;" and as the words resound through the dormitories, the response is at once made, "May the holy name of God be blessed!" Should a sister fail to rise at the first summons of the bell, or omit saying the aspiration, she is reported, and is required to do penance as for a great offense. In such cases one sister reports another, and is commended for so doing. All dress with rapidity and in perfect silence, and make their beds; then proceed down two pair of stairs to the wash-room, where the ablutions are performed without a word spoken.

Here some have to wait for others, and oftentimes all this has to be done in the dark. While in the wash-room, a bell is heard in a distant part of the building: this is called the warning-bell. After the lapse of a few minutes another bell is rung near the door of the room. Should a sister leave the room after the ringing of this second bell, she is marked and reported by one who acts in the capacity of a spy.

Each proceeds next to a dimly-lighted room under the chapel, and takes from a drawer, numbered for the purpose, her prayer-book, which she keeps there perhaps with one or two other religious books. The books, however, which a sister may bring with her on entering the institution are generally taken from her to replenish the library. A small volume, called the Community Book, or Formulary, is always kept in the pocket: it contains the prayers used by the sisterhood.

When all have reached their places in the chapel, a small clock near the door strikes the half hour, and should a sister enter after this period, she is required to go to the mistress of novices, kneel before her, and kiss the floor, in addition to which she may expect the infliction of some farther penance.

The sister who is appointed to read prayers now says, "My sisters, let us remember that God wishes to be adored in spirit and in truth, therefore let us pray to him with our whole heart, and with attention: In nomine Patris," etc. Then follows a prayer commencing thus: "My God, I believe that thou art here present," etc. A prayer is then said to invoke the assistance of the Holy Ghost in the performance of the morning meditation. After another short prayer, the first "point" of the morning meditation is read. This "point" is a short sentence, or a few sentences, mentioning some topic of devotional contemplation, as the circumstances of our Lord's Passion; the utterance of which is followed by a silent meditation, lasting half an hour. The second point of the meditation is read when the clock has struck the next half hour. It is observed in a kneeling posture, with the body perfectly erect and motionless, and the hands clasped in front of the breast. The position is most painful and fatiguing, and taxes the powers of endurance to a very trying extent. The slightest movement, while thus engaged, is severely punished, and not unfrequently the poor sister who is compelled to remain so long in this attitude of rigid constraint becomes exhausted and faints before the exercise is over. The hour completed, a sister says, "Let us thank God for the graces we have received during our meditation." Then follows a prayer—"I thank thee, O God, for the holy light," etc. Other supplications are added in English and in Latin. Soon the church-bell rings, and the *Angelus* is repeated. The sister who has been appointed to read says, "Angelus Domini nuntiavit Mariæ," etc. (The angel of the Lord declared to Mary, and she conceived of the Holy Ghost.) The community respond "*Ave Maria,*" etc. Then another sentence, "Behold the handmaid of the Lord," etc., followed by another Ave Maria. Then the sister says, "And the Word was made flesh, and dwelt among us," when every sister kisses the back of the seat before her. During Easter week the *Regina Cœli* (a hymn to the virgin

"Queen of heaven") is substituted for the "Angelus."

When the bell is heard again, a prayer is said, beginning, "Pour forth, we beseech thee, O Lord, thy grace into our hearts," etc. Then the "Litany of the holy name of Jesus" is repeated in Latin, several prayers follow, together with the Miserere, the Creed, the Lord's Prayer, the Hail Mary, and the De Profundis, which is said for the repose of the last Superior or priest, the directress, and the confessors.

These prayers being finished, the sister says, "Let us remember the presence of God, and the resolutions we have taken in the meditation we have made." The Superior's assistant then repeats one verse of the *Veni Creator Spiritus*, and the community respond, the whole terminating with a short prayer to the Holy Spirit. Then the "offering of the chaplet" (or rosary) is made, commencing "In nomine Patris," etc., and proceeding thus: "My God, I offer thee the chaplet I am going to say," at which words every sister takes her beads in her hands, "to praise and glorify thee, to honor thee; sixty-three years the blessed Virgin passed on earth; to beg of thee the grace to imitate her in the virtues which she practiced, particularly her humility, her charity, her obedience, her hidden and interior life; to comply with our holy rules and vows; and for our deceased sisters for whom we have not yet satisfied; for the wants of the Church, of the community, those of the seminary, and our own in particular; with the intention of gaining the indulgences attached to our chaplet, and for all those for whom we are most bound to pray, as well living as dead. I believe, etc. Our Father. Hail Mary. Glory be to the Father," etc.

The morning service concludes with a prayer to the "Mother of God" in these words: "Most holy Virgin, I believe and confess thy most holy and immaculate conception, pure and without stain. O most pure Virgin, through thy virginal purity, thy immaculate conception, thy glorious quality of mother of God, obtain for me of thy dear Son humility, charity, great purity of heart, of body, and of mind, holy perseverance in my cherished vocation, the gift of prayer, a holy life, and a happy death." From this prayer it will be seen that the sisterhood at St. Joseph's were a step in advance of the papal infallibility in the acceptance of the dogma of the Immaculate Conception before its promulgation at the court of Rome. "*V.* Behold the handmaid of the Lord. *R.* Be it done unto me according to thy word. *V.* O Jesus! be to me a Jesus. *R.* Now and at the hour of our death. Amen." Then the "mystery" for the day is said—that is, a short petition having reference to some part of our Lord's passion, as, for instance, "O Jesus, by thy prayer in the garden of olives, grant," etc. Each sister now kisses the seat in front of her, and the church-bell rings for the first mass.

Two masses are said every day at St. Joseph's, the second of which is attended by the boarders, and those of the community who are more privileged, being permitted to sleep until the "Angelus," or about two hours after the first bell. The first mass being over, the sisterhood proceed in rank, two by two, in perfect silence, to the novitiate and community-room. After entering the novitiate, every sister kisses the floor. Those wearing the *cornet*, however, kneel and kiss their crucifix, bending nearly to the floor, as their head-dress, extending to a point that projects over the face, prevents touching the floor in this ceremony. Then are said three times the *Ave Maria*, and seven times the *Gloria Patri*.

Prayers over, the sisters fall upon their knees, kiss the floor again, and proceed in rank to the refectory. Here all turn toward a crucifix that hangs upon the wall, kneel, and kiss the floor; then each says the *Benedicite*, kissing the floor; and seating themselves, they eat in perfect silence their morning meal. This consists of a morsel of bread, often without butter, and coffee and tea served in tin cups. Coffee is the beverage of the community, and no one can take tea without obtaining permission to do so. No spoons are used; the tea and coffee are prepared in the kitchen, and poured into each cup as the portion allotted. Breakfast concluded, each kisses the floor, again repeats the Benedicite, again kisses the floor, returns to the novitiate or community-room, and taking her prayer-book, places it in the drawer appropriated to her. Each then proceeds to her particular occupation—some to the dormitories, cells, kitchen, refectories, sacristy, cellars, clothes-room, wash-room, and other parts of the building; and those who teach in the academy to their classes when the bell rings. Silence and "recollection"* are required to be strictly observed.

* *Recollection*, in French *recueillement*, is used in the jargon of Romanism to signify a devout collectedness of mind—abstraction from the world.

In addition to all the religious observances and duties foregoing and hereafter to be related, there are prayers and "*aspirations*" to be said at every hour of the day, as follows: Whenever the clock strikes an hour, a sister rises, crosses herself, and says, in a loud tone, "Live, Jesus," and bows her head. Every sister responds, "Forever in our hearts." Then the mistress of novices repeats the "mysteries," of which there is a different one for every hour of the twenty-four. These are the mysteries of our Lord's Passion. When this is said, the sister who is standing commences a long prayer, "O sacred heart of Jesus," etc.; after which the mistress of novices makes an "*aspiration*" for the month, and the sisters respond. The sister then resumes her place. Every hour of the day or night the sisters thus "make the hour," as it is called, either orally or mentally, if they are awake.

The performance of *floor-kissing*, in token of humility, takes place, I venture to affirm, at least twenty times in the course of the twenty-four hours. One might suppose from this ceremony that some peculiar and magical property resides even in the senseless boards of this holy institution.

In addition to the religious exercises thus briefly described, from eight o'clock in the morning till nine at night an uninterrupted "*adoration*" before the altar is maintained. By this I mean that, during the time specified, some one member of the community must be constantly kneeling at the altar in the chapel and reciting prayers.* Each sister engaged in this office re-

* This perpetual adoration, as it is called, is in behalf of the extension of the congregation of the missions.

mains for half an hour in the attitude of devotion, when, as the clock strikes the termination of her duties, another sister who has just entered kneels behind her and takes her place. One of the sisterhood is appointed to see that this adoration be constantly kept up; and she must so arrange the succession of duties, that they shall not interfere with the other employments of those whom she calls upon to make this adoration. Severe penance is inflicted should she be remiss or unsuccessful in this charge; and it is a most burdensome one, as I have learned by experience.

Should a sister finish her work before the eleven o'clock bell, which rings for prayers, she goes to the novitiate, and takes some work from a sister having charge of the plain sewing; but this seldom occurs. At the first sound of the bell, each must leave her employment and come to the novitiate, kiss the floor, and take her place in rank. Should a sister fail to be in time to take her place in the ranks which are formed to proceed to the chapel, she goes to the side of the mistress of novices, kisses the floor, and is assigned a penance for her offense. This penance consists of a number of prayers.

In passing before a certain statue of St. Vincent de Paul, founder of the order, which stands in a corner of the corridor, the sisters invariably bow. In going to the chapel, as well as in returning, the rank must be preserved, and the sisters thus advance with eyes fixed upon the floor, repeating, at the same time, a "ten of the chaplet," consisting of ten *Ave Marias*, one *Gloria Patri*, one *Pater Noster*, and a prayer to the Virgin, commencing, "Most holy Virgin, I believe and confess thy holy and immaculate conception," etc.

All being assembled in the chapel, each sister kisses the back of the seat before her. The bell rings, and at the sound of it the Superior, or, in her absence, her assistant, says the prayer commencing "*Veni Sancte Spiritus*," etc. Then the "examination of conscience" is gone through, all kneeling with the hands clasped before the heart. This ended, the sister appointed to read prayers says, "For our deceased sisters and benefactors, the *De Profundis*;" and that psalm is repeated. A short prayer in Latin and one in English, addressed to the Virgin Mary, close these devotions, which are called the dinner-prayers. Before leaving the chapel, the Superior, or her assistant, raps loudly, when every sister kisses the back of the seat before her, and takes her place in the rank. Then, with beads in hand, and eyes cast down, saying another "ten" of the chaplet, they go to the refectory. Should any disorder occur during this procedure, the delinquent is reported by one of the sisters stationed as a spy for this purpose.

In the refectory are placed five tables. One is occupied by the vow-sisters, over which the Superior presides whenever she takes her meals in this hall. Habitually, however, she has them served in her own room. Another seat is taken by her assistant, another by the mistress of novices, another by an officer, and the remaining one by a novice, which was assigned to me. Dinner consists generally of soup—which is the chief article of food—meat, potatoes, and bread. Of vegetables a very few, and small variety. No fruit is ever allowed to the novices, and rarely to the vow-sisters, as far as I know.

Each sister has a napkin at the side of her plate, knife, fork, and spoon (which are of iron or pewter), and a tin cup. After the ceremony of turning to the crucifix, clasping the hands upon the breast, and saying the Benedicite, which is repeated by the Superior or her assistant, the meal is partaken of in silence by those occupying the tables, while a chapter is being read from the Lives of the Saints, or from a book entitled Christian Perfection, and another from the Roman Martyrology. This reading is performed by one of the sisters, who takes her own dinner when all have withdrawn from the refectory. Another waits on the tables, and, when all have finished, gives intimation of the fact to the Superior or her assistant by a bow in front of her; then, at a loud rap on the table, all rise, clasp their hands as before, and again repeat the Benedicite. The rank is again formed, the Superior going first with her officers, followed by the vow-sisters and novices or seminary sisters, saying, as usual, a "ten" of the chaplet, and bowing when they pass the statue of St. Vincent. As soon as all are seated in the chapel, the bell rings, and each, as usual, kisses the back of the seat before her. Several prayers are now said in Latin, after which the sisters retire to the community-room and novitiate. In the latter room several prayers are said before the altar of St. Joseph.

CHAPTER XIV.

ROUTINE OF A DAY—AFTERNOON.

THE prayers after dinner being ended, the sisters proceed to their respective duties, at which not an unnecessary word is to be spoken. Should any one finish her task before two o'clock, she goes to the novitiate, and then may obtain the privilege of conversing until two o'clock, but only upon permitted topics. This is termed the period of *recreation*.

To prevent the interchange of thought and opinion, very strict regulations exist on the subject of conversation. The only seasons allowed for this purpose are these few minutes after dinner and supper, and then, as I have said, only upon certain topics. Any observations or inquiries respecting the health and feelings of the sisters are especially prohibited. At their occupations or duties no talking is allowed, except so far as may be absolutely necessary for their proper discharge. In addition to this, as will be seen, there are seasons of positive and complete silence, during which not a single word is permitted.

Before the two o'clock bell sounds every sister gets her Catechism, and takes her seat in the novitiate*

* It will be observed that these statements of the occupations of the sisters are confined to the novitiate, where I had my place. Of what

with the work given her during the recreation-hour. From two to three o'clock is an interval of strict silence. Not a voice is heard throughout the entire building, and not a member of the community raises her eyes from the floor, the Catechism, or the work upon which they are fixed. Should any sister need a supply of thread, or another needle, or a pair of scissors, she is not suffered to ask another sister for what she requires, nor to receive it if offered, nor even to ask the mistress of novices, who is walking around the room. She must sit through the hour without being able to perform the work assigned to her, for which very failure she will assuredly be obliged to do penance. In such cases, a sister will often, for fear of discovery by the mistress of novices as she passes by, move her beads, or otherwise feign occupation, trembling all the while lest her want of employment be observed.

During this season the mistress of novices is continually perambulating the room, peering into each face; and should she observe the eyes of any sister in the least uplifted, or the face raised, she will put her hand on the head, and, with a sudden jerk, force it downward, saying, "Keep your eyes down." Sometimes she gives a lecture during this silence-hour, and at the close of it a spiritual reading is performed by one of the sisters appointed beforehand for the purpose. This reading is selected either from the "Life of Christ" or from the "Conferences," of which more hereafter. The sister appointed goes, at the close of

occurred in the community-room, among the "vow-sisters," I do not at present speak.

the lecture, to a table in the centre of the room. She then receives a signal from the mistress of novices, who nods her head, raises her hand, or raps upon the table, and then says, "*In nomine*," when the sister at once takes up the invocation, repeating it in Latin, and then adding in English, "In the name of our Lord Jesus Christ." Then she takes hold of the book with both hands and commences to read. Should any of these formalities be neglected, the mistress of novices advances to the sister and reprimands her severely.

The "class sisters," or those engaged in teaching in the academy, sometimes come in late, just after the ringing of the bell, being detained by their duties. In such cases the rules are more particularly enforced, and penance is enjoined; as also in cases of walking too fast, holding up the head, raising the eyelids, etc. This penance consists in kissing the floor, kneeling before the altar, saying prayers, etc. The Superior and the mistress of novices recommend that, in going to or from their duties at the silence-hour, the sisters should be engaged in "saying beads," or repeating the prayers customary in the use of the chaplet.

In one instance I was late at the silence-hour, and came in with a handkerchief in my hand, as it was a very warm day. The mistress of novices called me to her, rebuked me sharply, and made me kiss the floor, saying that it looked too worldly to have a handkerchief in my hand instead of keeping it in my apron pocket. She threatened me with severe penance if found guilty of such an offense again.

In the *community-room*, during silence-hour, the sisters have spiritual readings for about a quarter of an hour; the remainder of the time they spend in any kind of fancy-work that they may select. Their eyes are also kept down, but the Lady Superior does not, like the mistress of novices, move about to watch the countenances of the sisters; she remains in her own room, and reads or sews. At this hour silence is also observed in the *infirmary*. The sick read some religious book, and sometimes say a "ten" of the chaplet. At the close of silence-hour the three o'clock bell is rung, and the mistress of novices says a prayer called the "Adoration Prayer," the sisters responding. Those class sisters who leave the community-room and novitiate before the close of silence-hour, at half past two, say this prayer before the bell rings, in a small chapel of the academy.

After the three o'clock bell, as it is called, every sister goes at once to her usual duties. Silence and recollection are observed in doing this, as at other times. The utterance of a single unnecessary word is reported, every part of the building having its spy for that purpose.

Before five o'clock, those who finish their tasks resort to the novitiate, and take sewing from the sister who has charge of the work. When the clock strikes five, all in the room range themselves on one side in a row, and one takes a chair apart from the rest to "say beads." Six "tens" of the chaplet are then said, all responding. Then are repeated the Lord's Prayer, the Creed, the Litany of the Virgin Mary; and about the close of the prayers the bell rings for the evening meditation. After assembling as usual in the novitiate and community-room, the rank is formed, and the sisterhood proceed to the chapel, where half an hour is spent in meditation and prayer. After prayers the bell rings, and the sisters walk in order to the refectory for supper.

Supper consists of a piece of bread, with sometimes a small piece of butter, and sometimes molasses. After this meal a "ten" of the chaplet is said in the chapel. If it be the evening before holy communion, at least as often as three times a week, the sisters must obtain permission to receive the sacrament. The moment before leaving the chapel, the vow-sisters kneel before the Lady Superior or her assistant, and say, "Please, mother," or "sister," if it be her assistant, "let me go to holy communion," and then they kiss their crucifix. The Lady Superior sits near the door behind the sisters, and in this supplication they turn their backs to the altar. As the vow-sisters are rising from their knees and forming the rank, the novices, who sit between them and the altar, turn toward them, kneel, kiss the floor, and say, "Please, sisters, let me go to holy communion." On the day before communion, at silence-hour, the novices have also to obtain permission from the mistress of novices in the same manner, but without speaking. Then is said the usual prayer in the novitiate and community-room, after which all retire to their duties. A number of the sisters go to the refectories, where the tables are to be prepared for the morning meal. Should the work be finished before the bell for prayers, all go to the novitiate and community-room. This is also called the hour of "recreation," when such of the sisters are allowed, as after dinner, to converse upon permitted topics. At eight the silence-bell is rung. The meditation for the following morning is read in advance by a sister, to occupy their wakeful moments during the night.

I should say that, after supper, each of the sisters is required to take her knitting; no one sits idle for a moment, even during the so-called "recreation." After the reading of this meditation, the mistress of novices calls upon some sister to offer remarks upon the subject of the meditation. The sister called upon usually expresses her thoughts in a few sentences; sometimes several are called upon during the evening. At the ringing of the second bell, at eight and a half o'clock, the sisters form rank and proceed to the chapel, where night-prayers are said till about nine o'clock. These prayers are similar in a great degree to those of the morning.

Before the close of prayers, every light is extinguished in the chandelier which hangs from the centre of the chapel, and only one is left—that burns night and day before the tabernacle in the sanctuary. The sisters leave the chapel in the usual order, and retire to their cells. From nine o'clock till breakfast is over on the following morning, absolute silence is to be maintained. During this time it is not allowed to take a drink of water. No sister is permitted to see another after she goes to her cell; it would be a breach of the rule for one sister to see the head of another uncovered. While undressing for the night, "aspirations" are said by many, the practice having been recommended by the Superior and the mistress of novices.

If this narrative of a day's employment at St. Joseph's—embracing only the more "spiritual" and devotional occupations of the sisters—should appear interminably tedious to the reader at a single perusal, I beg him to estimate the weariness of body and soul that must be endured by the poor sufferers of this infliction, repeated from day to day, from week to week, with scarcely a variation in the monotony of its routine.

CHAPTER XV.

"DUTIES" OF THE SISTERS.

SUCH is the procedure of religious observances for a single day at St. Joseph's. Some portions of it are of course subject to deviation for the several feasts, Sundays, fast-days, and other special occasions. From this statement the reader may have obtained a faint conception of the incessant toils and fatigues thus imposed. But he must take into consideration, besides these "spiritual" exercises, those manual and menial employments in which the members of the community are daily engaged, and which are technically called their "duties." These consist chiefly of those labors that are generally performed by servants in a private family, but which, in so large an establishment, must necessarily be far more numerous and burdensome.

An "officer," as she is designated, superintends each separate department of the domestic economy, and exercises control over those employed in her service, by whom she must be implicitly obeyed, without murmur or hesitation. The kitchen, laundry, infirmary, refectory, meat-house, clothes-room, dormitories, scullery, etc., etc., have each its overseer, and those appointed to perform the appropriate duties. But besides these there are the teachers in the academy; the "angels," as they are styled, who watch over the boarders, and sleep in their dormitories; and the sacristan, who has charge of the sacristy, church, chapels, and confessionals. There is also a sister to wait on the Superior, and who is, in fact, her servant; one to keep the priest's room in order; and another—a young and handsome sister being always selected for this duty—to carry his meals to him. Each has her allotted task, which must be performed faithfully and strictly, and she must be ready at a moment's warning to assume a new duty, or leave her work when ordered. All the work of the academy and institution is performed by the members of the community, and between these occupations and those exercises already described, not a minute is lost, from four o'clock in the morning till nine at night.

Some estimate of the amount of individual labor accomplished by the sisterhood may be drawn from a relation of my own experience. For the first three weeks after entering the institution, I was employed in the refectory, where, commencing after breakfast, the following is an account of a day's duties: Brought in two tubs of water; washed the cups, bowls, knives, and forks; cleared off five long tables, and carried the plates, about one hundred in number, to the kitchen to be washed; swept, and sometimes scoured and scrubbed the floor of the refectory; brought back the plates, and arranged the tables for dinner; cleaned the knives and forks; kept up a fire in the stove, etc. After dinner, performed the same work, and prepared the tables for supper. After supper, washed and cleaned up every thing again, and prepared for breakfast. At the end of three weeks I was transferred to the academy, where I taught music and French, and worked in the refectory at night. My occupations then were varied. Sometimes I cooked and washed, at other times I was employed in the infirmary, waiting on the sick and making their beds, administering their medicines, and assisting in cupping, blistering, and other hospital duties.

It must be borne in mind that, besides the faithful execution of these requirements, the sisters are compelled to be punctual at all the devotional exercises already described.

The observance of these duties and devotions comprehends an aggregate of endurance and suffering such as will speedily exhaust the strength and destroy the tone of the most sturdy constitution. Numbers every day are so utterly overcome, that when the hour of repose arrives, it is with difficulty that they reach their cells ere they fall fainting to the floor. What a mockery of religion, as well as of mere humanity, to summon so often for acts of worship these poor creatures, whose limbs are writhing with pain, and whose frames are worn out with excess of weariness, especially when so many of those exercises are performed in postures more fatiguing than even the servile duties by which they have been preceded! How can the mind and heart be profitably engaged in circumstances such as these?

To illustrate the facts here stated, I may allude to the case of a novice who fled from the institution, notwithstanding the Mother Superior's assertion that all are at liberty to depart at will, and took refuge with a

Presbyterian clergyman in Emmettsburg. She had not abjured the Catholic faith, but made her escape on account of her inability to sustain the grievous burden of labor imposed upon her. "She had supposed," she said, "that the institution was a centre of holy influences, and that nowhere else could she serve her Maker with such entire self-consecration, but she found nothing like religion there." So deep was her disgust with her experience of the life in the sisterhood, that she declared, "If to continue a 'Sister of Charity' would certainly take her to heaven, she would not consent to remain." It must have been the recollection of great suffering that elicited such language. The case of this novice will be referred to again, when I come to speak of the Mother Superior's letter.

CHAPTER XVI.

THE "CONFERENCE."

THE order of observances here described is varied on Wednesday by a convocation of the sisters called the "Conference," or "Chapter." As already mentioned, postulants are not permitted on that day to remain in the novitiate during the silence-hour, which is from two to three o'clock in the afternoon. They are then sent to the kitchen or elsewhere, to be out of the way, while the sisters assemble in the novitiate and community-room.

It was after my "retreat" that I learned the nature of the performances on this occasion. The room having been darkened by closing the window-shutters tightly, so that the only light admitted came through the upper part of the Gothic arches of the windows, the sisters then assembled, and took their places arranged round the room, the mistress of novices being seated at a table at one end near the door. At first, all kneel, and say certain prayers, during which the "class sisters," or teachers in the academy—who, upon hearing the bell, repair thither from their duties—noiselessly enter, and kneel near the door until the prayers are ended. Every sister not so engaged must be in the room before the two o'clock bell rings. After prayers, all seat themselves and take their work, except four or five of the "cornet sisters," or sisters of the "holy habit," nearest to the altar of St. Joseph, which is at one end of the room. These continue kneeling toward the altar, each behind the other in a row, and in front of her own seat. The first sister in this row, after kissing her crucifix and crossing herself, places the palms of her hands together in front of her breast, and then "makes her accusation," which she does in the following form:

"My God, I most humbly ask thy pardon, and to you, my sister, I accuse myself of my faults. I accuse myself of having walked too heavily, or of making too much noise in shutting the doors; of giving my eyes too much liberty; of not accepting advice in a spirit of humility; of not being 'recollected,'" etc., etc. After specifying some such offenses, the accusation concludes thus: "For these faults, and many others of which I am guilty, I most humbly ask pardon of God, and beg you, my sister, that you will please to give me penance." Sometimes it is added, "I ask for spiritual charity in the next conference." Having said thus, the sister, before leaving the novitiate, will take an opportunity to whisper in the ear of a sister whom she may select, "I ask *of you* spiritual charity in the next conference."

The first sister, having finished her accusation, takes her seat, and the one immediately behind her commences. This continues until all the five have performed this duty. Just before the last one has concluded, the next four or five kneel in the same manner, each, when her accusation is ended, resuming her seat and commencing her work. This proceeding lasts till all have knelt and accused themselves in turn. Any sister who has accused herself and has asked for "spiritual charity" in the previous chapter, will say after her accusation, "I asked for spiritual charity in the last conference." Thereupon at once the sister whom she then notified will kneel and say, "In a spirit of humility and charity I accuse my sister of speaking in time of silence," or any other fault she may remember or please to imagine. She ends with these words: "I know myself to be guilty of these faults and many others, for which I most humbly ask pardon of God," and then resumes her seat. Penances, as punishments, are then inflicted by the mistress of novices.

Frequently it will happen that in making these accusations the sisters will speak in too low a tone. The mistress of novices will then give three loud raps, and say, "What sister is that speaking?" To which the sister must reply, giving her name. She is then awarded some penance, such as kissing the floor two or three times, as a punishment, and is commanded to speak louder. The sisters will often tremble with agitation during this ceremonial. The conscience is at work; and fears lest they should commit some error in the repetition of the formula, for which they would inevitably be punished, keep them in constant anxiety and alarm; more especially is this the case with those young novices who have heard the expressions but a few times, and are allowed no other way of learning them than by hearing the words repeated on these occasions.

The mistress of novices, before the commencement of this cruel process, opens a little black book, and reads a collection of reports made to her by her spies, accusing such of the sisters as they may choose to impugn of whatever transgressions they are pleased to ascribe to them; and the poor novices, who, perhaps, have never dreamed of the offenses which they thus find alleged against them, are not allowed to defend themselves, or make a word of reply, but must receive, silently and submissively, whatever reproof or punishment may be imposed. The opening of this little book spreads alarm and terror throughout the novitiate.

After the accusations, a small book is taken from a closet, which is read during the remainder of the silence-hour. This book contains the rules of the house. At three o'clock the great bell rings rapidly and loud, in remembrance of our Lord, who expired at that hour upon the cross, and every sister instantly falls upon her knees, each holding in her hand her crucifix, gazing intently upon it, and kissing it reverently and passionately; the "adoration" prayer is then said, and this closes the chapter. Conferences are held in the community-room also, but I do not know the forms used there, nor am I certain that the same day is selected for the purpose.

CHAPTER XVII.

CONSUMPTION AT ST. JOSEPH'S.

IT can scarcely be matter of surprise that, with so much labor and so little rest, the most robust health, subjected to the life of a convent, should be shattered, and the strongest constitution undermined; still less will it be wondered at that young girls of weak and delicate frames should speedily prove martyrs to a system so exacting. Even at night, when the wearied sister, on the hard couch of her narrow cell, woos the "sweet restorer, balmy sleep," to recruit her energies for another day of toil, it is often impossible to obtain repose. Many a time have I been awakened in the depth of night by shrieks and screams that made my very blood run cold. Often have I heard groans and exclamations of distress, and then, in sweet and tremulous tones, the warbling of some poor, heart-broken sister, who, perhaps, in dreams revisited the home of her childhood, but for whom the interests of real life were buried in darkness forever. Again would the silence be disturbed by the slow and measured footfall of a priest, summoned, perhaps, to administer the holy viaticum to some dying sister in the infirmary.

One night I was unusually alarmed by a loud and

prolonged shriek, proceeding from a neighboring part of the dormitory, and a heavy fall as of a body striking the ground. Immediately after I heard a person running past my cell toward the passage beyond. The sounds frightened me so much that I was unable to close my eyes during the remainder of the night. The following evening, during "recreation," a young sister who was seated next to me asked me if she could speak without being reported. I looked at her with surprise; but, seeing that she was pale and agitated, I told her, although against the rules, that she might speak without reserve, and tell me the cause of her distress, promising that I would not divulge it, but would serve her if in my power. She then informed me that she had been very much alarmed the night before, and asked if I had heard a strange noise and a loud shriek. Upon my assent, she stated that about midnight she had been awakened by a heavy step around the bed, and was so frightened that she could scarcely breathe. As soon as the sound had ceased, she felt something heavy at the foot of her bed, when she uttered a scream, and the person, or fiend, for she knew not which, rolled heavily to the floor, and, uttering a wild, demoniacal yell, fled rapidly down the cloister. So much had these occurrences terrified her, that she dreaded retiring to her cell, and was in a constant state of agitation and fear.

The very next night I heard a shriek, if possible, louder than the previous one. The following day I learned from a young sister that some one, at midnight, had walked round her bed several times, after which she had felt a pair of hands seize her by the throat, nearly stifling her for a moment, whereupon she uttered the scream I had heard.

Many an hour have I remained awake, revolving in my mind occurrences like these, for which I vainly endeavored to account. But more distressing than these frightful sounds was one far more common: the painful cough of the consumptive, which from more than one cell would be heard, announcing the presence of that fearful disease, elsewhere so dreaded, but here invited, and rendered almost inevitable by the course of life prescribed. I was told, and it was generally taught, that *consumption is a part of the vocation.* Sometimes I have found it out of the question to obtain an hour's repose, in consequence of the continual cough of some poor sister, who, wearied with the arduous duties imposed upon her during the day, would reach her cell with the help of others, in a few days more to be ordered to the infirmary, linger a little longer, receive the last sacraments, then welcome death as a release from her sufferings, and be carried to the graveyard near at hand.

One evening, while ascending the steps to my cell, I noticed a sister leaning against the wall as if for support, and breathing heavily. I imagined her unable to reach her cell, but could not speak, as it was silence-hour. Unwilling to pass her without notice, I offered my arm, which she accepted, and I assisted her to her cell. The following day she was sent to the infirmary, and soon after died.

Numbers die at the institution every year. I know of fourteen who died during the ten months of my stay in the community, and I saw at least twenty recent graves before I left. They are buried in regular rows. There are four infirmaries, in one of which there are several insane sisters. There is one for the old and infirm, who are totally unable to go about the institution, and who sometimes, though with great difficulty, reach the choir, which is very near, where they perform their devotions. The large infirmary connected with the house, though a separate building, is filled with the sick and the dying. It is divided into two departments: the lower, on the first floor, being occupied by the young sisters or novices; the upper, in the second story, by the vow or professed sisters. In this department there is a small chapel, where confessions are made by those who are unable to go to church or to any of the confessionals.

The lower infirmary is a large room, on each side of which is a row of small curtained bedsteads, about seven in number. At the end of a passage leading past the entrance to this room, there is a very small passage at right angles, connecting with a room where those who die in this infirmary are laid out. At the other end of the infirmary is a passage, on one side of which there are two doors, one leading to the refectory, and the other to the kitchen. On the opposite side is a store-room, where provisions are kept in small quantities for those who occupy the infirmary. In this passage a flight of stairs leads to the upper infirmary. At the top of these stairs, on the right, there is a sitting or work room for those sisters who, though ill, are permitted to walk about the upper infirmary—that is, to go from their apartments to the chapel, work-room, and medicine-room. Many of the professed sisters are allowed to take their meals in the infirmary on account of loss of appetite and impaired health, caused by the want of better fare.

The rules of the infirmary are framed and hung up in the work-room. Whoever transgresses these rules is reported by the "infirmarian," her assistant, and others. These rules are substantially as follows:

No sister is allowed to enter the infirmary without permission from the Superior, or other officer of the community. When entered, she must at once see the infirmarian, and act according to her directions.

She must ask for nothing, but receive whatever is given her without a murmur.

She must observe strictly the community rules—that is, must repeat her prayers, keep silence, and refrain from speaking to any other sick sister without permission.

When sent to bed, she is not to rise without permission, nor leave the infirmary unless directed to do so.

Those sisters who are allowed to take their meals in the infirmary-refectory are not permitted, when passing through the building, to speak to a sister who is sick, but must walk with eyes cast down, and hands folded across their breasts.

CHAPTER XVIII.

FIRST INDICATIONS OF DISFAVOR.

I HAD been in the community about two months when a letter from my family was received by the Superior. It was handed or sent by her to the mistress of novices for perusal in the novitiate. When the mistress of novices had finished reading the letter, she called me to her. I instantly obeyed, fell on my knees before her, and kissed the floor. She then told me that she had a letter for me from my family, and would not give it to me, but would read a few sentences of it aloud. She did so, and I was unable to control my emotion, or to restrain the tears that rushed to my eyes. Seeing me so agitated, she became very angry—for it is esteemed a step toward perfection to suppress all demonstration of feeling—and seizing me by the shoulders while I was kneeling before her, she threw me violently backward. My head striking the floor, I became insensible, and was taken, as I afterward learned, to the infirmary, where I was reported by the mistress of novices as detained by "ill health."

After leaving the infirmary, I was looked upon with an inquiring glance by many, who would fain have asked me respecting my health, but neither they nor I durst utter a word on the subject. It is positively forbidden to say any thing relative to one's feelings, or to make inquiries about any one who has been sent to the infirmary. Should any thing occur there, it is not to be spoken of in the novitiate or community-room; nor is any thing that happens in those rooms to be repeated in the infirmary.

Sometimes we would miss a sister for several days together; but we did not know where she was, and were not permitted to ask after her. It is forbidden to notice when any person comes or goes, or to inquire why such a sister is removed from one place to another; and before we would have farther tidings, she might be dying or dead in the infirmary without our knowledge.

But it was not long before other occurrences made me conscious of the fact that I had incurred the displeasure of my superiors, and that I must expect the strictest surveillance and punishment for the least omission of duty or infraction of the rules. Unintentional errors, such as in others would be overlooked, were sure to be visited upon me; and every word I uttered was duly reported by spies set to watch my conduct. One evening, exhausted by the labor undergone during the day, as I was carrying a tub of water from the kitchen to the refectory, I remarked to a sister, "How very hard we have to work!" This was, of course, reported to the Superior. While at breakfast on the following morning, I was sent for to come to her room. I went, and found her much displeased. She threatened me with condign punishment in case another word of complaint were spoken relative to the labor imposed. She said that "if I should ever again complain, I would get myself into trouble." I left her room with the determination to be silent in future. At this period I did not know the rules, having not yet made my retreat. I was often rebuked, and more than once threatened with arraignment before the "council" by the sister who had charge of the refectory.

One night, having been sent by the mistress of novices to the infirmary on account of some indisposition during the day, I asked permission of the "infirmarian" to retire before night-prayers, being unfit for the fatigue of kneeling during such a length of time. She answered, "No; I had come thither to suffer and do penance," and might return to the infirmary after prayers. I did so, but was told that I must rise from my bed at the ringing of the first bell—at four in the morning—and must attend morning-prayers and the first mass. This infirmarian was ere long, however, succeeded by a new one, to the great satisfaction of the young novices, as she did not enforce the rules with the strictness of her predecessor.

One evening, about this time, after duties, having been sent to the infirmary to watch by the bedside of a sister who was very ill, I noticed in a bed near by a young sister apparently dying of consumption. She was beautiful; her large dark eyes shone with unearthly brilliancy; her face was very pale, save one bright spot on each cheek, that spoke plainly of her approaching doom. Once or twice I noticed that she sighed heavily; and, watching her more closely, I discovered the tears trickling down her cheeks. My sympathy was roused, and, crossing the room to her bedside, I inquired how long she had been in the infirmary, and whether she were improving. She had been there, she said, all winter, and was no better. Raising her hand, which was covered with a handkerchief, she told me that she was in great suffering. I saw that the hand had been opened, as by a surgical operation. She did not know why it had been done, and felt sure that she would lose it. A few days later she was sent away from the institution, nor did I learn for some months after where she was. I shall have occasion to speak again of this sister in another place.

The Lady Superior, mistress of novices, and infirmarian had, particularly the two latter, since the reception of the letter from my home, manifested toward me a severity of character which alarmed me. The Lady Superior, even in her rebukes, would usually close by some mild and persuasive remark, which went far to alleviate my wounded pride and lacerated feelings. I had no reason to believe that she had any hostile feeling toward me, except on account of my evident and still strong attachment to my family.

The treatment I received, however, produced a great change in my outward conduct. Fear, a sense of duty, and the cherished hope of obtaining permission to depart, all combined to induce me, at least apparently, to submit with perfect patience and resignation to the will and wishes of my superiors; and although my heart ached for that lovely and suffering sister, and my curiosity was aroused to the utmost to know more of her, yet I dared not prolong the interview at this time for fear of the infirmarian.

CHAPTER XIX.

THE ILLUSION AND THE REALITY.

HAVING made my retreat as a postulant, when, for the first time, I learned and fully comprehended the nature of the sacrifice demanded of me, I saw that the chief requirement was an abject submission to the will and commands of the superiors *in every respect;* that their dictates must be regarded with the same reverence as the voice of God himself; that the highest holiness was made to consist in an entire surrender to their control—physically, spiritually, and morally, as to the Almighty; that this obedience required a renunciation of father, mother, sister, and brother; in whose stead the Father and Mother Superiors of the institution, the members of the community, and the priest, must thenceforth be regarded with filial and sisterly devotion; that every affection of the heart must be stifled, every earthly tie broken, and an eternal farewell bidden to home, friends, and country.

As these considerations crowded upon my mind, I became terrified at the prospect. I determined to write home and declare that my resolution was altered, and that I no longer desired to follow the life of a Sister of Charity.

It did not occur to me for a moment that any obstacle would be interposed to prevent my withdrawal from the community. I had been told that this was not a "close convent;" and even from such it is *publicly* declared that a novice is at liberty to depart at any time before assuming the black veil. I was still attached to the Roman Catholic faith, but I found it impossible to reconcile myself to the idea of subjecting my will and affections to the slavery enforced by the vows of the society. I was self-convinced that my "vocation" for such a life was a figment of the imagination, and that my spiritual welfare would not be promoted by a forced obedience to rules abhorrent to my nature. But, alas! I was soon made to feel that already the chains of a cruel servitude had bound me hand and foot; that already I was under the full control of a heartless organization, whose only motives of action were its own aggrandizement, and a base subserviency to the ambition of an unscrupulous priesthood.

In accordance with the resolution thus formed, a few days before the time appointed for my reception into the sisterhood, I wrote to my father announcing my intention to withdraw from the institution and return home. This letter, as is customary, was read by the mistress of novices, and afterward submitted to the Mother Superior. I was soon summoned to her presence, where, on my knees, I was asked, sternly, why I had perpetrated such a piece of folly. I told her, in brief and respectful terms, of the change in my views, and of my desire to return home.

No sympathizing reply, nor even a mild dissuasion, followed this statement; but, to my astonishment, the Mother Superior, tearing the letter to pieces and throwing the fragments into a stove near by, harshly answered that, having renounced my own will in this matter, I must persevere to the end for the good of my soul, and God would bless my determination. No remonstrance on my part was listened to, but I was compelled to write another letter, *at her dictation*, declaring my happiness in my present condition, and my entire contentment with it, and adding that I would accordingly remain and make my vows at the institution. I was completely cowed, and obeyed in fear and trembling, with the certainty that even if I should then resist, I should be finally constrained by punishment to obey. How trying the alternative! What more painful and revolting to the feelings of a daughter than thus to be compelled to write a lie to her parent—to persuade the loved ones at home that she was happy and contented, when her heart was torn with anguish, and when the first symptoms of despair, like a gathering cloud, shut out those bright anticipations she had been forming of a speedy reunion with the family circle. I retired from the interview with sensations that no language can express, and such as I trust never to experience again. That night was spent in silent tears and bitter thoughts.

After this rebuff, a settled feeling of despondency took possession of my mind, though I was constrained, through fear of punishment, to avoid a betrayal of my sentiments. My highly-wrought expectations had vanished; my prospects of happiness were scattered to the winds. At this time, too, my faith in popery received a shock; my eyes were partially opened to the rashness of forsaking the church of my fathers, and attaching myself to a system whose crooked policy was now in process of development before me. An honest self-examination, serious reflection, and the influence of events that followed this first display of intrigue and deception, completely uprooted every vestige of my previous preferences, and enabled me both to appreciate my own folly and to perceive the distorted lineaments concealed under the attractive mask that had allured me. If I have suffered—and God only knows how poignantly—from the injustice and malevolence of my oppressors, still am I deeply grateful that these sorrows should have been the means of awakening me to a sense of my error, and of disclosing the truth in its purity to my perception.

All this, however, did not take place at once; and though, as I have said, my enthusiastic anticipations disappeared, and a thick cloud overspread my spirit, there came as yet no thought of rebellion against the control of my superiors. I resolved to perform the duties allotted me, and submit patiently to the consequences of my own rashness, until, as I still vainly hoped, I should be permitted to depart in peace. Not the remotest idea of escape was then cherished, and it was not till circumstances occurred, the recollection of which even now causes an involuntary shudder, that I was rendered desperate, and determined to brave every consequence, and even death itself, sooner than remain incarcerated in a prison such as this.

CHAPTER XX.

POOR JULIA.

I HAVE said that disease and death are busy actors among the inmates of St. Joseph's. Consumption, that dread yet insidious foe of the young and innocent, stealing, like the tiger of the jungles, with noiseless step and remorseless purpose on its unsuspecting victim, and fastening its deadly grasp ere the approach be suspected, makes sad ravages here. Worn out with incessant toil, and with an unremitting observance of the oppressive routine of useless forms; subject, also, to frequent exposures to changes of temperature, not only in passing over the porches to and from the academy, but also from a frequent lack of clothing, and sleeping in cold cells without sufficient covering, to say nothing of the effects of sudden prostration of the body upon the cold floor at four o'clock every morning, it is no wonder that the sisters, and especially those of them who are most conscientious in the discharge of their laborious duties, should often fall a prey to this fell destroyer.

But a short time after my admission to the sisterhood, I entered the novitiate one morning at an earlier hour than usual, and saw a sister sitting before a table with her head resting upon her hands, and violently weeping. No one being present, I went up to her, and kneeling at her side, asked affectionately why she wept so bitterly. She answered that the cause of her sorrow could not be revealed; that she would fain speak to me without reserve, but could not do so; and added, "Sister, I was for many years a boarder here, and received my education from the sisterhood; but I did not dream of what a religious life is. I can not tell you how I have been deceived. I do not care to live." Hearing steps in the adjoining corridor, we separated for fear of being observed, and at her request I left by a side door.

This young lady was the daughter of a wealthy Southerner, who had placed her at an early age in the academy, where she had remained several years, acquiring all those accomplishments that were suited to fit her for the sphere of society in which she was expecting to move. Having completed her studies, and spent a couple of years at home, she urged her father to permit her to revisit with him the peaceful vale where she had passed so many happy days of her childhood. As he intended to take her younger sisters to the same institution for their education, he consented that this eldest daughter should accompany them, and make a short stay at the institution. Her purpose in this request was to enter the sisterhood, should opportunity present itself; but this design was, of course, concealed from her father, who would have opposed it at once. Upon arriving at St. Joseph's, the daughter spent much time in the company of those who, no doubt, had persuaded her to embrace this resolution, and on the eve of the father's departure it

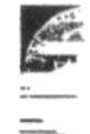

was for the first time made known to him. Upon hearing of her determination, he became greatly displeased, and demanded that she should be called to speak with him, but he was told that he could not see her, as she had gone over to the house occupied by the sisterhood. There her beautiful long hair was severed from her head, and sent to her father as a parting gift, and the white cap of the postulant was put on. A few weeks elapsed; her health began to fail, and soon after becoming a novice she was so unwell as frequently to be sent to the infirmary. Often, when coming with her from our duties in the academy, have I seen her cling to the railing of the porches for support, while the tears were streaming from her eyes.

Though unable at first to draw from her the cause of her distress, at length, one evening, as I urged her to confide in me, she took from her pocket a tiny stocking, and said, with much emotion, "This is the only relic I have of my little baby brother." She had brought him with her to the institution, as she could not bear the thought of parting with him at home. "It was a bitter trial, sister," she continued, "when my mother died, a year before I entered the community; but it is harder yet for me to give up all hope of ever seeing my little brother again."

A few days after this conversation I missed her from the novitiate, and learned that she had been sent to the infirmary. I asked permission of the mistress of novices to visit her, scarcely expecting, however, that I should be allowed to do so. To my surprise, leave was granted for a short interview. I found the sister in bed, supported by pillows, her face flushed with fever, and evidently in deep distress. No one being near us at the moment, I took her slender hand, thin almost to transparency, and asked if she were better. "No, my dear sister," she replied; "I am worse; I am dying;" and she inquired whether I too were sick and had come for medicine. "Do not take a cold, sister, for *it is always fatal here.*"

I could remain but a short time, and when I left, promised to seek a speedy opportunity of visiting her again. A week or two passed, during which I made many inquiries concerning her health, but could learn nothing. When again allowed to see her, I was alarmed at the change a few days had wrought. She was then but the shadow of her former self, and could scarcely speak above a whisper. Since her first illness she had refused to take any nourishment, or any thing that was thought calculated to afford relief. She would wipe the blood from her lips, and, smiling sadly, say to me, "I shall soon be gone, and my poor father will not know of my death."

One evening, as I was passing through the infirmary, carrying a message from the mistress of novices, she called me, and though it was a breach of the rules, I went to her bedside. She requested me to hand her her knitting. I refused to do so, as she was scarcely able, from extreme debility, to raise her hands. Said she, "Sister, did I say *my* work? mine? *What* is mine?" Then making an effort to rise from her bed, she fell back fainting on her pillow. When consciousness returned, she burst into a flood of tears, crying, "My poor father! my mother!"

She was ill two months, during which time she did

not rise from her bed. She would often say to the infirmarian, "Sister, what is the matter with me? Please to tell me." The evening of her death she had several convulsions, and after recovering, asked where she had been. She then said to one of the officers at her bedside that she had seen her mother, who had come for her, and she could stay no longer. The officer, supposing that she alluded to the Mother Superior, was about to send in haste for her. "No," exclaimed the poor sister, "I mean my own dear mother." The words had scarcely passed her lips when she expired, without having received the last sacrament or made her vows.

She was laid out in her novice's dress; her beads and crucifix were laid upon her breast. As usual, a sister watched by the corpse until morning, when mass was said for the repose of her soul. She was placed in a plain wooden coffin, of dark color, and beautiful indeed was this unfortunate girl in death. A white rose had been laid upon her bosom by some member of the community, perhaps by the sister whom I overheard making the following remark, which showed that she at least was not utterly devoid of feeling: "Yes," she murmured, gazing upon the fair remains, "she came to us a bud; now she has gone, a rose in perfect bloom."

Her coffin we covered with a black pall and bore to the chapel, where, as I have said, mass was sung for her repose. Beside the corpse six lighted candles were placed. The altar and paintings were shrouded in mourning. After mass, while the chapel bell was tolling, six novices carried her to the grave-yard near by, and the community followed two by two in the usual manner. Thus the once admired, accomplished, and beloved Julia was committed to her final rest.

During her illness, her sisters, who were in the academy, were permitted to see her but once, a few moments before her death, when she asked to see them; nor were they permitted even to write to their father of her illness. He knew nothing of it until subsequent to her decease, but not long after he sent for his two daughters from the academy. He was a Roman Catholic.

CHAPTER XXI.

SISTER SERAPHIA.

As I have stated, the novices at St. Joseph's have occasion frequently to remain at night with those who are ill. It is also their duty to carry the coffin of the dead, and watch through the night at its side. This they sometimes do quite alone in the chapel.

The former of these offices I have many a time performed, among the sick and dying in the infirmary. I was for some time an assistant in that department of the institution, having been put on duty after a very severe illness, and as soon as I was sufficiently strong to walk from one bed to another.

One night, during that illness, hearing a strange noise in a neighboring passage, I arose, and went to the door of the infirmary. It was dark. I walked on a few steps, when I fainted, and fell to the floor. I know not how long I remained unconscious. Upon my recovery, it was some time before I could find the door, and when I did so, I ascertained that the lamp, which burns through the night, hanging from the centre of the room, had gone out. It was with difficulty that I reached my bed, which I accomplished by feeling on the floor for a register near it. I remained ill for many days, and much of the time unconscious of all that passed around me.

On a bed opposite to mine lay a young sister, who had the consumption, and was pronounced incurable. The second winter after her admission she had taken a severe cold, which received no attention. At length she was sent to the infirmary, but there found no relief.

When, after my recovery, I was placed on duty in the infirmary, I took particular care of this sister. A short time before her death, she said to me, as I was arranging her pillows, "Sister, you have been so very kind to me, that I wish to see you after I die; and if Almighty God will permit, I shall come back to you, and tell you of the unknown world." I told her that I hoped she might do so. I prepared her to receive the last sacrament, arranging the table, and placing upon it the candles and crucifix. She received the extreme unction, made her vows, and expired.

The day subsequent to Sister Seraphia's death, I received a message from the mistress of novices directing me to keep watch alone in a small chapel on one side of the sanctuary in the church. Entering that chapel, I was startled at the sight of a coffin covered with a black pall. At once I imagined that it was the corpse of the young lady who had died on the preceding day. I seated myself by the coffin, and in perfect silence began my lonely vigil. My thoughts could not but recur to the circumstances of her decease—to her exclamations in the conscious approach of death, when she cried out, "I am going! I am going!" and called on the names of the saints to help her in that extremity. I remembered also, as I sat keeping solitary watch by the side of the dead, that strange promise which she had made me; and my mind, already growing superstitious under the influence of constant meditation upon supernatural occurrences, was now uneasy at the slightest sound. I had been thus engaged for about an hour, when suddenly the folding doors between the chapel and the sanctuary, which had been locked, burst violently open, with so loud a noise that I uttered a scream, and rushing to the door, held one side, while the other, striking the table as it flew open, overturned it, with the candle and the crucifix. Then, seizing both leaves of the door, I held them till the sacristan, who had doubtless heard my scream, if she did not hear the noise made by the doors, came in. She asked me, in a whisper, what was the matter. I told her I was greatly alarmed, but did not explain the particulars. She closed the doors, relocked them, and left me. I then arranged the table and crucifix, relighted the candle, and seated myself once more by the side of the corpse. I fully expected every moment to see her rise from the coffin. As she had promised to revisit me, now, I thought, was the moment; and, possessed with this idea, I placed my hands across her breast, and called her several times by name. I should not have been surprised if she had answered me, nor, indeed, at any thing that might have happened; for, during my stay in the infirmary, I witnessed scenes and heard sounds for which I was unable to account. Soon another sister came to relieve me; and, as I was about to leave, I said to her, "Should you hear or see any thing, don't be alarmed, sister." She asked me if I had been frightened; I made no reply; and she then could not be persuaded to remain. I staid therefore alone until the morning, but heard nothing else to disturb the still repose of death.

CHAPTER XXII.

MYSTERIOUS SOUNDS.

I HAVE said that many things occurred during my stay at St. Joseph's that seemed strange at the time, and, however easily to be explained as machinations of miracle-working priestcraft, caused much alarm and excitement among the community where they were enacted. This will scarcely seem matter of surprise when it is considered what an atmosphere of superstition and what a world of imaginary fears surround the poor inmates of a convent.

One of the older sisters, having died, was committed to the grave with the usual ceremonies, and the members of the community retired from the spot, leaving the sexton to complete the interment. When he had commenced to fill up the grave with earth, a loud and distinct rapping was heard to proceed apparently from the interior of the coffin. The sexton was surprised, but thought his ears deceived him, when, the sounds continuing, he became greatly terrified, dropped his spade, and ran in haste for the priest. It was only after much solicitation that the latter would consent to accompany the sexton to the grave, not believing his story; but finally he was persuaded to do so, in order, as he said, to convince the frightened man of his folly.

On arriving at the place of burial, the sounds were still heard, and, by command of the now apparently startled priest, the coffin was taken out and opened, and the cornet raised from the face of the sleeper to see if any signs of life remained. But she lay in the stillness of death, and the rapping had ceased. The coffin being again committed to the grave, the sounds were resumed, more loudly than before, and then continued to be heard, fainter and fainter, till smothered beneath the weight of earth, as the priest hastily directed the sexton to fill up the grave.

Around the walls of the cell where this sister died, knocks were repeatedly heard. A sister who was ill, and who slept there, told me she could not rest for the loud rapping that occurred, and begged me to get her a lamp to burn at night; but lights are not allowed in the cells of the institution, and no one, with the exception of a few who have special charge, is permitted to possess a candle or a match at any time.*

* Miracles have been rife at the institution of St. Joseph's. "On the 10th of June, 1820," soon after the death of Mother Seton, the founder of the establishment, "one of the sisters, who had been reduced by an accumulation of diseases to the very verge of the grave, was *suddenly restored to health,* immediately after receiving the holy communion. For thirty-six days she had not been able to retain the least particle of food on her stomach; and whenever she attempted to take any nourishment, it was ejected with such violent sufferings as to create the apprehension of immediate death. The physicians having exhausted all the resources of their art, and the case having been pronounced desperate, she was advised by Mr. Dubois to make a novena, or nine days' devotion, in honor of the holy name of Jesus, in union with Prince Hohenlohe, who, on a previous occasion, had announced that on the tenth of each month he would pray for the intentions of those living out of Europe. On the last day of the novena she received the blessed sacrament at the hands of the Reverend Superior, and all her

CHAPTER XXIII.

GRADES IN THE SISTERHOOD.

It is time that I should endeavor to explain the meaning of the several terms that have been here used in designation of the several grades that exist in the sisterhood at St. Joseph's; those, namely, of *Postulant, Novice,* or *Seminary Sister,* and *Professed Sister.* The explanation will exact of my reader some little patience and attention. I shall, however, make it as plain and brief as possible.

A Postulant is one on probation in the community. She wears in general a plain black dress with a cape, and on the head a white cap, concealing a part of her face. The period of postulancy is seldom protracted beyond the space of three months. It may be less than this, according as the Superior shall determine. I myself took the habit before the expiration of that period. The postulants are not all retained in the institution; many are sent away within a few days after their arrival. But, though they may be turned off, they can not leave of their own accord. This depends upon the will of the Superior alone, their own will being renounced at their entrance.

morbid symptoms instantly *disappeared.* On the 10th of August, another case of disease, but of a much more aggravated character, was also suddenly cured by performing a similar novena in union with Prince Hohenlohe."—*Life of Mrs. Seton,* p. 444.

The rules and regulations of the sisterhood are not fully made known to a postulant until the period of her *retreat.* The purpose of this retreat, indeed, is chiefly to acquaint the postulant with the nature of the three vows—those of poverty, chastity, and obedience—and the obligation she then assumes is expressed to her in language somewhat as follows: "You do *now* bind yourself to keep forever these vows," etc. No response is required, but in silence, total, abject silence, all is to be listened to with the most thorough acquiescence. This retreat lasts from five to eight days. The time is spent in silent prayer and meditation, nor is the postulant allowed to utter a solitary word during this period. At its close the "habit" is received. The postulant then becomes a NOVICE, or "Seminary Sister." Such she continues to be until the expiration of five years, when she "takes the vows." These vows I believe to be none other than those communicated in the retreat of the postulancy. These once assumed, she becomes a Professed Sister.

The "*holy habit,*" which is worn by the professed sisters, is given to the novices whenever the Superior may please to grant it. I had been measured for my own shortly before my escape; this, probably, was owing to the fact of my employment in the academy, and my subordinate charge of the novices in the novitiate at "adoration," and in the refectory.

The "*novitiate-room*" is occupied by the postulants and novices, the former being seated on benches in the centre, and the latter in seats along the walls, facing the postulants.

At the termination of the five years when the "vows

are taken," the novice does not gain access to the community-room among the "professed;" although she is then a professed sister, she is still called a novice. A farther probation is required before admission to that room. Three years at least, amounting, with those already spent in the novitiate, to eight, and sometimes even to ten, must yet elapse before these sisters, now called "novices professed," can become occupants of that higher sanctuary called the *community-room.*

Thus it will be perceived that there are in what is termed the novitiate-room three classes of sisters—postulants, novices not professed, and novices professed; the last, and some of the second class, wearing the holy habit. The term sister is applicable to all the grades in the community; and when we speak of the community generally, we mean the entire body or sisterhood.

The three to five years that are spent in the novitiate before admission to the *community-room*, besides the five years above mentioned, constitute, doubtless, a sort of probation, during which it may be ascertained whether the sister be qualified by natural capacities, or by acquirements of education, for the duties of a "sister of charity," or whether she be sufficiently reliable to be intrusted with the secrets of this higher grade before she can be sent abroad into the world on a mission. This is particularly requisite in the case of those who are designed for teachers, and for "sister-servants" to take charge of the mission houses, or to perform other duties that demand more or less ability. Such a probation is not required, however, of those sisters who are ignorant or of homely appearance. These are often sent out at an earlier period to fill subordinate places, as servants in mission-houses, and for other stations.

It will be seen, then, that in the *community-room* none are admitted as inmates until they have spent at least eight years in the institution. This is the rule, and no exceptions are, to my knowledge, allowed. There may be other vows beyond those which were communicated to me, and much also concerning the vows I have named; the latter, doubtless, is the fact. These vows are more strictly to be kept by the novices than by the "professed" in the community-room.

I have noticed that each PROFESSED SISTER, as well as each of those who intend to assume the vows, when approaching the time of that assumption, carries in her pocket a small black book, tied with black tape, which is attached to it at the pointed end of a lappet of some black material, extending beyond one cover, and folding over it like a pocket-book. Should this book fall, or be left by accident lying in any place, its contents would thus be concealed unless the tape were unfastened. I always supposed, from the care taken to keep this book out of view, that it contained something of an improper nature relative to the vows assumed, a supposition which was engendered by reading in the books of the conferences. The sisters generally read this book before confession.

I am aware that after the first five years the sisters are required to *renew* their vows yearly, on a certain fixed day, and in words they do make the vows from year to year, but in heart they bind themselves forever. At these appointed periods of renewal, the sisters respond to their vows in an audible tone of voice. This is done at high mass, just before communion, and with the remembrance that those who perform the act *have no longer any will of their own.* The rule declares that they can not leave the institution during this interval of renewal, nor during the course of the year. And the vows must be thus renewed yearly, on the day set apart for the purpose. Before entering St. Joseph's, I was told that I could leave at any moment at my pleasure. I was assured that, not only before the expiration of the five years of novitiate, but even after that period, I should only be bound to remain for a year at a time, being free to renew my vows at the end of each period or not, as I might choose. This I found to be all fraud and deception.

CHAPTER XXIV.

COSTUME OF THE SISTERS.

It may be well here to describe, in a few words, the *costume* of the sisterhood, before farther explanations respecting the vows. The dress of a novice consists of a black gown, a dark blue apron, with a boddice covering part of a small white shawl, falling gracefully over the shoulders, and not concealing the form. On the head is worn a closely-fitting cap, made of white muslin, covering the ears and concealing the hair, which has been cut short. Over this cap is worn a white "bonnet," the "bobs" of which fall over the shoulders to the waist behind. Over the "bonnet"* again is the black "capot," a kind of silk veil that hangs over the shoulders, extending nearly to the feet. This dress is also called the sister's habit, or the seminary dress.

The "holy habit," or dress worn by the older sisters, consists of a gray cloth gown, an apron of the same material, loose hanging sleeves, and beneath it a white linen sleeve that fastens around the wrist. Over this is drawn in winter a close worsted sleeve. Around the neck is worn a broad linen collar, falling nearly to the waist in front, where the ends overlap each other slightly. The head is shaved close, and is

* Pronounced bonné.

covered with a closely-fitting cap called the touquoir. Over this is worn the "cornet," which is a broad piece of linen, fashioned into a species of bonnet, and drawn to a point above the face; it projects in front over the forehead about six inches. The sides, or "wings," droop to the shoulders, but do not touch them. The sisters often say, "These are the wings that will carry us to heaven."

Large heavy beads, with a crucifix attached, are worn at the left side, and constitute a part of the dress. These are to be distinguished from the chaplet beads,* which, when not carried in the pocket, are worn on the right side. Some of the sisters possess, attached to the chaplet, a small crucifix, said to be made of the wood of the tree under which St. Vincent was in the habit of sitting. The holy habit, when put on or taken off, is always reverentially kissed. The costume at first adopted by Mrs. Seton for the institution of St. Joseph's is thus particularly described in her life: "A black dress with a short cape, similar to a costume that she had observed among the religious in Italy. Her head-dress was a neat white muslin cap, with a crimped border, and a black crape band around the head, fastened under the chin."—P. 253.

The shoes worn by the sisters are of the coarsest kind. Speaking of them, I may mention, as an illustration of the petty annoyances which are designedly practiced upon the younger sisters, for their *spiritual* advantage no doubt, the following incident. Shortly after my entrance as a postulant, Sister J. P—— met me in the corridor, and, looking down at my gaiter-

* *Chapelet*, French; rosary.

boots, she said to me, "You must not wear such shoes as those; come with me." I followed her to a room on the ground floor, partly paved with bricks, used for bathing, and also as a shoe depository. Having seated me on a small bench, the sister said, "Put out your foot here;" and then, for a long time, looked for a pair of shoes to fit me. They were all too large; and as I expressed my dissatisfaction, she said, "It's no matter; you don't want your feet to look small; you are not 'in the world' now;" and so saying, she took the smallest pair she could find, and placed them on my feet. These shoes, like all the rest in the room, were made of leather, with a strap on each side of the instep, and tied with a leathern string. The soles were about half an inch thick. Once a week we blacked our own shoes in the same room. A few days after this, the same sister met me limping, and asked me what was the matter. I told her that my feet were chafed by the slipping of the shoes up and down when I walked, and by the binding or cord around the top. She then went with me into the refectory, and cut the binding, which somewhat relieved me. It was long before I could accustom myself to the use of these shoes. A few weeks before I left, I had a new pair given me, having worn the former through on one side. That pair was then given in my presence to a postulant; whether they were mended or not afterward, I can not say. The Lady Superior wears morocco buskins.

CHAPTER XXV.

THE VOW OF POVERTY.

THE first of the vows taken in the institution, namely, that of poverty, is of sufficiently plain significance, its purpose being evidently to enrich the establishment by so much property as the members of the community may possess, as well as to derive from their manual labor all their earnings, over and above the amount required for their own support. As members of the community, they would naturally be more likely to donate their possessions to the institution than otherwise to dispose of them. But, moreover, their vow of poverty not only precludes them from retaining this property within their own hands, but actually places all they possess at the disposal of the Father Superior, as declared by the "Rules," and as stated in the "Conferences," which are read when the sisters assume the habit.

A sister breaks the vow of poverty should she see upon the floor a pin or a needle, a piece of thread or cotton, or any other trifle, and fail to take care of it. Economy is carried even to parsimoniousness for the advancement of the order. Under this vow, a sister can not wish for any object, even though it be a new habit; in case that the one she wears has been worn threadbare, or is torn or patched, she must wait and be contented till another be given her.* The work from which the note below is taken was often quoted from for our edification.

When speaking of the habit, shoes, or any other article of apparel, a sister must not say "my habit, my shoes, or my pencil;" she is not permitted to consider herself the owner of any thing, not even of her own person. She must feel that she belongs, soul and body, to the service of the community; her will pertains to the Father Superior. The mistress of novices once told me that my body was not my own, but be-

* "The second degree of poverty," says the Roman Catholic Textbook for Nuns, "is to deprive yourself of whatever is superfluous, for the smallest superfluity will prevent a perfect union of the soul with God. St. Mary Magdalene de Pazzi went so far as to strip her little altar of all its ornaments except the crucifix. St. Theresa relates of herself that, knowing God to be most jealous of religious poverty, she could not 'recollect' herself in prayer so long as she retained any thing which she thought to be superfluous. If in your convent there is not a perfect community of property, endeavor at least to imitate the poverty practiced by the most exemplary and exact among your companions, as well in dress as in food and furniture. But you will perhaps say that whatever you possess is retained with the leave of the Superior. Permission to keep superfluities may save you from the punishments inflicted on '*proprietors*,' but will not secure to you the merit of perfect poverty. Again, you will perhaps say that you have no attachment to what you keep; but whether you have an attachment to it or not, the possession of what is not necessary will always prevent you from attaining the perfection of poverty. You may imagine that a certain sum of money or a certain amount of property will enable you to relieve the poor or to assist your companions, but I repeat that it is the nun who has nothing to give, and not the religious who has the means of distributing alms, that edifies the Church.

"ABOVE ALL, SEEK TO BE POOR IN MONEY."—St. Alphonsus Liguori. "*The Nun Sanctified;*" translated and published *for the use of English Nuns and Postulants.* 8vo. Dublin, 1848.

longed to the community. The community is called "our mother;" and every sister is bound to love and cherish it as a daughter.

Some of the sisters have constant hemorrhages from the lungs, and such are required to carry, wrapped in a pocket-handkerchief, a small square bottle, which is kept corked. This is used by all who raise blood even occasionally; for, should they use their handkerchiefs to wipe the blood from their mouths, it would be an infraction of the vow of poverty, as it would tend to wear them out, and also cause a waste of soap and a loss of time in washing them. The handkerchiefs used by the vow-sisters in the community-room are about thirty inches square; they are of fine linen, imported from France in the piece, and are cut so as to form a square according to the width of the piece. The novices, however, use cotton handkerchiefs.

The vow of poverty prohibits a sister from using any thing to gratify the senses, such as perfume; or to wear any ornament as such, or to partake of any luxuries, such as cake, preserves, custard, or whatever pleases the palate. Should any such article be offered, it must be refused. It is not allowable to *desire* to eat any thing but the most common food, and that only when given. A sister breaks her vow of poverty when she gets hungry and desires to eat between meals. At the table she must eat what is set before her or go without eating, and she is taught to take food only with a view to strengthen the body for the performance of duties, and to take no pleasure in it.

She may not accept the most trifling present from any one without permission of the Superior or the mistress of novices, nor can she give away any object without first obtaining permission. It is not allowed her to receive from a boarder even a flower, though it be presented by a pupil under her own tuition.

It is a mortal sin for a sister to use perfume, and the use of looking-glasses is entirely prohibited; not even the boarders are permitted to use them. They would sometimes keep a small piece concealed, and I have known some of them to bury their perfume-bottles in the play-ground, because it was a forbidden article.

One day, as I passed a boarder who had been arranging her hair, she said to me, in a playful manner, "Sister, what is this on my hair?" I stooped my head, and, smelling the perfume, smiled, but said nothing. An old sister, coming along at the time, observed the movement, and said, lifting up her hands in holy horror, "Why, sister, why did you not practice mortification?" It will be remembered that to touch or notice any person, even a boarder, in the way of a pleasing attention, or for any other purpose than the performance of the "duties" assigned, is a mortal sin. The person of a sister is considered sacred and holy, and this impression is to be made and kept in the minds of the boarders.

A few words in relation to our conduct toward the boarders of the academy may not be out of place here.

As a young novice, looking so sanctimonious, so sad and dejected, I was often regarded by the mischievous girls of the academy with doubt and incredulity as to my fitness for the life of a convent, and frequently they would say to me, "Sister, what did you come here for? Sister, you ought to be in the world; you can not be happy here; you will certainly die if you stay here; I believe you are dying with the consumption; you look like a saint, sister, but you are too young to be here; this is not the place for you," etc. Yet, though such kindly-meant remarks might be made to me by the boarders, it was never safe to communicate with them or to corroborate their surmises, lest it should reach the ear of the Superior, and bring upon me the infliction of penances as well as more strict confinement and more onerous "duties." Had I given to any one of them a hint of dissatisfaction, she might have repeated it in another class-room, or at least have allowed some allusion to escape, upon which I would have been immediately arraigned. The necessity of such strict surveillance over those sisters who have duties in the academy will at once appear. Any such intimation of dissatisfied feeling might alarm some boarder who was seriously thinking of entering the community; hence none but those whose exemplary conduct recommended them to the officers as reliable in this particular were permitted to teach the boarders.

To stop in the corridor for the purpose of looking at or smelling a flower, whose fresh bloom and delicate odor might occasionally tempt to a momentary indulgence of innocent enjoyment—this would be a loss of time, and thus would amount to a breach of the vow of poverty. Not an instant must be wasted in any sort of pleasurable occupation. Secular music is never allowed in the community. It is *work*, or *worship*—"duties" of some kind or other, and that *continu-*

ally. When lying upon the bed at night, every wakeful moment must be employed in meditations on the subject assigned before retiring, in the recitation of prayers, or in "making aspirations," that is, uttering some ejaculatory expression, such as "Sweet Jesus! Sweet Mother! Holy St. Joseph, pray for me! My blessed Mother! Holy Virgin! Mary my Mother!" etc.

Even during sickness, a sister is not permitted to have or to desire any article, such as ice, that might be grateful to the taste, and add to her comfort while the fever is upon her. Of this I will relate a single instance. It is that of the sick sister in the infirmary, by whose appearance I had been particularly struck during my postulancy, and who had subsequently been sent away from the institution. I now saw her again. She had been to Baltimore for the amputation of her arm, and while absent, prayers had been said for her, that she might survive the operation. She had now returned, the arm having been taken off below the elbow. I saw her in the infirmary, where I was also, ill. After my recovery I was put there on duty. Among others I attended her, dressing her arm, changing her clothes, and administering her medicine.

She was placed in a small room adjoining the main apartment, and was the only patient there, although the infirmary was not at that time full. It was the room that I have elsewhere mentioned as used for the purpose of a "dead room," bodies being laid out there previous to the funeral service in the chapel and the interment. At this period I slept in the infirmary. One night I was awoke by a furious storm that moaned and whistled round the building. Hearing steps in the passage near the infirmary door, I rose, and went to ascertain the cause. There is no door between the infirmary and the small room before alluded to, but the doors of both rooms open upon one passage, as before related. I saw a figure in white leaning against the wall. It was the poor sister, who had come out into the passage. She appeared exceedingly agitated and alarmed, and entreated me to accompany her to her room, stating that she had been so startled by extraordinary sounds that she should certainly die with terror. Supposing that the storm had thus frightened her, I went and remained with her till it was over; but she could not be pacified. She afterward declared that these noises had been heard before the storm, and were still repeated nightly; and as evening approached, she seemed in an agony of distress, beseeching me to procure a light for her. The room was, I think, the same with that in which had died the *religieuse* from whose coffin the sound of rapping appeared to proceed.

In assisting one day to change her clothes, I was surprised to observe a large swelling on her right side. I asked her the cause of it. She told me that she had been in the institution about eight months, when she was sent from the refectory one evening for some plates. She was bringing an armful from the kitchen, and was crossing the porch, covered at that time with ice and snow, when she stumbled and fell, her side striking across a tub which stood in her way, and thus the swelling had been occasioned. She had been sent to the infirmary, but nothing was done for her side—

no application whatever having been made to it. Her health had been bad ever since, and she had been repeatedly sent to the infirmary. I touched the lump, and it appeared to me like a projecting portion of bone. I continued to attend her for some weeks, and about a fortnight after I had left the infirmary she died. She was not allowed a light at night, though more than once she pleaded for it. She asked for ice to put in the water she drank, and was refused. I made the same request in her behalf, but could not obtain it. She solicited some little delicacies, such as a lemon and an apple, but they were denied her. No sick person is permitted to ask for any thing; I never dared do so when ill. The very things desired were generally the last to be granted.

This sister had a cough, and was, as I supposed, in the consumption. Her arm was never entirely healed. She was a native of Switzerland, and spoke broken English. She told me she had come to this country with her sister and her sister's husband from France. They placed her at St. Joseph's, and left her there; she had never seen or heard from them since. I inferred at the time that, in all probability, she had been wealthy, or had been brought there for some wrong motive, instead of being left at the Mother House in Paris; and she often expressed the wish that she had been so left, instead of being brought to this country. Some mystery was connected with her case. I frequently saw her weeping; she would refuse medicine, and say she did not wish to live. I helped to lay her body in the coffin; I watched by the side of it, and assisted two other novices in carrying it to the chapel door and placing it upon the bier. Under the weight of the burden in so doing, I was almost bent to the ground, and thought I should have fainted with the effort. This sister's name was Neomesia; her age I should judge to have been about twenty to twenty-three years.

CHAPTER XXVI.

VOWS OF CHASTITY AND OBEDIENCE.

THE other two vows, or obligations of CHASTITY and OBEDIENCE, when fully explained in their relations with the peculiar ideas inculcated by the priests concerning their breach and observance, will doubtless prove novel and startling to the unsophisticated denizens of "the world" without, to whom Jesuitical casuistry and doctrine are unknown pursuits of study. These vows will be treated in connection.

A sister or *religieuse* breaks the vow of chastity by looking a man or woman, and even a "sister," in the face, unless *required* by duty.* She must not

* St. Alphonsus Liguori, one of the most eminent saints of the Roman Catholic Church in modern times, in his work entitled "The Nun Sanctified," thus dilates on the "sanctification of the eyes:"

"A deliberate glance at a person of a different sex often enkindles an infernal spark which consumes the soul. The first dart which wounds and frequently robs chaste souls of life finds admission through the eyes. St. Bernard, after being a novice for a year, could not tell whether his cell was vaulted. In consequence of never raising his eyes from the ground, he never knew that there were but three windows in the church of the monastery in which he spent his novitiate. The saints were particularly cautious not to look at persons of a different sex. St. Hugh, bishop, when compelled to speak with women, never looked at them in the face. St. Clare would never fix her eyes on the face of a man; she was greatly afflicted because, when raising her eyes at the elevation to see the consecrated Host, she once invol-

raise her eyes to a sister, nor when speaking to or addressed by the Father Superior, her confessor, or any

untarily saw the countenance of the priest. St. Lewis Gonzaga never looked his own mother in the face. It is related of St. Arsenius that a noble lady went to visit him in the desert to beg of him to recommend her to God. When the saint perceived that his visitor was a woman, he turned away from her. She then said to him, 'Arsenius, since you will neither see nor hear me, at least remember me in your prayers.' 'No,' replied the saint, 'but I will beg of God to make me forget you, and never more to think of you.'

"From these examples," proceeds the saint, "may be seen the folly and temerity of some religious, who, though they have not the sanctity of a St. Clare, still gaze around from the terrace, in the parlor, and in the church, upon every object that presents itself, even on persons of a different sex; and notwithstanding their unguarded looks, they expect to be free from temptations and from the danger of sin. For having once looked deliberately at a woman who was gathering ears of corn, the Abbot Pastor was tormented *for forty years* by temptations against chastity. St. Gregory states that the temptation, to conquer which St. Benedict rolled himself in thorns, arose from one incautious glance at a female. St. Jerome, though living in a cave at Bethlehem in continual prayer and macerations of the flesh, was terribly molested by the remembrance of ladies whom he had long before seen in Rome. Why should not similar molestations be the lot of the religious who willfully and without reserve fixes her eyes on persons of a different sex? . . . . Father Manarco, when taking leave of St. Ignatius for a distant place, looked steadfastly in his face; for this look he was corrected by the saint. From the conduct of St. Ignatius on this occasion, we learn that it was not becoming in religious to fix their eyes on the countenance of a person even of the same sex, particularly if the person is young. But I do not see how looks at a young person of a different sex can be excused from the guilt of a venial fault, or even from mortal sin, when there is proximate danger of criminal consent.

"Except in looking at such objects (sacred images, etc.), a religious should in general keep the eyes cast down, and particularly in places where they may fall upon dangerous objects. In conversing with men, she should never roll the eyes about to look at them, and much less to look at them a second time.

"St. Francis of Assisium once said to his companion that he was

other priest. She must not suffer her thoughts to dwell upon any individual of the other sex. She must not touch a sister's hand, nor her habit, nor allow herself to be touched by another. Persons "in the world" she must neither look at nor touch, nor may she permit them to touch her hand or her habit. If allowed to see a father or a brother, she must not take his hand. Sisters may not see one another with their heads uncovered. A *religieuse* must renounce all curiosity, never look around her, nor through a window, nor toward a door when it is opened, to see who enters. She must walk through the cloisters and corridors with downcast eyes, and hands folded in her sleeves in front of her breast, passing and repassing the sisters without a word or a sign of recognition.

Should a sister be seen conversing with a boarder, she would be reported to the Superior, severely repri-

going out to preach. After walking through the town with his eyes fixed on the ground, he returned to the convent. His companion asked him when he would preach the sermon. 'We have,' replied the saint, 'by the modesty of our looks, given an excellent instruction to all who saw us.' It is related of St. Lewis Gonzaga that, when he walked through Rome, the students would stand in the streets to observe and admire his great modesty."

How unlike the real quality, we may add, is this sham modesty that says, *Come and see how modest we are!*

"To be faithful to her spouse," says St. Basil, "a virgin must be immaculate in her tongue by the delicacy of her language, *and by abstinence as much as possible from conversations with men;* she must be immaculate in the ears by shunning, like death itself, all worldly discourses; immaculate in her eyes by the modesty of her looks, always restrained so as never to fix them on the face of a man," etc.—*St. Basil, de Vera Virg.*

Injunctions of this character were frequently repeated to us by the priests and mistress of novices for our instruction.

manded, and assigned a penance. Often have I veiled, by a powerful effort, my unhappiness from the boarders, but they could not help observing and marking at times the paleness of my countenance, which bore traces of the agony that shook at times my very soul. Yet I durst not appear otherwise than calm and collected, nor say one word about the cause of my unhappiness, nor even raise my eyes, while walking through the academy.

Sometimes, indeed, I would venture to answer the voice of some gentle girl, who would speak to me in passing, and whose sunny smile would cheer my sad and lonely heart, but from the clasp of whose hand I would be forced to recoil as from a serpent's touch. I was narrowly watched, and frequently reported as guilty of "impropriety," and many a reprimand have I received for speaking on such an occasion, or for suffering my hand to be taken, or my waist encircled by the arm of a pupil, an offense which would be reported by spies of the community, who are ever on the alert. Indeed, the rule requires that any such transgression be avowed in confession, and that penance be solicited in expiation of it.

But in regard to the observance of these and all other rules, it must be borne in mind that, should the Superior at any time command the contrary, the sister must OBEY. Should a priest, and particularly a priest of the Order of St. Lazare, take her hand, with whatever intention, she may not withdraw it. *The vow of* OBEDIENCE *here has supremacy over the vow of chastity.*

Should her thoughts go out into the world, should

memory call up a friend of the other sex, should the mind overleap prescribed limits, especially with reference to a priest, she must make known that thought at the confessional. Yet if the Superior, her confessor, or any other Lazarist, should direct her thoughts to such topics, she would be commendable in so doing, for she would prove her obedience.

In the books of the "Conferences," so called, which are occasionally read to the community, particular directions are given by the founder concerning the vows, rules, and regulations of the sisterhood. These books are kept locked in a mahogany box, and are only taken out to be read to the community during annual retreat. When reading these "Conferences," as translated from the French original, I have frequently been made to blush at what I was reading. In one of these books the sisters are told not to fall in love with a priest; but should they do so, to tell him of it, and obtain his advice. Should a sister on a mission chance to entertain such feelings toward a priest, she is instructed at once to inform the Superior, and ask for a change of place. Sometimes this request is granted.

And here I would solicit the earnest and candid attention of the reader to the infamous craft exercised in these regulations. A young girl, thoughtlessly betrayed into an infraction of the rules, such as that just mentioned, discloses her error as required. The priest thus informed can either take advantage of her confession or not, as he may feel inclined, or as his judgment of the character of the sister may determine. Sometimes policy will induce him to express a holy horror at the offense, with a view to the exalting of his own superior sanctity, and this especially if he should entertain an aversion for the penitent, or should he deem her an unsuitable subject for his purposes. On the other hand, should his own evil heart suggest to him the moral destruction of this sister, how great the advantage he possesses for its accomplishment, in view of this doctrine of passive and meritorious obedience.

In a word, the sisters are taught that their vow of OBEDIENCE is supreme; that the expressed will of the Superior must be regarded as the voice of God, and *that in case the vow of chastity be violated by those exercising authority over them, no sin can be imputed to themselves, because they are doing right by maintaining inviolate the vow of* OBEDIENCE.*

* If the testimony of personal observation on this subject needs to be confirmed, it will only be requisite to quote a few words from the highest authorities. "The principal and most efficacious means of practicing the obedience due to superiors," says St. Alphonsus Liguori, "and of rendering it meritorious before God, is to consider that, in obeying them, we obey God himself, and that by despising their commands we despise the authority of our divine Master, who has said of superiors, 'He that heareth you, heareth me.' When, then, a religious receives a precept from her prelate, superior, or confessor, she should immediately execute it, not only to please men, but principally to please God, whose will is made known to her by their commands. In obeying their directions, she is more certain of doing the will of God *than if an angel came down from heaven to manifest his will to her.*

"It may be added that there is more certainty of doing the will of God by obedience to superiors, *than by obedience to Jesus Christ,* should he appear in person and give his commands. Because, should Jesus Christ appear to a religious, she would not be certain whether it was he that spoke or an evil spirit, who, under the appearance of the Redeemer, wished to deceive her. . . . In a word, the only way by which a religious can become a saint, and be saved, is TO OBSERVE

HER RULE; FOR HER THERE IS NO OTHER WAY THAT LEADS TO SALVATION!"

Awful blasphemy! Yet Jesus said, "I am the way; no man cometh to the Father but by me."

"The fourth and last degree of perfect obedience," observes this saint elsewhere, "is to obey with simplicity. . . . St. Mary Magdalene de Pazzi says that '*perfect obedience requires a soul without a will, and a will without an intellect.*' . . . . To regard as good *whatever* superiors command is the *blind obedience* so much praised by the saints, and is the duty of every religious. . . . . To try the obedience of their subjects, superiors sometimes impose commands that are *inexpedient, and even absurd.* St. Francis commanded his disciples *to plant cabbages with their roots uppermost.* He obliged Brother Matthew to continue turning round till he fell to the ground."

Copious directions are given to nuns by St. Alphonsus as to the necessity of blindly following the confessor. "Obey him, then," he says, "not as man, but as God, and *you shall never err.* In the beginning of his conversion, St. Ignatius of Loyola was so violently assailed by scruples, and so encumbered with darkness, that he found no peace. But because he had true faith in the word of God (*he that heareth you heareth me*), he said, with great confidence, 'Lord, show me the way in which I ought to walk, and, though you should give me a dog for my guide, I will faithfully follow him.'"

But lest it be supposed that any exercise of judgment be allowed the nun as to what is divine guidance and what is not, St. Alphonsus takes care to add: "To nuns who begin to censure the decisions of their confessors, we ought to say what the learned Monsignior Sperelli wrote to a religious who had accused him of heresy because he had said that the sins which she had confessed were not sins. 'Tell me,' said the learned bishop to her, 'in what university have you studied theology, that you know better than your confessor how to decide on sin? Ah! go to spin, and do not give ear to such follies.'"

Such are the perils of a loose morality—should we not rather say of a gross immorality?—to which a young girl is exposed, in our own Christian land, who gives herself to the guidance of corrupt and corrupting priests. The voice of conscience, that monitor of God's own appointment in every human bosom, is silenced by the vile utterance of a sinful man. The "more sure word of prophecy," which God has put into our hands as all-sufficient for doctrine, for reproof, for correction, for instruction in righteousness, that the man of God might be perfect, thoroughly furnished unto every good work, is laid aside for the authority of the confessional and the lying wonders of tradition.

CHAPTER XXVII.

MORALS AT ST. JOSEPH'S.

As the result of these pernicious and utterly demoralizing doctrines, a lamentable state of things, I grieve to say, existed among a portion of the community at St. Joseph's. It was some time—so little suspicion of the truth was entertained—before I understood and appreciated the symptoms of the evil that raged around me. When, at length, the light dawned upon my mind, it was accompanied by a shock as of electricity, that paralyzed me for the moment. I almost doubted the evidence of my senses; but with the reaction came the strong resolution to leave at all hazards the precincts of such an establishment; a resolution only hastened in its accomplishment by subsequent events.

And here let me add—for I would not be so misunderstood—that I have no intention to include the whole sisterhood in one sweeping charge of immorality. Far from it. Many are unquestionably pure in their feelings and sincere in their desires to serve God, however mistaken and ill founded the views which they have learned to entertain. Many would be glad to be freed from their bonds, and, like a liberated bird, sing rejoicingly at their release; but others are infatuated with their lot, and no inducement could be offered that would tempt them to leave it.

Infractions of moral duty and departures from rectitude are the legitimate consequences of the system from which they spring, and whatever errors may be committed by the sisters are justly chargeable to the reverend guides and directors who inculcate such mischievous tenets.*

* That the Church of Rome knows well the danger rising from the confessional, and the law of blind obedience, to priest and penitent both, is clear from her instructions on the subject addressed to confessors. Thus Dens's work on Moral Theology, the text-book at Maynooth and at other Roman Catholic seminaries, has a clause on just causes for permitting feelings of a sensual nature. And here it is distinctly stated that just causes of this sort are the hearing of confessions ; the reading of cases of conscience drawn up for a confessor ; necessary or useful attendance on an invalid. "The effect of a just cause is such," he proceeds to say, "that any thing from which such sentiments arise may be not only lawfully begun, but also lawfully continued ; and so the confessor, receiving those sentiments from the hearing of confessions, ought not, on that account, to abstain from hearing them, but has a just cause for persevering ; provided, however, that they always displease him, and there arise not therefrom the proximate danger of consent." And the theologian proceeds to mention cases in which confessors, in the performance of their office, were accustomed to fall into sin as often as two and three times in a month ; adding, that it is the duty of the confessor, in such a case, notwithstanding, to persevere in the discharge of his calling ! See *Dens*, tom. i., p. 299, 300, Coyne's Dublin edition, 1832.

But more than this : St. Thomas Aquinas, "the Angelic Doctor," states as a thesis, that "a 'religious,' violating the three primary articles of his rule, viz., poverty, chastity, and obedience, sins *mortally*." This thesis, however, is not laid down to be maintained, but to be disproved, and St. Thomas proceeds so to do :

"The state of a 'religious' is a *safe* state.

"But a 'religious' is exposed to many temptations to break his rules, and if to break his rules were mortal sin, then the state of a 'religious' would be dangerous instead of safe.

"THEREFORE it is *not mortal sin* for a 'religious' to transgress his rules !"—*St. Thomas Aquinas*, Secunda Secundæ, Quæst. clxxxvi., art. 9.

The power conferred upon the fathers by the rite of confession affords them great facilities to accomplish their purposes. The highest importance is given to a strict and punctual attendance at the confessional, which may truly be denominated the throne of the Roman Catholic ecclesiastic; for there, armed with the assumed authority of God, in whose stead he officiates on earth to the suppliant slaves prostrate before him, he deals the terrible anathema of the Church to the disobedient and refractory, dispenses his "absolution" to the faithful and submissive, and awards the "penance" to be observed in expiation for sin. Seated at the confessional, he is empowered, by virtue of his self-arrogated position, to propound queries which, from the lips of others, would be deemed flagrant insults. Kneeling there, the young maiden answers questions calculated to eradicate every feeling of modesty, woman's highest charm, and lays bare to the inquisitive search of her "spiritual director" every secret thought, every incipient emotion, every impulse of her being. How easy, then, for an evil-disposed confessor stealthily to infuse into the innocent and trusting heart, taught to consider blind obedience a virtue, thoughts, whose growth, cherished by his daily care, shall soon fill it with a diseased vegetation. If any distrust betray itself—if any hesitation appear to the answering of these artfully-framed inquiries, the objector is readily quieted by an assurance that it is the confessor's duty, for her soul's sake, to propound these queries; that he is the authorized medium of communication between her soul and Heaven; that he occupies the place of the Almighty in reference to her spiritual wants and requirements, and must be so regarded if she wishes to avoid purgatorial fires and secure future felicity. Is it, then, a matter of wonder, that those brought up within the pale of this Church, and whose every thought and feeling from childhood to maturity has been watched and directed by such a "spiritual guide," should yield themselves entirely to his control, and even see no danger in their abject submissiveness, nor evil purpose in his exercise of unlimited power?

But if "in the world," as it is technically termed, the confessional may be such a source of perilous and demoralizing influence to the youthful mind, and so potent an agency for the subserviency of guilty designs, it may easily be conceived that in a religious community, whose members are secluded from public observation, and given over, bodily and spiritually, to the charge of priests, its control must be more absolute, and more unscrupulously exercised.* Shut up and

* This inevitable result is eloquently set forth by the able author of *Mornings with the Jesuits at Rome.* "In these nunneries," he says, speaking of the convents of Tuscany, "there are sometimes thirty, sometimes forty, sometimes fifty, and in many even one hundred nuns. And these nunneries have almost always convents near them, more or less large, for those monks who are to be the confessors of those nuns. And living, as these nuns always do, in a state of seclusion and dullness; living, as they do, a life of hopelessness and monotony, without the interests of mothers, for they have no children; without the interests of children, for they have no parents; without the interests of sisters, for they have no brothers; without the interests of wives, for they have no husbands, they are thrown upon their own confessors for society. And the visits of the monks from the adjoining convents break the tedium of their lives; break in and while away their hours of idleness, bring to them the gossip of the neighborhood, and reveal to them the news of the outer world. And the result is, that from the rising

deprived of intercourse or communication, even by letter, with parents, relations, and friends, and taught by the invariable law of human instinct to seek direction and sympathy from other minds, the inmates of these institutions submit implicitly to the guidance of their confessor, and regard his injunctions and admonitions as "oracles divine." To him they resort in every trifling difficulty; to him they go with every petty trouble; and accustomed to view him as a wise arbiter and an infallible monitor, no limit, at least, is placed to their confidence and obedience until they become the pitiable victims of their black-robed and black-hearted betrayers.

My recollections of my novitiate at St. Joseph's will ever be associated with a feeling of contempt and abhorrence for those men who use their advantage of rank and position to the basest ends, and with deep thankfulness for my own escape from their insidious snares. It was a contemplation of the peril to which I was exposed that first suggested the idea of escape, at any risk, from the institution. I could have borne toil, privation, and bodily maltreatment as the consequences of my own rashness and ill-advised impetuosity, but the future wore too dark and terrible an as-

to the setting of the sun, the visits of these monkish confessors are the objects looked for in the morning, and remembered in the evening. Now it is only in human nature to suppose that, under such circumstances, attachments may spring up between the younger nuns and the younger monks. It is no unkindness, it is no scandal to say it—it is only what nature seems to dictate. The real unkindness, the real scandal is that the Church of Rome interposes a law, and forbids the consecrating of these attachments by the bonds of holy wedlock."—Rev. Mr. HOBART SEYMOUR, *in a Lecture on "Convents or Nunneries," at Bath, Eng., June 7th,* 1852.

pect, that I should resign myself with quietness to its horrors. Although the conversations and the acts of individual members of the community, the secret mysteries of the confessional, and other circumstances besides, were ample evidence to my own judgment of the alarming position I occupied, yet, as it may be contended by those interested in concealing the truth that my mental vision was distorted, and that my prejudices were too strong to admit of a calm, dispassionate induction from what I saw and heard, I feel most reluctantly compelled to state an incident concerning which there can be no misconception.

A priest, who had been engaged in exercising his pastoral functions at St. Joseph's, was about to leave the institution, and, as is customary, the sisters were directed to enter the room where he was stationed, and ask a blessing at his hand previous to his departure. When my turn came, I went in, with downcast eyes and clasped hands, as required, and knelt to receive the expected benediction. But instead of the pressure of his hand upon my head, I felt the impression of a kiss upon my forehead. Startled and confused by a salutation so unexpected and inappropriate, I staggered to my feet, and ejaculated, almost unconsciously, the words, "Oh! Father!" But before I could recover my composure, seizing my wrist with his left hand, and encircling my waist with his right arm, he drew me toward him, and imprinted several kisses on my face before I was able to break from his revolting embrace. Yet I was compelled, from prudential fears of the consequences, to be silent respecting this insulting treatment. What could I do? to whom should I

apply for redress and protection? If I had complained to the mistress of novices or to the Mother Superior of the outrage to which I had been subjected, I should have been denounced as a base calumniator of the "*holy father*," and punished for the offense. There was nothing left but to wait in silence for some other means of redress.

"*I must quit this place!*" These words were now continually in my mind. But how? was a question difficult to be answered. I could not communicate with my family through the authorities of the institution. This privilege had been denied me before, and I had suffered on account of my expressed desire to do so. Having experienced the evil results of the failure of this first attempt, I feared to make a second effort, lest worse should follow, and a stricter surveillance be kept over me. I could not procure the transmission of a letter by means of the boarders, even had I been enabled to write one without detection, for all the letters they send home are examined and read. This method of communication had been attempted by others, but the plans were discovered and the offending sisters punished. A secret escape was the sole alternative, and this I resolved, if possible, to accomplish. I was fully aware of the difficulties in the way, and the fearful issue of a failure; but this thought only nerved me for the trial, and led me to use every exertion that secresy and caution could suggest to insure success. Having formed the determination, my first endeavor was to banish all traces of nervousness and anxiety from my features, and compose them into an expression of calmness and resignation, that no mistrust of my intention might be entertained. This effected, I patiently awaited a favorable opportunity to execute my design.

CHAPTER XXVIII.

RELATIONS OF THE LAZARIST PRIESTS TO THE SISTERHOOD.

In the books of the "Conferences," to which I have already referred, the founder directs that a priest shall not be permitted to enter the apartments of the community unless accompanied by a sister. The devil, he remarks, is always at work, and even angels have fallen; and yet the novices are accustomed to sleep in cells with curtains instead of doors! Farther, it is forbidden that a sister should see a priest alone in a parlor; there must always be two. Nor is it allowed that she should visit a priest alone; yet she may remain at the confessional for any length of time alone with her confessor—nay, she may see him in his own room in case of indisposition. In fact, the priests do often enter the rooms of the sisters, and remain there for a considerable time; nor is any one permitted to open the door (for the rooms of the vowed sisters have doors) or enter the room during their stay.

When the Father Superior enters the room of the Lady Superior, should a sister be present at the time, it is her duty to withdraw at once; nor is any one allowed to enter while he remains.

A sister never enters the room of the Father Superior so long as there is another sister in his room. There is one who attends to his door, and informs the applicant whether he be engaged. When a sister is particularly anxious to see him, she writes her name upon a slate, and is sent for at his option.

Sisters are also advised, in the "Conferences," not to attend persons of their own sex when solicited to do so in certain cases of sickness while on their missions "in the world," lest they might have bad thoughts.

One day, while on duty in the room of a professed sister, I heard groans proceeding from an apartment nearly opposite, and noticed the infirmarian passing up and down before the room. I was then commanded to close the door opening into the passage, in order to prevent the sound from reaching a neighboring corridor, which led to the building occupied by the community. Having done so, I returned to the duty in which I was engaged.

After a few minutes I was called by the infirmarian to the medicine-room. She said to me, "Be quick, and pour out ten drops from that vial," pointing to one in the medicine-case. In my agitation and alarm, instead of dropping the liquid, I poured it out with a trembling hand—I knew not how much, perhaps a tea-spoonful. With this I was sent to the sister's room, and administered it as directed. The sister was propped up with pillows, extending from the shoulder downward. She was deadly pale, with dark circles around the eyes, as I have seen persons appear after convulsions. Her feet were resting against the foot of the bed, as if for support. The infirmarian soon followed me into the room, and I saw no other person there. I retired at once, and resumed my duty with the sick sister in the opposite room. A short time after, I heard a priest's voice in the apartment in question, but did not distinguish the conversation. The groans increased until they became shrieks, at intervals of about ten minutes, and then more frequent, until almost continuous, when they ceased altogether.

This happened in the course of an afternoon, including a period of about four hours. I left the sister's room opposite about three hours and a half subsequent to my hearing the first groan, and when in the infirmary below could plainly hear the shrieks described.

I had never seen this sister before, except two or three times within a month previous to this occurrence, when I had noticed her accidentally in the same room as I passed the door. On those occasions she was sitting in a rocking-chair, dressed in a loose wrapper. After this I saw her occasionally, at first in bed, and later in a chair. Shortly after, my duties in the infirmary ceased, having continued only some seven weeks, and I saw no more of her. This took place about three months before I left the institution; after this I visited the infirmary but occasionally, when sent on transient duties.

Shrinking as I do most painfully from the statement of any thing that may seem to throw a shade upon the perfect sanctity of those retreats, where I myself long imagined the very embodiment of excellence to dwell, the task I have conscientiously undertaken compels me to withhold nothing that shall acquaint my countrymen with the reality of those dangers to which their daughters may be exposed within these guarded precincts. It has been my duty to declare, for their warning and determent, some part at least of that which I have seen and heard as a personal witness. Yet I can not bring myself to recount in detail the instances of undue familiarity which have fallen under my own notice, and the evidences of it that have forced themselves upon my own conviction. I hasten to close what it has been necessary to state on this subject.

When I first visited the institution, before entering the community, I had in my possession a letter which I had been told to deliver at once upon my arrival into the hands of the priest. Accordingly, it being about nine o'clock in the evening, I asked to see him. The sister who was present, raising her hands and eyes to heaven in holy horror, exclaimed, "A priest does not remain here at this hour of night—never!"

After my entrance into the community, as I was one day walking upon the corridor, I saw a room adjoining the priest's room, through a window which looked out upon the corridor. In that room I saw a bed. And I know that a priest once slept there, for I heard it said that it was too cold for him to come so early in the morning to say first mass. I have also heard priests walking through the institution at night. I am convinced, from these and other considerations, that priests do sleep there.

I was invited one evening to go with some six or eight vowed sisters to a place called the Grotto. This is a spot surrounded by lattice-work, in the centre of which stands a statue of the Virgin. There are seats around it, and a delicious spring of water gushes forth near by. Soon after we entered, an Italian Lazarist, or priest of the corresponding institution of St. Lazare,* came into our midst and took a seat. The sisters clustered around him, kneeling, and conversing freely with him. Looking up earnestly into his face, they would exclaim, "O father!" with a tone almost of adoration. I know of no words to express the intensity of feeling thus manifested, beaming from every countenance, and exhibited in their actions; fascination does not seem strong enough to convey the idea. Had the Savior himself been present in person before them, they could hardly have shown more reverence and love. Every soul appeared to gaze upon him with its most ardent affection.

* The "Catholic Almanac" for 1855, in a list of the religious institutions of the archdiocese of Baltimore, illustrates very forcibly and pithily, in the following extracts, the connection between these two establishments. We quote verbatim:

"ST. JOSEPH'S SISTERHOOD, Emmettsburg, Md.

"This is the Mother-House of the Sisters of Charity in the United States.

"Very Rev. F. Burlando, *Ecclesiastical Superior.*
Rev. H. Gandolfo, *Chaplain.*
Sr. M. Etienne Hall, *Mother Superior.*"

"CONGREGATION OF THE MISSION, Emmettsburg, Md.

"Very Rev. Francis Burlando, C. M.
Rev. Hippolytus Gandolfo, C. M."

CHAPTER XXIX.

MONTHLY AND ANNUAL RETREAT.

ON a particular Sunday of every month there is observed at St. Joseph's a "*monthly retreat.*" That day is spent in prayer and meditation, in spiritual reading, in saying the litanies of the Holy Ghost and the blessed Virgin, in "preparation for death," and other religious exercises, terminating with a "repetition of the meditations" made in the course of the day.

These meditations are divided into three periods. The "repetition" of them consists in kneeling at the centre of the room before the assembled sisterhood, and repeating the thoughts that have occupied the mind during each period given to meditation throughout the day, all of which is rehearsed for the edification of the community.

Those gifted with a ready flow of language of course make beautiful "repetitions," as they can easily fabricate them for the occasion; but others not so endowed will naturally blunder through the performance in such a manner as often to excite the risible sensations of their hearers. All alike, however, conclude with the following formula: "I will place my resolutions in the sacred heart of Jesus," or "of Mary;" "I will practice some virtue, and the resolutions I have made for future conduct." Then kissing the floor, the sister returns to her seat. No one is allowed to speak during the whole day, save as called upon in this exercise.

The "preparation for death," a formulary read aloud to the community, is calculated to produce emotions of intense grief, anxiety, and distress, amounting almost to derangement. I have seen sisters weep and tremble, and have heard them groan as if in the deepest agony of mind. These demonstrations are considered highly commendable, and are particularly encouraged. My own feelings were never thus manifested, for the reason that I felt as though I could welcome death with all its bitterness. It had no fears for me, and especially since my mother's death I have had little desire to live.

These readings commence as follows: "Let me die, O my God! let me die! Let my body be eaten by worms, in punishment for my pride," etc., etc.

On the days which are thus occupied by special observances, the regular work and "duties" of the establishment must be dispatched with great speed, to allow time for these unusual engagements; and if not accomplished in due season, they must be finished after night prayers.

The Lady Superior does not go into this retreat. It is made by the novices in the novitiate-room, and by the professed in the community-room. No one can leave the room on these occasions for any purpose whatsoever.

The monthly exercises which I have here described, attended as they are with such evidences of great depression of spirits, and exhausting as they do the physical energies, are not the only seasons when these effects are apparent. In the *daily* meditation similar scenes not unfrequently occur. Upon one occasion, during meditation in the chapel, a sister, overcome by her feelings, fell to the floor, and, striking against a settee, cut her face in a shocking manner, so that she was at once taken to the infirmary. Fainting and falling to the floor are no uncommon events during the meditation-hour. When a fast-day happens upon the day of the monthly retreat, the exercises prove especially exhausting.

The "ANNUAL RETREAT" is a period lasting from eight to ten days, and spent in silent prayer and meditation in the chapel, during which time not a word is spoken. Several priests are in constant attendance to hear confessions.

The "meditations" during this retreat are very exciting. Frequently will the sisters break forth into screams; often, faint and worn out with prayer, vigils, and penances, many of them become ill, and are sent to the infirmary. One of these meditations, the subject of which was "a sister in hell," seemed sufficient of itself to cause insanity. It was awful in the extreme. It represented a sister who had broken her holy rules and vows, as asked by the Lord after death for her habit, when she would scream and say, "Give me back my holy habit!" but would be thrown into hell to howl and rave with the devils.

During this annual retreat the Superior gives "conferences" in the chapel, consisting of discourses or lectures on such topics as the three vows—Poverty, Chastity, and Obedience; and the three virtues which are to be practiced in connection with these—Humility, Charity, and Simplicity.

A *general confession* is made in the course of this annual retreat. On this occasion the sisters have the choice of their confessors, for there are several Lazarist priests who are invited to the institution for that purpose. Sometimes the sisters will remain at the confessional for two hours, and leave it weeping. I have seen them enter the confessional much agitated; often they will lean against the wall for support.

During one of these retreats, which happened while I was in the institution, I was, of course, obliged to resort with the rest to confession. I went into a little chapel on one side of the "sanctuary," entered the confessional, and knelt before the lattice-work. The priest drew the curtain that covered it on the opposite side; then, walking to the window, raised the curtain, so that the light shone directly in my face; and seating himself at the confessional, with his head resting on his hand, and close to the bars, said, "Sister, draw aside your veil, that I may see whether your countenance betokens sorrow for your sins." I complied reluctantly, and commenced the *Confiteor*—"I confess," etc.

When I had repeated this, he asked me how old I was; how long I had been in the institution; why I entered it; if I was in love with any one when I entered; if I loved any one then, and whether it was a person in the world, or one consecrated to God. Of course I was unprepared for questions of this nature, and, instead of answering them, said, "Father, I am ready for confession." He then remarked, "When I entered the community (that of St. Lazare), I thought I had done much for God, but now I find that I have done nothing." He proceeded to counsel me to imitate the example of St. Theresa. "You must persevere," he added, "in the service of God; it is a blessed thing for a young person early to devote herself to the service of God, and enter such an institution." He bade me open my heart to him, and tell him every thought and feeling. I should state that this priest was about twenty-three or four years of age.

This conversation continued for a length of time, and I became exceedingly fatigued in my kneeling posture. I mentioned this to the priest, begging that he would defer my confession till some other time. Had I not done so, I know not how long he would have kept me in the confessional. When I had promised him to come again on the following morning, he permitted me to leave, telling me that in the mean time I must think of him and pray for him. I saw this priest but once again as he was passing through the institution. One evening, shortly after this incident, I met a "vowed sister" walking upon the corridor. She inquired of me, "Have you been to confession? and to whom?" I told her; and she then asked, "Did he put many questions to you?" I replied that he did. The next day I observed that she went to confession to this priest, and no doubt she was highly pleased, for she remained in the confessional three hours. Probably she wished to go to a person who would address to her such questions as she would take satisfaction in answering. This sister was a French person, and one whom I had often noticed in the corridor conversing with the priests; she also frequently visited their apartment. I have many times seen her and others walking in the passage on the ground floor, as the priests passed to and from their room. Repeatedly have I observed the vowed sisters with the priests, walking up and down this passage, talking and laughing with them, and retiring with them to their room. Sometimes, when the door chanced to open, I have seen one of them in a kneeling posture before the priest, and talking with him.

Sometimes one or two priests and several sisters take supper together in the community-room, and I have overheard them talking and laughing in a very loud tone. On one occasion I was asked by a professed sister to visit with her the house for the Lazarists in Emmettsburg, but I was not permitted to go near that place.

The sisters frequently went to St. Lazare. This building belongs to the institution, and is about a mile distant. During vacation several of the sisters spend their time there. They have a very beautiful chapel in the house, where they perform their devotions. Novices are not permitted to visit here, but the priests are allowed this privilege. I visited the place three times in my occasional carriage-drives, and once breakfasted there. I have never heard that any other novice did so.

In addition to the lectures given by the Superior in the chapel, conferences are also *read* at these annual retreats by a sister who stands at a table. In the retreat which I attended about three months before my escape, the Father Superior, during one of these conferences, took occasion to expatiate on the troubles that threatened the Church, remarking that there were enemies who were endeavoring to destroy its servants; that the Pope was fearful that the avowed opponents of the Church were about to make a determined effort to break down its power and destroy its institutions. He appeared extremely solicitous about this danger, and requested the prayers of the sisters that the Church might be protected from these anticipated efforts. I did not then comprehend his meaning, for he seemed to refer to a special movement of which I knew nothing; but, since my departure from St. Joseph's, I have concluded that he made allusion to the American movement, which I have learned was at that time rapidly growing and gaining strength throughout our country. Nor do I imagine that any other sister understood the allusion, as we were never permitted to see a newspaper, except occasionally one lying on the Lady Superior's table, which it was not allowed to read or touch. I have, however, seen the Lady Superior attentively reading newspapers.

At the close of the annual retreat, the sisters are invited to come to the Lady Superior's room, where she presents them each with a picture; to some she gives more than one, and sometimes a "Litany" in French or English. From the Lady Superior's room they repair to the Father Superior, before whom they kneel, and obtain his blessing. He questions them as to the manner in which they have passed the retreat, their feelings, etc., and encourages them to keep more strictly their holy vows and rules. Sometimes, too, he presents some of them with a picture, a rosary, a medal, or other small gift.

CHAPTER XXX.

ANOTHER VICTIM.

It was very shortly after the annual retreat, the nature of which I have now explained, that a letter was one day received by the Mother Superior from a young lady, whose parents resided in Virginia. As she had been a particular acquaintance of mine, I was summoned to the Superior's presence, and the letter was handed to me. It had already been opened and read, doubtless by the Superior, whose practice it was to do so whenever a letter was sent to any member of the institution. After reading the contents, which were addressed to me, inquiring how I liked the life of the sisterhood; if I was happy; what were the duties; whether I thought the writer competent to perform them; and expressing a desire to enter a religious house, the Superior put certain questions to me respecting this young lady. She asked me if her father and mother were living, how many children they had, if they were wealthy, if she was accomplished and pretty, etc. These interrogatories being answered to her satisfaction, she directed me to sit down and write in reply, "Come and see." "Tell her," she added, "that I invite her to visit the institution; say that you are happy and contented;" in short, she dictated a letter which I wrote, and handed to her on the spot.

Three or four weeks elapsed, and I was again sent for to come to the Superior's room. I observed on entering that there was a lady present; but, not being allowed to raise my eyes to her countenance, could not distinguish her particularly. The Superior said to me as I advanced, "Sister, do you know this young lady?" I raised my eyes, and behold it was my friend. Very coldly and calmly I replied, "Yes, mother." Upon this my friend sprang toward me with outstretched arms. I drew back, my hands clasped upon my breast, according to the rules. The Superior meantime closely watching me, I did not allow my friend to touch me, but looked at her calmly, as though it were no surprise or delight for me to behold her again. In all this concealment and repression of feeling we were trained; and they who best perform their part, and exhibit least emotion, are most highly commended, while such as are unable to govern the natural outbursts of affection are required to do penance.

My friend, evidently grieved and wounded at this cold reception, after a short pause, asked me how I liked the religious life, and whether I was happy. The Superior, too, put similar questions; to all of which I dared make no other reply than that I was delighted with the mode of life; that the duties were easy, and such as she could readily perform; and that I was perfectly happy. After this the Superior told me to leave, and I accordingly retired to my duties.

The next day, at recreation-hour, I was permitted to go and see my friend, accompanied by an elder sister, and I then learned the state of her mind. She was in raptures with the place; and after some conversation with her, I was sent for by the Superior to report these expressions of her feelings. After supper I again saw her, and we had another conversation in company with an elder sister; and, as I had been instructed, I endeavored to increase her interest in the institution.

On the following day she went into a "religious retreat." Two days subsequent, while on my way with the community to chapel, in my place in the *rank*, or order of procession, I was sent for by the Lady Superior. Somewhat alarmed, I hurried to her room, and was ordered to have the dinner of the young lady taken to her apartment. I was told to give directions for a "nice dinner," as, for some reason which I did not learn, the young lady had not dined. I waited on her at table, and, though she pressed me to partake, I durst not do so, as it is against the rules to eat with a person of "the world." There was, besides, an officer sitting in the apartment adjoining, with the door partly open: this door had a glass sash, and the officer was doubtless placed there for the purpose of watching me. The dinner was not such as we ordinarily partook of, but of a tempting character, such as we never saw in the refectory.

Dinner over, I reported to the Superior what had been said by my friend at the table; among other remarks, that she "had come prepared to enter the community," which seemed greatly to gratify the Superior; and that "the only tie that now bound her to the world was her affection for her parents, and particularly for her father; but this difficulty she intended to settle by ascertaining from the priest her true vocation." This news greatly pleased the Lady Superior; and it was arranged that my friend should visit the priest—the Father Superior—that same afternoon. I was appointed to accompany her to the presence of the father, who was duly informed of this conversation; and when she made her appearance in his room, he seemed delighted to see her. He took her hand as I passed, and said, pointing to me, "You see we never shake hands with a sister."

I staid a few moments in the room, until, at a signal from the priest, I left, having first obtained his blessing. I went to the novitiate, and there watched the door leading to the priest's room to see my friend come out. I did so, not by order from the Superior, but from my own anxiety to know whether, after this interview, she would still remain determined to enter the house, and with but a faint hope that she might not be prevailed upon to do so. From that interview, however, she went directly to her own room. During recreation after supper, I was sent to visit her with an elder sister, being directed to conduct her over the beautiful grounds of the Superior to a fine grove of trees, in the midst of which there is a mound covered with shrubbery. Upon this mound stands a very large cross, surrounded by symbols of the passion—the serpent, the ladder, the hammer, the sponge, the spear, the crown of thorns, the scourge, etc. This last was painted to represent blood upon it. At the foot of the cross there was a statue of the Virgin Mary, upon which the sisters, when permitted to walk over the grounds, sometimes put wreaths of flowers, and before which they make their orisons. The stillness and seclusion of the spot, the perfume of flowers, the balmy atmosphere, the solemn and holy calm, gave to this place the charm of an earthly paradise. It is called "Our Lady of the Fields;" and hither the priests frequently resort to sit in quiet, decorating the statue, or employing themselves as they please.

On the next evening I was again called to the Lady Superior's room. My friend was there, clothed in a black dress, with the officers of the institution standing around her. The Superior commanded me to lead her to the novitiate and introduce her to the mistress of novices, whom she had not yet seen. It is usually the duty of an officer to take a postulant into the novitiate, but an exception was made in this instance. My friend was much agitated. I left her with the mistress of novices, to whom I communicated my errand.

Her first duties were in the refectory. Often have I seen her carrying plates and other crockery on a large "round"—a circular piece of wood with a handle—to and from the basement-room below. Once I saw her crying with the great exertion required in this duty, and the pain it occasioned her.

After this I frequently saw her in tears, and sometimes going in that condition to the Father Superior's room. I noticed that she looked delicate, and wonderfully changed in appearance. She used to be called upon to read aloud on successive days, for a week at a time, during dinner and supper, out of the Lives of the Saints, the Roman Martyrology, and other books—a duty which the mistress of novices, who never entertained any special regard for me, desired me to perform, but the Superior would not indulge her in this wish. At other times, and in addition to this duty, she was obliged to wait upon the table. Once she was sent to the infirmary in consequence of a cold taken from sleeping in the dormitory without sufficient covering in winter, and when I left she was again there.

CHAPTER XXXI.

TOKENS OF SISTERLY REGARD.

It will be readily imagined that the unnatural state of things prevailing under the conventual system is calculated rather to promote than prevent the rising of those petty jealousies and dislikes which must be incidental to such an association. Without the strong ties of kindred or friendship to bind them one to another, it is not likely that the poor prisoners of a convent will spend in perfect harmony the tedious hours and years of their compulsory seclusion. A single incident may let the reader into the realities of that relationship which Rome pretends to constitute among the unhappy inmates of a nunnery, and which she designates by the deceptive name of "sisterhood."

Having been sent one evening to work in the boarders' refectory, instead of that of the sisterhood, while standing near one of the tables at which the boarders were seated, I took up a basket and carried it to the scullery for some bread. Scarcely had I entered the room and handed the basket to the sister who had charge of the department, when I felt myself seized by the arm, and, looking round, saw the angry countenance of the sister who presided at the boarders' table. She asked me, in a passionate tone, by whose authority

I had taken that basket for bread, and whether I had been appointed waiter by the Superior. I answered no, and that I would not have taken the basket had she not ordered me, the night before, to do so when she had said that bread was wanting upon the table.

The sister told me that I had no authority of the kind, and that she would report me to the Superior, and have me brought before "the council." I replied that I was not conscious of having done wrong; but she followed me into the porch, talking in a loud and angry tone. I dreaded the "sacred council," and went at once to the novitiate, and told the mistress of novices what had just occurred. She answered me that I had "many a cross to bear."

That evening, while on the way to my cell, I noticed in one of the cloisters a sister leaning against the wall. She beckoned me to her, and then made a motion for me to follow her. I soon found it was the sister who had ill-treated me in the refectory. I became alarmed, as she was leading me to a balcony beyond the cells. I whispered that I must go to my cell—that I would be missed. By this time we had reached the balcony. She insisted that I should wait, closing, at the same time, the door after us. Just then, hearing a noise near by, as if some one was crossing the porch to the infirmary, we walked on a few steps to escape observation. The sister then fell on her knees, asking my forgiveness for having abused me, and begging me not to speak of what had occurred should I have an interview with the Superior priest. I would here state that, in those interviews, a sister is questioned as to any difficulties she may have had with others in the community. I promised secresy, and went to my cell.

Wearied and exhausted with my duties in the academy, besides my evening work, an irresistible oppression of soul weighing down my powers of mind and body, I tried in vain to sleep. I thought of my ill health, caused by the laborious exercises I had to perform, and the sufferings and sorrows I had undergone since my reception in the community. I looked out upon the future: it appeared to stretch before me, even into eternity, a drear path on which no beam of sunlight would fall to cheer, and in which no voice of kindred love would breathe its music of consolation to my heart. I sighed for my home. In desolation of spirit, I mourned for its remembered love. But the fearful consciousness came to me that I was severed eternally from all that made life dear. At length I arose, dressed, and groped my way along the cloister leading to the choir, and from thence down the narrow flight of stairs into the chapel. It was dark, save for the few rays that streamed from the solitary light which burned dimly in the sanctuary. Kneeling before the altar, I fastened my eyes upon the crucifix above it. Long and earnestly I gazed, but the feelings that filled my soul were too deep to find repose in the contemplation of any material object. I bowed my head upon the railing, and wept. Ere long, the image of HIM who had suffered arose to my view; the pure and holy Savior of the world, whose mild, benignant eyes, in their pitying tenderness, penetrated to the depths of my wretched heart, and shed a blessed hope upon its gloom. I prayed—prayed earnestly, and from the heart; my desires flowed from its inmost depths. With streaming eyes and unutterable groans, I asked Him, the Savior of the world, to deliver me from this prison, this den of cruelty and hypocrisy. I believe it to be the only time I prayed from my heart while in the institution.

With this outburst of emotion, this pouring forth of my grief to God in spirit and in truth, I found relief, and became composed and calm.

I know not how long I had been keeeling, when I was startled by deep-drawn sighs and sobs, proceeding from the direction of the "seven dolors" altar,* which is at one side of the chapel door, under the choir. Fearing observation, I arose, and hastening down one side of the chapel, reached the stairs leading to the choir. As I entered the choir, I saw a dark figure glide past me, and go into a small passage behind the organ. Probably this person was in search of the poor heart-broken creature whom I had left weeping so bitterly at the foot of the "seven dolors" altar. Fortunately I escaped notice, and, softly closing the door behind me, reached my cell just before the bell rang for morning prayers in the chapel.

* An altar, that is, dedicated to the "seven sorrows" of the Virgin Mary—"septem dolores."

CHAPTER XXXII.

CRUELTIES INFLICTED.

So far as my own observation and experience can attest, nothing is more mistaken than the notion which has led so many to the cloisters, namely, that the holy and religious life of the nun, or, as at St. Joseph's, of the Sister of Charity, delivers her from the liability to fall into the grosser passions of the world, such as envy, malice, hatred, jealousy, anger, passionate love, etc. These evil susceptibilities of human frailty exist in their fullest perfection and development among the inmates of the convent.

The even rule of justice is not more rigorously carried out there than among men in general, nor do the heavenly dictates of pure charity always animate and control the Superiors of that "house of charity," but partiality, favoritism, prejudice, and cruelty exhibit their baleful influence throughout the community. Of this, if it were necessary, numerous instances might be recounted—acts so oppressive and severe that I verily believe they were performed with the purpose of destroying the health, as well as of cowing the spirit. If in this suspicion I do wrong to the perpetrators of those acts, God, who alone reads the heart, and knows what my sufferings have been, will, I trust, forgive me.

It would be natural to expect that a system of favoritism would extensively prevail within the walls of such an institution, not only as regards the Mother Superior, who dispenses her indulgence and partiality among those upon whom she can rely, or whom she wishes to attach to herself, but also with respect to the priests and certain members of the community. Jealousy also exerts a potent sway throughout the sisterhood. It is no rare thing to witness the features of a beautiful girl convulsed and distorted with passion when she passes a rival, who exults for a season in the triumph she has achieved, but who, poor deluded victim! soon is brought to experience like sensations of anger and thirst for revenge upon her own desertion for more attractive objects of priestly favor and desire.

Here I shall mention occurrences as they come up to my remembrance, with a view to illustrate the power and disposition of those who exercise authority in the institution to annoy and oppress such individuals as may have displeased them.

The intensity of these passions can be only augmented by the necessity of keeping them pent up and disguised from perception and discovery, or by their uncontrolled violence among those whose rank elevates them above the need of disguise. When occasionally permitted to manifest themselves at a fitting opportunity, they burst forth in redoubled vehemence. I myself have frequently been made the subject of these exhibitions. Regarded from the outset with jealousy as "the *pet* Josephine," I was visited with every annoyance that could be devised by certain individuals in the community. At one time, on the pretense that

I had knelt and kissed the floor too near the door in the novitiate, I was reported by a sister to the mistress of novices, who made me do penance by kneeling before the altar until permission should be given me to leave, and I was kept in that painful posture nearly three hours. Another time, as I was passing by the side of another sister through a doorway, she thrust me violently against the jamb, pressing with her whole strength upon me, and with such force as to break my beads to pieces, the crucifix and other pieces falling to the floor, scattered in every direction. In a third instance, I found myself watched and persecuted without intermission by a sister who had charge of the sewing. She would consequently assign to me the worst and most difficult work she could find, telling me to perform it in a certain way; then, when done, she would say it was wrong, and order me to pick it out and do it over in some other way. This accomplished, she would finally report me for doing it improperly, and tell falsehoods to substantiate the accusation.

One morning, a slip of paper, containing the names of those who had been called upon to make the "repetition" of their meditations, was found upon the table, torn across the middle. A sister came to me and said, "You tore that piece of paper; you had no right to do so; I will report you." I denied the charge, knowing nothing of the deed, and not having been near the table. She insisted on criminating me, and reported me accordingly.

Going up stairs one evening to my cell, I discovered something like a heap of clothes lying on one of the broad steps; I heard, also, moans and lamentations. There was but one lamp burning very dimly in the cloister, and putting out my foot to ascertain what the object before me was, I discovered it to be sister J. P——, of *shoe* memory. Giving her no very gentle kick by way of retaliation, I passed on to my cell. She was indeed ill, as I afterward learned, and needed commiseration; but the feeling was one which had not obtained much cultivation in my breast since entering the institution, where it was very seldom exercised by others.

About a quarter after nine o'clock one very cold evening, the mistress of novices came to me in a state of unusual excitement, and said, "Sister Josephine, I want you to go to the chapel, and see if all the doors are closed, and if every thing is right there, and if nothing is missing about the altar." To do this, I would have to grope my way through a dark passage in the basement to the stairs leading up to the chapel. Somewhat terrified at the thought of performing this errand alone, I obeyed nevertheless. On reaching the lobby that led into the church, I found the inner door open. I walked slowly to the door, and looked into the church, when I heard a noise like the sullen growl of a dog, and a rattling as of a chain; and by the dim light of the lamp before the altar, I saw a dark form before the altar of the "seven dolors." I ventured to approach, and found it was a member of the community; who, I knew not then, nor have I since learned; but it was one whom I have seen at other times. She was old and decrepit, and nearly blind, and used to go, about that hour of the night, to pray in the chapel and say her rosary. She always carried her books with her, wrapped in a yellow pocket-handkerchief, though she could not see to read.

Not observing any thing else of an unusual character in the chapel, I turned to go out, groping my way back. I closed the door after me, and reached the brick corridor. When near the statue of St. Vincent, by a light in the novitiate I could see the mistress of novices coming out of that room, and approaching the spot where I stood. Though I saw her, she could not see me. At once I determined to frighten her, in return for sending me upon that errand. She was walking very lightly, as though in fear of something. I stationed myself on one side of the statue, and, as she drew near me, rushed out against her, and crowded her against the stone wall on the outer side. She uttered a cry of terror, and I fled rapidly down the corridor, and thence to my cell.

Although the mistress of novices seemed to entertain an aversion for me, yet the Mother Superior treated me at times in a very different manner, showing me marked favor, and this may have instigated the hatred manifested toward me by the former.

I was several times sent for by the Lady Superior to accompany her as a companion in her drives. On these occasions she had an attendant in the carriage and a colored driver on the box. Once or twice we passed through the town of Emmettsburg, but I was not privileged to look out of the carriage, which was a close one, and was directed to keep my eyes cast down. The impossibility of an escape at such times will be apparent. The town of Emmettsburg is chiefly Roman Catholic; many of its inhabitants are dependent on the institution for support. The Lady Superior is a great favorite among them. She did not stop any where to make visits on these occasions. An attempt to leave the carriage would not only have proved useless at the time, but would have subjected me to severe punishment, and exposed me to closer confinement. We wore, in driving out, the habit usually worn by the community. My place was at the Superior's side on the back seat, the front seat being occupied by the other sister or attendant accompanying us. We entered the carriage from the Superior's room, near which it had been driven up to an inner gate situated in a wall between two buildings; through this gate we passed into the carriage, and there we left it on our return. I was never permitted to leave the Superior's side during this time.

For these marks of favor bestowed by the Lady Superior I have noticed that the jealousy of some was awakened, as also when a medal of the Virgin Mary, called the "medal of the immaculate conception," was presented to me by a priest. This medal was placed upon my beads, and thus worn in sight; and the sisters would say, as I passed them, "The Superior's pet; the priests' pet; I know where that came from," etc. They would take hold of the medal and examine the inscription, which read as follows, in French: "O Mary, conceived without sin, pray for us, who have recourse to thee."

This medal, I may state, was the second of the kind presented in the institution. It was made, I think, of gilded brass. The first one was given to a novice who had been converted to the Catholic persuasion, and was older than myself in that faith. Many of the sisters showed evident signs of jealousy toward her, which I observed the more, perhaps, from being on the alert when placed in the same category, and made the object of similar remarks, looks, and actions, small in themselves, but indicative of spiteful feeling.

Several of the vowed sisters wear a medal of St. Dominic, the virtues of which are said to shield the wearer from sickness, peril, and other injuries. It is worn as a charm to secure this protection. The inscription is in four letters, with a cross, the meaning of which I did not know, nor did any of the sisters within my knowledge. These medals were given by the Superior as tokens of regard.

CHAPTER XXXIII.

TRIAL OF MY VOCATION.

It was about two months previous to my escape from the institution, when, entering the corridor one day on my way to the chapel, I observed a spy who had been placed there to watch those who were going thither. As I approached, she rushed toward me, and pinching me by the arm, she said, hissing through her closed teeth, "Didn't you hear the bell?" Though it was silence-hour, I answered her, "Yes, I heard the bell." This offense was reported, and I was punished for it. I supposed the sister to be jealous of me, but for what cause I knew not.

At another time—it was on Sunday, at the close of the silence-hour, and the bell was ringing for vespers—an act of cruelty was perpetrated toward me, which likewise I have been unable to account for. The sisters had formed the rank to proceed to chapel, and I was in the rear. The mistress of novices came forward, and struck me upon the forehead with her clenched fist. I looked with amazement into her face, but durst not speak, as it was a season of strict silence. She bade me keep my eyes down, at the same time repeating the blow; then catching hold of the ends of my black silk "capot," which were tied loosely under my chin, she drew them so tightly around my throat as for a moment to deprive me of breath. I struggled to get free, but recent illness had rendered me very weak. I then fell on my knees before her, and uttered a loud scream, for I began to fear she would take my life. There was no one to help me. The last novice who had passed through the door, in the rank, did not dare to turn and see what had occasioned the scream.

When I could speak I begged her to spare my life, and asked what I had done to merit such treatment. She answered not a word, but dragged me across the novitiate to the passage beyond, loosening and drawing alternately the ends of my "capot." As soon as she released her grasp I arose, but was forced to cling to the railing of the stairs for support.

She then said to me, "*I did not think you would take it so well.*" I begged her again to tell me what I had done, but she did not reply. I told her that I would go to the priest's room, and see the Superior about it; when she rushed toward me again, and taking me by the arm, shook me violently, saying, "Go if you dare, and I will follow you." She then ordered me to the chapel, where all the community had by this time assembled for prayers.

Trembling and weeping, I obeyed; and after service I spoke to the Mother Superior, but could obtain no satisfaction from her. Shortly after, I saw the Superior, and told him my trouble. Patting me on the head, he said, "I must not mind it; it was *only a trial of my vocation*—a trial sent from God; I should like the life after a while;" and thus, while he endeavored to soothe my wounded feelings, he justified the act.

I have said that I had reason from the first to regard myself as an object of peculiar hatred on the part of the mistress of novices, and I may here remark that she was of foreign birth, very astute in her perceptions, keen, shrewd, and penetrating, and had doubtless discerned, or thought she discerned, in my character a trait of firmness amounting to obstinacy, which would develop itself whenever I should be convinced of the duplicity practiced in that institution, and therefore I would never be a *reliable* "Sister of Charity."

The Lady Superior, a perfect lady in her deportment, and possessed of a powerful intellect and a profound knowledge of the human heart, mild, bland, and, withal, very discriminating, I have reason to believe had not so read my character, but persuaded herself that I would yet become a willing and perfectly obedient "daughter of St. Vincent."

CHAPTER XXXIV.

HUMILITY.

I WAS ordered one day by an officer of the institution to scrub some stains from the floor of the porch, where grease had been accidentally spilled by a sister. The day was intensely cold, and at first I was inclined to refuse; but the order being reiterated in an authoritative tone, I dared not do so. Frequently have I seen the blood oozing from the chapped hands of those engaged in laborious duties under similar circumstances.

It was in consequence of such a want of "humility"* on my part that the mistress of novices once remarked to me she wished I had been in the community during the life of Sister Daserai, who had died a short time before my entrance, and whose grave was yet fresh in the cemetery. This person was a native of France, the daughter of a marquis, and is said to have been very beautiful, of a noble and commanding appearance. She was dressed, on her arrival, in black, having been but a short time a widow. Though per-

* How strikingly is this false sentiment rebuked in those prophetic words of the apostle, where he condemns those things "*which have indeed a show of wisdom in will-worship, and humility, and neglecting of the body;* not in any honor, to the satisfying of the flesh."—Col., ii., 23.

suaded to enter St. Joseph's, she would not at first comply with the rules of the community, which were not strictly enforced by the officers in her case, owing to the high station she had occupied in society, and her great wealth. She could not bear the idea of drinking out of a tin cup, or of washing her hands in a tin basin, and positively refused to do so. Her arms, from unaccustomed exposure, having become rough, she would often endeavor to hide them with her hands and sleeves.

The Superior, seeing that this sister lacked "humility," determined to set about humbling her pride. She was assigned the most laborious work in the house. In exchange for the silk dress she wore on entering, a coarse, patched habit was given her. Soon, finding that her will was held in subjection, and that she must renounce it entirely, she became convinced "that Almighty God would be pleased with her spirit of humility," and no longer refused to comply with the wishes of her superiors.

Her duties were increased daily, and were performed to a greater extent even than required. She would scrub the floor until the blood streamed from her hands, and would say to a sister who chanced to be passing by, "See the blood streaming from my hands—it is all for our Lord." Her mind was in such a state that she believed every untoward event to happen by the will of God. Should a fly alight on the bread, or the molasses, or the soup she was eating, she would not brush it away, but would eat it, because she thought such to be God's will. While at her duties she was constantly saying her prayers, making aspirations, fasting, etc. "She lost her health," said the mistress of novices to me, "because the Lord loved her, and wished to take her to himself."

Often would she rise at midnight to pray, and pass the entire night at her devotions. If a member of the community spoke to her, she would utter no reply. When taken ill and sent to the infirmary, she refused to take the medicine given her, and requested to be put on duty there. Work was assigned her, which was faithfully performed, as the mistress of novices said, "in a spirit of mortification and penance."

Soon after entering the infirmary, on account of the heavy work she performed, as well as the prayers and penances she continued to observe, she was compelled, in an almost dying condition, to take to her bed. There, however, she would not recline upon her pillow, but, supported in a sitting posture, would pass her time in sewing and knitting, until she became too weak to hold the needles in her tremulous and almost transparent hands.

Here, as the mistress of novices narrated these facts to me, I remarked, "She must have had the consumption, mother."

"Yes, my child," replied she, in her blandest tones, and gazing into my face; "'tis a part of our vocation."

During her illness in the infirmary she would often decline taking any nourishment, and when she consented to do so, she ate the food with a number of flies that had alighted upon it. "This she did for mortification," said my informant. She would lie awake all night, making such aspirations as these:- "Sweet Jesus! Holy Mother! Holy St. Joseph! pray for me." "I wish you could have seen her," said the mistress of novices, "when she died. Her large black eyes were fixed upon the crucifix, and she requested us to light the candles upon the table at the foot of her bed, on which the crucifix stood. O sister! she was a living saint, and at her death was admitted at once into the presence of our Lord and blessed Mother; she melted away like a print of butter!"

Such was the example I was desired to imitate.

CHAPTER XXXV.

SELF-MORTIFICATION.

THE foregoing narrative will serve to exemplify the nature of the subjects to which our contemplations in the community were habitually drawn as worthy to be admired and followed. I may now mention some few of the historical models whose characters we were accustomed to study with peculiar veneration.

The life of St. Theresa, founder of the Order of reformed Carmelites, was often rehearsed for our special edification. She was a Carmelite nun, a native of Spain, and undertook to revive the former austerities of the community to which she belonged. Her history, written in French, was in the library, and was frequently read. This order is the most strict of all except the Trappist. There is but one Carmelite nunnery in this country—that, namely, which is located in Aisquith Street, Baltimore. I have already given some account of its severe discipline.

A favorite theme of narration at St. Joseph's was the life of the Princess Louise, daughter of Louis XIV. of France, who became a Carmelite nun in her father's palace.

By the aid of a maid-servant and a nun who were in her confidence, she made her profession, and having procured the tunic worn by the sisters, she wore it in order to accustom herself to its use. After this she obtained the hair shirt, and wore it also under her princely robes, without the knowledge of her royal parent. She had an utter dislike to the odor of tallow; but, as the Carmelites use tallow candles, she caused her servant to procure some, and every night would burn one—at first for a short time, as the smell sickened her; and thus she accustomed herself to it. In a very small room near her own she had placed an iron bedstead, with a hard mattress, and, before retiring to her own apartment, she would recline for a while on this Carmelite bed, until so used to it that she could there pass the whole night. Thus it was that she practiced mortification of the flesh. She afterward entered the nunnery, and it is related that on one occasion she was sent to scour the pots and kettles in the kitchen. She was robed in a brocade, "couleur de rose," and this dress has been preserved, to show that even a princess could perform menial offices. Not knowing how to do such work, she ignorantly cleaned the outside of the vessel; but, when told that it was the inside that should be cleaned, she cheerfully scoured that also.

These instances of humility on the part of a princess were held up for our instruction; and my own feelings, in view of such relations, were at times deeply exercised, as I was urged to emulate this spirit of so-called humility and mortification of the flesh.

CHAPTER XXXVI.

INSANITY AT ST. JOSEPH'S.

Sister John Patientia, as she was called, was a person considerably past the period of youth, and somewhat faded in aspect, but still retaining the traces of extraordinary beauty. She would often break the rules of the institution, but would receive no punishment for the offense. She would sometimes speak in time of silence, and try to make the novices laugh. Entering the novitiate with a mischievous glance around her, she would utter some humorous remark, provoking almost irresistible mirth.

If, as the wise man says, there be "a time to laugh," it is assuredly not during any portion of a novice's life. The rules forbid any approach to merriment; a serious face is continually to be worn, and any thing like levity would be severely punished.

This alone, it might be supposed, would of itself impair the health of an individual endowed by nature with a lively and cheerful disposition. But, as I am not qualified to judge of this effect, I simply state the fact, and leave physiologists to determine.

Sister Patientia was very talented and highly educated. She spoke several languages fluently, and had formerly been a teacher in the academy. Her duties at present were to attend to the corridor, or outer gallery; sweeping the brick floor, brushing the windows, and removing the dust from the leaves of the plants; scrubbing the platform and steps, and washing the windows. It was her duty also to ring the great bell of the cloisters for the devotions of the community. This is the sister who had charge of the shoe-room, and of whom I have elsewhere spoken.

Sometimes, as the sisters were passing her in the corridor, she would rest her chin on her broom, look facetiously at them, making faces, and stationing herself in their way to obstruct their progress. She did not take her meals with the community, but breakfasted at about ten, and dined at four. Her portion would be placed upon the corner of the table, near the door. She would remove the plate that covered it, and then perform her devotions before the crucifix in a manner calculated to excite merriment, making the sign of the cross with a rapid jerk. Then, looking significantly upon her food, she would go away and leave it untouched; or, perhaps, taking a mouthful, make a grimace, mutter to herself, and walk hastily away through the corridor. I seized an opportunity one day to ask her why she did not take her meals more regularly. She replied, "One should take more care of the soul than of the body;" and her tone and manner were so ludicrous that I could not help laughing.

Sometimes, on meeting the Superior in the corridor, she would kneel down, and kiss the hem of her habit with an air of the most devout worship. One day she took me with her to her cell, and commenced to give me a short history of her early life; of the wealth of her family; how she entered the institution, leaving home without her parents' knowledge or consent; how she came to this country, etc. Fearing lest I should overstay my time, I attempted to leave. "Wait a little," she replied, "till I tell you how much I have suffered and am suffering now." Pointing to her bed, she said, "I have not rested on that bed for years, but am forced to remain in a sitting posture all night, on account of a large ulcer on my side, and a difficulty in breathing that will not suffer me to lie down."

There was another sister in the house who was also said to be insane, yet was allowed to go about the house, and to attend mass and confession. I remember meeting her once on the corridor, when she came rushing toward me, and, shaking her clenched fist, shrieked, "Novice! get out of my way!" I jumped over an oleander box to avoid her, in great alarm.

The reader will not be surprised to hear that there are insane inmates of these institutions. There is an apartment for the insane which I have never entered. I have occasionally seen insane persons come rushing out of a door at the foot of a stairway leading to that apartment, muttering and talking wildly. The unnatural life they lead is, perhaps, the life of all others most calculated to produce such effects.

Infirmity of body and insanity of mind I consider the *natural results* of convent life.

CHAPTER XXXVII.

ORDER OF "SISTERS OF CHARITY."

THE institution of St. Joseph's is not one of those establishments denominated "close convents," in which the nuns, having once assumed the veil, are perpetually immured. Its ostensible purpose is the education and training of its inmates for deeds of charity and mercy. These persons, having received the requisite instruction and discipline, are, *when they can be trusted*, dispatched to various stations, with the object of exercising their functions and of attracting notice to the order to which they belong. They constitute a striking feature in the Roman Catholic Church, and offer a continual and living text of laudation to the priests, who point to them and to their "labors of love" as beneficent fruits and appropriate illustrations of the holy character of their religion.* There

* In so far as this order claims to be a voluntary association of women for charitable purposes, under the title of *Sisters of Charity*, it is no original creation of the Roman Catholic Church, but has actually been borrowed from Protestantism. Among the Waldenses, the "Bohemian Brothers," and the Moravians, there is a record of the existence of "deaconesses," as they were termed in the primitive age, as early as 1457; but it was in the sixteenth century that Robert von der Mark, Prince of Sedan in the Netherlands, founded the institution of Protestant "*Demoiselles de Charité*," as he called them, and to this institution he granted the revenues of suppressed monasteries. The

are forty-one mission-houses attached to the order in the United States, numbering about five hundred

office so founded received a formal ecclesiastical recognition in 1568, from the General Synod of the Reformed Church of the Lower Rhine and the Netherlands. It was not until 1633, or *sixty-five years later*, that Vincent de Paul established his order of Sisters of Charity. There are now institutions bearing the title of houses of Protestant Sisters of Charity, or Deaconesses, at Paris, Strasburg, Echallens, Berlin, Utrecht, Stockholm, and Kaiserwerth. There is also one at Pittsburg in our own country. Acting as nurses to the sick, teachers of reformatory schools, guardians of females released from prison, visitors of the poor, and in other spheres of usefulness, these excellent women are *bound by no vow* or obligation of obedience, but serve God with the freedom and voluntary earnestness of intelligent Christians. They number now many hundreds, of whom several are engaged at the present moment in caring for the wounded and dying of the allied armies before Sebastopol. The institution of Kaiserwerth, on the Rhine, under the direction of the Reverend Pastor Fliedner and his excellent wife, has sent forth no fewer than one hundred and eighty of these deaconesses to different parts of the world. Its hospital contains one hundred and twenty patients, its training institution for deaconesses seventy-seven probationers; the entire household, with orphan asylum, infant school, etc., numbering three hundred and ninety inmates. But while we cite these facts to show that the idea of such charitable enterprises is not peculiar to Romanism, we would not lay any great stress upon such developments of Christian charity, remembering that the glory of our Protestantism resides not in a multitude of formal organizations for the professed relief of human miseries, but consists rather in those numberless, quiet, and unobtrusive channels of individual beneficence which in Protestant countries now, as in the primitive days of Christianity, carry material succor and spiritual consolation to the abodes of the destitute and friendless. And while, thanks to the healthful tendencies of a pure religion, which elevates the masses in mental capacity, and social comfort, and political well-being, there is far from the same amount of physical distress to call for alleviation in Protestant lands as in those where Romanism has combined with civil despotism for ages past to crush the intellect and degrade the life of the masses, we do not covet, in any sense, the help of these conventual systems and establishments, which undertake, by a mechanism controlling individual wills under a stern law of

members, including those at the central institution. These are scattered in various cities and towns of the country. Where there are but two sisters in a city or town, they have their mission-house, their chapel, and their separate confessional, at which the priest on the station is always a frequent visitor. When their services are not too constantly in requisition, they generally open a school, at which the children of the poor are taught free of charge, and by which means many proselytes are won to the Roman Catholic faith. These communities are all under the control of the Superior of St. Joseph's, which is the "mother-house," as it is styled, in this country. But this mother-house is connected with the house in Paris, which is the centre of the whole order throughout the world, comprising some five hundred and fifty-three establishments, with nearly nine thousand members. This is according to the best statistics I can obtain; but in the institution of St. Joseph's I was informed there was a much larger number.

The fact that sisters are sent from the mother-house to the different towns and cities throughout the country to exercise their vocation as nurses for the sick, has been enlarged upon to refute and ridicule the idea of any restraint or coercion to prevent members from leaving the institution; but this assertion must be received with a considerable degree of allowance. It should be recollected that the sisters who are thus sent abroad go forth to establish new communities ("mis-

obedience to authority, the performance of those offices of mercy, which, to be truly Christian, must be the dictates of a free and cheerful piety.

sions" they are called) subordinate to the principal one, where the same rules are observed as at head-quarters. On these missions only the *trustworthy*—those, namely, upon whom the Superior can implicitly rely—are sent. But a little reflection will convince the reader that, even if so disposed, it would be a difficult thing for a sister to escape from her bonds. A constant supervision is kept by the priest and the sister-servant on the station, who would instantly report any refractory symptoms, and she would be recalled. In a strange place, too, far from her friends, it would require a strong resolution to desert her charge, and appeal to the public, especially when she knows that the entire Catholic population would combine to discredit her statement and destroy her character. Few would dare to contend with such considerations as these. By far the greater number would prefer to endure evils with which they were familiar rather than encounter unknown trials in a new position.

The number of inmates at St. Joseph's, including postulants, seminary sisters or novices, and professed sisters, is about one hundred and forty—often more, but seldom less. This number, of course, does not comprehend the boarders in the academy, of whom there are sometimes as many as one hundred and fifty. From this mother-house, members are transferred, at the option of the Superior, to the corresponding institutions in different parts of the United States—even to California, and also to France. This removal is in order to supply vacancies occasioned by sickness or death in the subordinate communities, and sometimes to establish communities in places where their existence may be deemed politic or necessary, as the means of increasing the influence of the Church in such localities.

The Sisters of Charity have for years constituted a theme of enthusiastic praise and commendation, even on the part of many Protestants. Their purity, their self-devotion, their self-denial, their courage in exposure to disease while ministering to the wants of the sick and dying, in crowded hospitals, whose fetid atmosphere is full of peril, have been lauded to the skies. Turgid eulogies of their gentleness and beauty, their tender ministrations, the soft touch of their white hands, and the sympathetic tear called forth by the sufferings of their patients, have been so often the subject of newspaper paragraphs and sentimentalities of novels, that public sentiment has been warmly enlisted in their advocacy and defense. But it may be asked, in all candor, is there any need of the show and parade with which the good deeds of these sisters are exposed to the views of the world? Are they the only beings who tend the bed of sickness, or assuage the pangs of disease? Are those only to be regarded as acts of Christian benevolence which are accomplished by drilled and disciplined cohorts, who, like the soldiers of an army, resign themselves to the government of a single will, and mechanically or slavishly obey it? Is this method so infinitely superior to that of the numerous Protestant associations throughout the length and breadth of our land, and the far more numerous individual missionaries of mercy, who not only tend the sick in the hospitals, but, far more, who search out the poor, the widow, the fatherless, and let in the light of charity upon their comfortless abodes? who instruct the ignorant, comfort the desponding, and reclaim the fallen, and this of their own free, heaven-inspired choice and uncontrolled purpose, and without regard to sectarian limits, but rather extending to all, of every name and nation, an equal share of generous relief? The appropriation of all these high-toned panegyrics to a vowed community of Roman Catholics, whose main design is avowedly to proselyte by means of their various enterprises of benevolence, reflects an indirect slander upon the charity of Protestants, as though their less ostentatious course were actuated by inferior motives.

I entertained formerly the same extravagant ideas of the pure and unselfish life of this order, but experience and observation have dispelled the illusion. The fact is, that the whole system of popery is one of proselytism, toward the fulfillment of which every instrument is brought to bear; and the Order of "Sisters of Charity" forms not the least efficient part of the forces employed by Romanism, certainly not the least influential of the appliances by which the doctrines of popery are infused into the breasts of the credulous and unwary.

The community of St. Joseph's is under the direction of two superiors—the "Mother Superior," and a priest of the Order of St. Lazare. It would be an anomaly in Romanism for an institution to exist without the participation of the "holy fathers" in its government. The Lazarists have a "house" at Emmettsburg, and pay frequent visits to St. Joseph's to hear confessions and for other purposes. They are styled in the community the "sons," as the sisterhood are the "daughters" of charity, regarding each other as brethren and sisters of one great family. The two orders are thus nearly allied, and operate in association. They are governed by the same religious authorities, the ecclesiastical superior of the one being the director of the other, and both having the same chief confessor. They affect a community of interests, and mutually extol each others' merits, and commend the piety, devotedness, and purity of each others' lives. One of these priests is always at the institution, where he is regarded with the utmost reverence and affection, and his counsels are appreciated as the commands of Deity.

CHAPTER XXXVIII.

THE ACADEMY.

CONNECTED with St. Joseph's there is a school for the instruction of young ladies, at which the most accomplished and reliable of the sisterhood are teachers. The academy is a separate building, but attached to the other edifices by covered porches, and the pupils have their distinct refectory and sleeping apartments, which are presided over by sisters appointed for the purpose, and denominated "angels," as before stated.

This school is managed with consummate dexterity and ability; so much so, that, with few exceptions, the scholars become ardently attached to their teachers, and are warm advocates of the interests of the community. This is no matter for wonder, as they see only the bright side of the picture, and have not the most remote conception of the privations, the intrigues, and the horrors within. They behold an assemblage of pious recluses, who have parted with all the vanities of the world, and are preparing themselves, by patient and meek self-denial, to assuage the sufferings of their fellow-creatures on earth, and render themselves meet for heaven. So fair is the light, so attractive the coloring of this poetic scene, that many, having passed through their educational course in the academy, return to the institution, and enter upon their novitiate, discovering too late their mistake, and the terrible reality of the life before them.

Both the Jesuits and the "Sisters of Charity" are adepts in teaching the young, having reduced the practice, by long experience and study, to a system almost perfect. They know especially how to blend strictness and discipline with kindness and indulgence, by observing the characters and dispositions of those under their charge. The pupils are taught well, according to the capacity of each, that their parents may be satisfied with their progress and attainments, and may speak in approving terms of the institution. At the same time, every exertion is made to win the affections and secure the confidence of the scholars, that they may stamp their young and impressible minds with the doctrines of the Roman Catholic Church, and, if possible, allure them within the pale of the community. Rarely do these attempts prove unsuccessful, at least in creating a strong prepossession toward those doctrines; and the ideas implanted at the school become deep-rooted and fruitful, unless checked in their growth by the watchful care of parents and friends, even this proving often unavailing.

At St. Joseph's *all* the pupils, or boarders, as they are called, are required to attend mass once a day, and to go through all the genuflexions and other forms usual at that service. They do not, however, witness those other religious exercises of the community, in which devotion is made a pretext for the infliction of torture; they hear nothing of the rigid penances enjoined for the slightest and most unintentional infraction of the rules; they are ignorant of the unjust favoritism and the flagrant partialities exercised by those in power. All is fairy-land to them. And should a charge be made to this effect in the presence of a graduate of the academy, by a sufferer from these practices, she would be denounced, as I have been, as a fabricator of falsehoods, and a calumniator of the holy sisterhood.

The extent to which the affections of the boarders are gained, both by the Lazarist priests attached to the institution and by the teachers of the academy, including the Mother Superior, is scarcely credible. I have known instances in which boarders have refused to go home with their parents; and one in particular, in which a father visited his daughter at St. Joseph's, when she manifested the most complete indifference to his attentions, and even showed repugnance at his caresses, weeping bitterly when told of his intention to take her home, and angrily desiring to be left, even when appealed to in the name of her mother. More than once have I seen, with the blood tingling in my veins, and the flush of indignation on my cheek, a young girl of fifteen or sixteen reposing her head on the breast of a young "Lazarist" as they walked together, his arm thrown over her shoulder. This, no doubt, was innocent on her part, at least. She regarded him in the light of a father; but what pernicious consequences might ensue from this familiarity! And was he performing the office of a holy guide?

And yet Protestant parents will send their children to be educated at Roman Catholic institutions, deluding themselves with the idle and silly notion that no effort will be made to indoctrinate them with popish errors. Are they not aware that this religion is one of exclusive pretensions, and that, believing all without its pale doomed to sure perdition, its members, if sincere, are bound to use every effort for the conversion of heretics, and their rescue from destruction? If ignorant of this, their ignorance is unpardonable, for it is the result of sheer indifference, or disinclination to inform themselves on the subject; and thus to hazard the temporal and eternal welfare of their most precious jewels in slothful disregard of this all-important issue is a crime beyond excuse. The whole paraphernalia of popery, from its enthroned vice-god at Rome, to its humblest lay-member cringing at the feet of his priest, is perpetually engaged in the business of making proselytes: the clergy, to swell the ranks and augment the influence of their fraternity; and the laity, aside from all other motives, because they believe that in so doing they are saving souls. Schools and colleges afford the widest scope and the readiest means of realizing these ends; and hence the great number of these institutions that have sprung up of late, in every section of the land, attached to Jesuitical communities and convents, where the craft of man and the gentle persuasion of woman unite in bending the tender character of youth, that the matured tree may develop in accordance with popish distortion and disease.*

* While the influences brought to bear at these institutions upon the pupils are generally such as to attract their affection, and render them contented, there are cases in which a sterner course is followed, and in such cases the oppression is evidently irremediable. Coercive means, as well as those of a persuasive character, can be used, in the

When will American parents learn wisdom? If they consider it indispensable that their children be sent from home for their education, are there not hundreds of Protestant schools, where every branch of knowledge is taught by intelligent and experienced teachers; where every elegant accomplishment can be acquired, and all valuable instruction obtained? At all events, let not the susceptible mind and heart of a young girl be intrusted to the charge of Catholic nuns and their clerical directors. Let not the precious ob-

academy as in the sisterhood, to accomplish the work of bending the will and the faculties to the purposes of Rome. Inquiries have often been addressed to me with reference to the opportunities of novices for sending messages to their friends by means of the boarders. All such modes of communication are precluded by the watchful care of those in charge. The directress has the perusal of all letters written by the boarders or sent to them. Protestant parents should understand that their children are not allowed to correspond with them in an unrestrained manner. Small, however, as the chances of any communication with friends may be in the academy, I feel assured that if any suspicion of my discontent had been entertained, I should not have been permitted to enter the academy for the purposes of teaching.

I may here mention the case of a child under my instruction at the academy—a case which I am confident is only one among many: Josephine Picuabia (such, I think, was the name) had been placed at St. Joseph's by her parents, who were from Cuba, at a very early age. She would frequently come to her lessons in tears, and, resting her head on my bosom, would give vent to her sorrow, after exclaiming, "Oh, sister, you are the only one that is kind to me!" She complained of severe treatment; that she was whipped and beaten, and was in terror of her life, yet could not inform her parents, as the directress would not let her write home.

This child first became attached to me more particularly because my name was the same with her own. I always treated her kindly, and sympathized deeply with her distress. We were frequently left alone in our music-room, and I had occasion to hear her grievances as I endeavored to soothe her into composure for her lessons.

jects of parental solicitude and love—the Cornelian jewels of American homes—be placed where their lustre will be tarnished and their value lost; when, in this Protestant land, so many institutions have been founded where the youthful mind may be properly trained, and the gem, skillfully polished, may be returned to adorn society and the world.

CHAPTER XXXIX.

NUNNERIES AND SCHOOLS.

It is proper that some explanation be given at this point with reference to one of the objects of these Roman Catholic institutions of learning, as it is one not generally understood by the Protestant public.

Schools are first opened in connection with a new enterprise of the Sisters of Charity, at their mission-houses, for the reception of children belonging to the poorer classes. This course at once establishes the reputation of the order for benevolence and charity, and serves to ingratiate that part of the population, who do not fail to speak in terms of eulogy respecting their amiable and disinterested benefactors. The sisters have among them teachers highly competent to give instruction in all the branches of female education, even for the highest departments. Such teachers can always be procured from the older and well-established houses of the community, and that without cost, save their maintenance merely. Very soon they add "pay-scholars" to the number of their pupils; and, as the school becomes better known, the proportion of such scholars augments, while the number of those who are taught gratuitously diminishes. At length there are none at all of the latter class, and then the institution assumes the character of a select school. Even though the prices of tuition may not greatly increase, a selection will be made from the more wealthy families, and such as will best suit the purposes and designs of the managers. Next it becomes a boarding-school; the prices are advanced; and in the course of time a more strict discrimination is made in the reception of pupils. The number is more and more limited, until, a sufficient amount having been realized from the proceeds of instruction, the object is attained, and the school is abandoned altogether.

Collections are often made among the scholars to add to the funds of the institution. At St. Joseph's this was frequently done for some special purpose, as, for instance, to beautify the grounds of mission-houses.

At the Visitation Convent in Baltimore, on the corner of Park and Centre Streets, the sisters had formerly a very extensive school, with a large number of boarders. When I visited that convent prior to my entrance at St. Joseph's, I was informed that the number of boarders was then limited to sixteen, and that the school would soon be discontinued. I was also told that a sufficient amount had been acquired for the purchase of Mount de Sales, a beautiful and most valuable property, which cost over a million of dollars, and is now, I learn, the residence of Father Deluol, the Superior General of the order of Jesuits. The carriage of that institution was to have been sent for me to visit Mount de Sales in company with a priest, but I did not remain in Baltimore long enough to avail myself of the opportunity. At the Carmelite nunnery there was formerly a school, but not, I believe, a boarding-school, that institution being more strict and private than others. The school is now given up altogether; so, at least, I was informed at St. Joseph's.

While on the subject of the accumulation of money in these Roman Catholic convents, I may advert to the fact that there is at St. Joseph's a *treasurer*, who occupies a small apartment adjoining the stationery-room, and in which she sleeps at night. I have often been sent to that room, and have there observed an iron chest, in which I have seen a quantity of gold coin and jewelry. Many of the statues are decorated with valuable ornaments, such as diamond-rings, necklaces, gold crosses, etc. These are presents from visitors and other friends. I knew one sister who wrote to her parents for certain gold and silver articles of great value, which she designed as presents for one of the statues of the Virgin Mary. If the sisters individually are poor, in accordance with their vow of poverty, the community as a whole is wealthy, and the Superiors exercise entire control over that wealth. They have also an immense farm connected with the establishment.

CHAPTER XL.

FOUNDERS OF THE INSTITUTION.

THE "Conferences" have frequently been mentioned in these pages, and in connection with them the "rules" laid down by the founder of the community. These rules, which are contained in small books kept under lock and key, have been handed down from St. Vincent de Paul, who communicated them to the sisterhood.

A large and finely-executed portrait of this saint, who was also the founder of the congregation of missions known as the Order of St. Lazare, hangs in the chapel at St. Joseph's. He is there represented as holding a foundling in his arms, while at his side a sister is seen taking another infant out of a basket.

The lives of St. Vincent de Paul and St. Francis de Sales were frequently given us to read, as well as that of Mother Seton, who originated the institution at Emmettsburg. Mrs. Seton had been a Protestant lady, the daughter of an eminent physician in New York, and the wife of a merchant of high character, a member of the Protestant Episcopal Church. In 1803 she accompanied her husband to Italy for the benefit of his health; he, however, expired shortly after reaching Naples, and she was at once received into the family of an Italian gentleman who had long been in commercial correspondence with her husband. This gentleman, a zealous Roman Catholic, undertook the conversion of Mrs. Seton to his own faith. His influence over her mind continued after her return to America, and in 1805 she joined the Church of Rome, and was rebaptized in St. Peter's, New York.

Being in a great measure deserted by her relations, and obliged to resort to teaching for support, Mrs. Seton removed shortly after her conversion to Baltimore, where she opened a school, with the hope that, in process of time, it might grow into "a society whose members would be specially consecrated to God"—that is to say, into a convent. She was joined by her sister-in-law, and by a Miss Conway, of Philadelphia; and soon after this was invited by the priests of Baltimore to commence a "religious" establishment, for the foundation of which a legacy of eight thousand dollars had recently been left.

The vicinity of Emmettsburg having been selected for the location of the projected sisterhood, a piece of land south of the village was bought. At that time the only tenement on the farm was a small stone building, forming part of what is now used as the wash-house of the institution. It stands at a short distance from the main edifice, and is called the cradle of St. Joseph's.

Mrs. Seton now assumed for herself and those who joined her the title of "Sisters of St. Joseph," placing themselves "under the protecting care of St. Joseph, the faithful guardian of the Son of God upon earth." In their new residence—a small house containing only one story and an attic, with two rooms on each floor—sixteen persons were soon crowded together. They were often reduced to the poorest fare, such as "carrot-coffee, salt pork, and buttermilk." Thus they "labored at the work of their sanctification." "Consequent upon this style of living to persons mostly reared in luxury, the sisterhood was for several months an infirmary." Miss Harriet Seton was the first victim. She was shortly followed by her sister Cecilia. Mrs. Seton's eldest daughter, Anna, soon after sickened and died of consumption. Her death was probably induced by acts of violent mortification, which the biographer characterizes as "heroic." "I half reproached her," said her mother, "for her little care of her health: rising at the first bell, ever being on the watch to ring it the moment the clock struck; washing at the pump in the severest weather; often eating in the refectory what sickened her stomach."

The next who fell under this course of life was a Miss Murphy. "On one occasion she was directed to put her feet in warm water; which the sister infirmarian having brought, she put her feet into it, and immediately withdrew them, observing that the water was too hot; but her attendant insisting that it was not too warm, she returned her feet into the vessel, and kept them there as long as she was required, although it caused her intense pain, and produced an inflammation, from which she suffered for a long time after." By such "assiduous practices of the virtues of her state," we are told, "she soon became ripe for heaven."

In July, 1813, the society was regularly organized, eighteen individuals taking upon themselves the vows of "poverty, chastity, and obedience." Meantime, large additions were made, and continued to be made, to the buildings and conveniences of the establishment. The asylum, in which about fifty orphans, as near as I can judge, are now kept, was the next building erected. It was at first occupied by the community. A marble tablet in the wall of a room in this building marks the spot where the bed of Mother Seton stood, and where she died.

Although at this early period the natural fruits of the system were produced in the suffering, sickness, and death of the inmates, carrying out the idea which, as I have already had occasion to observe, is still inculcated—that "consumption is a part of the vocation of the sisters"—yet it seems that the system failed then, as it does now, of producing that superior sanctity of life and character which are perpetually claimed as its result. So much may at least be inferred from the following extract from an address of Mrs. Seton, who was now called the Mother Superior, to her sisters in profession: "How is it," she asks, "that many of us keep the rule as to the letter of it, and also look pious enough? There is no want of good will, nor idleness indulged; and in a house where it would seem so easy to become saints, you would say, What is the matter? Why are we not saints? Why is there so little progress in perfection? Or, rather, why are so many *tepid*, *heavy*, *discouraged*, and going along MORE LIKE SLAVES IN A WORK-HOUSE than children in their own homes, and the house of their Father?" The answer would seem easy for any one at all acquainted with the spirit of Gospel obedience:

Because the position, and the relations, and the occupations pertaining to this unnatural mode of life are such as Heaven has not chosen to ordain and bless for the religious development and sanctification of human souls.

One morning, meeting after mass a young sister who had been absent from the service, Mother Seton looked her steadfastly in the face, and asked, "Why did you not come to our Lord for a recompense this morning?" "Mother," answered the sister, "I felt a little weak, and took a cup of coffee before mass." "Ah! my dear child!" said Mother Seton, "how could you sell your God for a miserable cup of coffee?" Nothing, it has been well said, weakens the moral sense more than hair-breadth distinctions and minute observances. Mother Seton's life for a series of years was full of these. She rivaled the Hindoos in self-mortification. She would deny herself fine writing paper, and for pens she used the stumps of quills abandoned by her pupils.

Another death soon succeeded in the institution: it was that of the Mother Superior's second daughter, a lovely girl in her fourteenth year. In her last moments she cried to her confessor, "Father, is there any harm to hope that I shall go to heaven as soon as I am dead?" He replied, not if that hope was grounded on her own merits. "What merits," she cried, "can such a child as I have?" So little comfort can the contemplation of our own good works afford in the dying hour! Again she exclaimed, "I hope that my sufferings will be accepted as my penance without going to Purgatory. *Oh! how I would like to go to heaven!*"

In 1816 two more of the sisters died; one, only twenty-one years of age, brought up in luxury in the West Indies, and whose delicate hands often bled from exposure during the winter in performing the work allotted to her. The following year witnessed the death of four more of the sisters, and the next year three more. How the austerities which hastened the deaths of so many young persons affected the health of the Mother Superior herself, may be inferred from the following confession, in a letter of hers to the Rev. M. Bruté: "Rules, prudence, subjection, opinions, etc., are dreadful walls to a burning soul wild as mine. For me, I am like a fiery horse I had when a girl, whom they tried to break by making him drag a heavy cart; and the poor beast was so humbled that he could never more be inspired by whips or caresses, and wasted to a skeleton till he died!" Mrs. Seton's death occurred in 1820.

CHAPTER XLI.

THE FEAST OF CORPUS CHRISTI.

BEFORE reaching the closing circumstances of my stay at St. Joseph's, I may pause to describe the ceremonies performed at that institution in commemoration of a festival of peculiar solemnity which was celebrated during my residence there. It was the day of Corpus Christi, or the Feast of the Blessed Sacrament, termed, according to the tenets of the Roman Catholic Church, the Body of Christ.

On the morning of that day the sisterhood assembled in the community-room and novitiate, and, at the sound of the bell, formed themselves in the "rank," and walked in procession to the chapel. Each sister held in one hand her chaplet beads, and in the other a candle taken from a box near the door as she went out. During this space of time all were engaged in saying, in a low tone, the "Ave Maria."

Arriving in the chapel, after the usual ceremony of kissing the back of the seats before them, a chant was commenced by the choir; and the Superior, attended by two other Lazarists, entered the sanctuary, clothed in rich and costly vestments. The altar had been splendidly decorated for the occasion, and the statue of the Virgin wreathed with flowers. The Host was then for a moment elevated and exposed to view; then it was veiled from sight with a covering, on which was inscribed, in Latin, "Behold the Lamb of God."

After the saying of a few prayers, one of the priests took the sacrament and advanced to the railing which separates the sanctuary from the chapel. There he was joined by the others in attendance. Several altar-boys raised above the heads of the priests a magnificent canopy. The choir again commenced a solemn chant. The sacristan then advanced from the sacristy, and lighted the candle held by that one of the sisters who sat at the end of the nearest bench. The next sister then lighted her candle by means of her neighbor's, and so on, until the whole number had done likewise, and all the candles were lighted in the hands of the kneeling sisters.

This completed, the priests, carrying the Host, with the canopy elevated above them, marched slowly down the aisle, while every head was bowed in silent adoration. When they had reached the door, a rap was given by the Mother Superior, upon which the whole assemblage, after kissing the seats as usual, rose and walked in procession, each sister with her lighted candle, the choir accompanying them and chanting, in which the priests joined.

The procession crossed the Superior's garden and the adjacent grounds to a small and beautiful chapel,* which the priests entered, placing the sacrament upon the altar while the "Benediction" was sung. During

* This is a small chapel in the boarders' play-grounds, called the Chapel of Sister Bernardine, it being built by her when she was directress in the academy by donations obtained from the scholars.

this period the sisters knelt upon the ground, kissing the earth as they knelt and before they rose. The sacrament was then taken from this chapel, and the procession moved on to that of St. Joseph, which is situated in another part of the grounds, called "The Sisters' Garden," or the community-ground. "Benediction" was sung here also, and the same form was observed as before, both in and out of the chapel. Then the sacrament was carried through the community-room and the novitiate, a path being formed in one of the rooms, bordered with rose-leaves and evergreens, through which the procession walked.

After crossing the corridor and entering the chapel of the institution, the ceremonies were there ended with a benediction. The lights were extinguished, and, after the usual form of kissing the seats in front of each, and repeating a few prayers, the community once more arranged themselves in the rank and proceeded to their respective rooms.

The boarders of the institution followed in the rear of the procession of sisters throughout the whole of these imposing ceremonies.

CHAPTER XLII.

A SECOND LETTER FROM HOME.

A SECOND letter was at length received at the institution on the —th of September, 1854, from my relatives, and upon its receipt I was ordered to appear before the mistress of novices. Kneeling at her feet, I listened to the letter as she read it aloud. It was from my sister. She stated that she would come for me in a few days, and that I must return home with her.

This information excited greatly the displeasure of the mistress of novices. Having finished its perusal, she seized me with a tight grasp by the arm, saying, "Do you think you will *ever* return home?" I answered that I did not know, and began to tremble violently, as well with agitation as with dread, such is the awe that an official inspires at the institution. This enraged her. She struck me upon the forehead, and, roughly thrusting me from her, she ordered me to go and kneel before the altar of St. Joseph at one end of the room, and repeat some prayers as a penance.

I obeyed mechanically, but no prayer, no tears came to relieve my feelings; cold and almost stupefied, I remained motionless as the statue before which

I was bent. An hour and more passed ere I was roused from my stupor; but a stormy conflict was raging within my breast. The agonizing consciousness had a second time with terrible force come upon me that I was eternally severed from all that made life dear.

The bell rang for meditation in the chapel, and this call I must obey. Had it been some other kind of punishment that was allotted me, this would have given variation to my employment, and relieved the fatigue; but the signal only called me to renew the exhausting effort of maintaining for a long time the same painful posture. I rose, took my place in the rank, and repaired to the chapel, where another hour was spent on my knees in prayer and meditation, as far as bodily constraint and mental distress would permit the exercise of thought.

A week elapsed, and on Sunday I asked permission to reply to the letter received from my friends. As it was a day usually appropriated in part to the writing of letters—which, however, must be written after high mass, and submitted to the inspection of the Mother Superior, by whom they are forwarded at her pleasure —I had some hope of obtaining my request. But permission was denied me, with an assurance that it would be but a loss of time, and useless for me to do so. I was ordered to the refectory for the purpose of cleaning knives and forks. I had been but a short time engaged in this employment, when the "religieuse" who had charge of this department suddenly rushed toward me, and seizing the knife I was cleaning, drew it through my hand, commencing an angry rebuke for some pretended fault, and threatening to report me. This unprovoked cruelty so startled me, already enfeebled as I was by severe labor and protracted fatigue, that I fell in a spasm on the floor, striking my head against a bench. A young novice, who had seen me fall, dragged me into the passage, supported my head, and sent another to report to an officer my situation. Before the officer came I had revived, and was proceeding down the corridor, aided by two sisters, when I met her. She conveyed me to the infirmary, asking me, at the same time, what was the matter. Fearing to tell her, I remained silent; but as she insisted on an answer, I related to her the occurrence. She made no reply, and did not seem to entertain much sympathy for me. She left me on a bed in the infirmary, but soon after returned, and made me get up and go back to my work in the refectory.

I ought to say that a sister must obtain permission to write on the Saturday preceding; should she fail to do this, it is not allowed her to ask the privilege. But often, when this is done, the request is refused, and the petitioner is told that it would be "a loss of time." I have more than once received this answer. All letters written by the sisters are given to the mistress of novices for her perusal. Many of them never reach their destination, being destroyed by her on the spot. Others are sent to the Superior's room, but the writers never know what becomes of them. I have seen the mistress of novices engaged in reading and tearing to pieces letters which have been sent to the novitiate, but were never destined to reach those who perhaps were anxiously awaiting their arrival at home.

Many a time have I seen sisters kneeling before the mistress of novices, the tears streaming from their eyes as they listened to letters read by her, but which they were not permitted to hold in their own hands, nor look at, to trace the beloved characters of a mother's or a sister's writing.

CHAPTER XLIII.

MORTALITY AND DEATH AT ST. JOSEPH'S.

It is on all hands acknowledged that the life of monastic and conventual establishments is most unfavorable to bodily health. Those even who are chiefly interested in upholding these institutions make no attempt to conceal the fact. On the contrary, I have shown, and of this farther evidence will be given hereafter, that from the very outset the system adopted at St. Joseph's has been disastrous and fatal in the extreme, so far as sickness, disease, and death are evidences of its workings. In the second year after the foundation of the society, which commenced with only eighteen members, three of them died; in 1816, two more; the following year, four; and the next, three. I have already testified that, within the ten months of my sojourn at St. Joseph's, no fewer than fourteen deaths, to my personal knowledge, occurred. Nor does the Mother Superior, in her remarkable letter written after my escape, controvert this point; she maintains only that this excessive mortality is the result of the pious and charitable exertions to which the sisters devote themselves in attending hospitals and ministering to the sick. I leave it for an impartial judgment to decide whether it may not much more rationally be ascribed to the exhausting and depressing effects of unremitted and laborious servile "duties" and devotional exercises, the forms and attitudes of which resemble rather the varieties of torture than the employments of Christian meditation and worship. I leave it for a candid discrimination to say whether such be not the inevitable result of protracted and reiterated vigils, of exposure to a damp and chilly atmosphere, of mental excitement fed by superstitious fears and apprehensions, of unnatural severment from all the attachments of life, and seclusion under perpetual restraints.

I myself, while a member of the community, was often sick, worn down and utterly prostrated by the services daily and uninterruptedly required of me. Even while engaged in performing the duties, comparatively lighter, which were enjoined upon me as a teacher in the academy, it would frequently happen that the lassitude of body and mind became almost insupportable. In addition to instructing a class of pupils in the French language, and teaching others in music, I was required to perform a similar task for such of the novices as evinced any talent for vocal or instrumental music, in order that the vacancies occurring from time to time in the choir might be appropriately supplied. I have often sat for hours, without a moment's intermission or rest, at the piano, and after that have been occupied at work in the refectory or other departments.

If illness and a shattered constitution—the ordinary and necessary results of such a system*—had been

* The Rev. M. Hobart Seymour, a distinguished clergyman of the

the only suffering brought upon me by the endurance of these inflictions, I might still be an inmate of St. Joseph's—an unwilling inmate, doubtless, since I had become thoroughly convinced of my own mistake in entering that institution. But this alone would not have proved sufficient to impel me to the desperate venture of an attempt to escape from its walls. I call it a desperate venture, because the failure to accomplish my object would have been attended with the most bitter consequences. But other apprehensions were combined with those of bodily suffering to impel me in this effort to flee from a place the atmosphere of which was dangerous and contaminating.

I entered the institution of St. Joseph's under the complacent impression and belief that among the "Sis-

English Church, stated in a lecture some time since, that a gentleman, high in official position at Rome, who had been a visitor with the Cardinal Vicar in the various nunneries of that city, gave him the following facts from his own positive knowledge. He remarked that, "entering these nunneries at the early age of sixteen or eighteen, for a few years the nuns seemed sufficiently happy; but that afterward, having discovered the extent of the step they had taken, some of them pined, and drooped, and withered, and died; while others, struggling against it for a time, in the end gave way to despair, and died of madness. He stated that, of his own experience, *the majority of these young nuns* DIED DERANGED BEFORE TWENTY-FIVE YEARS OF AGE!"—Lecture at Bath, England, June 7th, 1852.

In the concluding portion of this volume we shall have occasion to give the statement of an unimpeachable witness, the excellent Dr. De Sanctis, now a minister of the Waldensian Church in Piedmont, but formerly a Roman Catholic priest of distinction, curate of the Magdalene at Rome, and confessor at a number of convents in that city. In a communication made expressly for the present work, he gives it as the result of personal observation, that "a very large proportion of the nuns die in their youth; and a great part of the rest drag a miserable existence in continual disease and suffering."

ters of Charity" I should find an entire devotedness, a pure and unselfish dedication to the service of the Almighty. I had heard and read so much of their pious lives, their earnest efforts to comfort the afflicted, relieve the sick, and console the dying, that I entertained the most exalted ideas of their Christian perfection. During the short time of my visit as a visitor, my limited observation, together with the assurances of the Superior, confirmed these favorable sentiments, and I became a member of the community, prepared, under circumstances the most propitious, to look upon every thing with an admiring eye. Gradually this illusion was dissipated. The rose tint gave place to the sombre hue of the reality; my golden anticipations one by one were falsified; and the ardent enthusiasm with which I entered, from fever heat cooled down to zero.

I had no doubt that the great number of individuals in the sisterhood were perfectly sincere and conscientious in the practice of their devotions and the discharge of their duties. But among these, so much superstition, weakness, and folly prevailed as to excite contempt, or at least pity. The idolatrous worship of the Virgin Mary was carried to such a pitch as could not fail to shock a mind that retained any vestige of scriptural belief and conviction.* The re-

* The impulse that has been given of late years by the Romish priesthood to what they call "the devotion to Mary," has carried that worship to an excess and exaggeration almost inconceivable. Connected with this increase of a blasphemous homage is an endeavor to represent the Virgin Mary as, in a peculiar sense, the DEITY *of women*, and, of course, especially of *nuns*. Thus the famous M. de Genoude, one of the most eminent ecclesiastics of the Romish Church in

spect paid to pictures and images, though designed, according to the doctrines of the Roman Catholic Church,

France, has expressed this tendency in these remarkable words: "MARY was the *repairer of Eve's offense*, even as OUR LORD was the *repairer of the offense of Adam!*" ("Marie fut la réparatrice de la faute d'Eve, comme Notre-Seigneur fut le réparateur de la faute d'Adam."— —*Tableau historique du premier siècle de l'Eglise.*) Another writer, M. Oswald, professor of theology in the Roman Catholic Seminary of Paderborn, in Germany, makes the following more full statement of the same idea: "Mary was not a human creature like ourselves; she was *The Woman*, as Christ was *The Man*. The work of redemption revolves upon two names—Jesus Christ, the God-Man, and Mary, the Virgin-Mother of God. *For this reason we are disposed to erect by the side of Christology a Marialogy, of which this should be the creed:* I believe in Mary, born without sin, and exempt from faults throughout her entire life; the Virgin-Mother of the Lord by the grace of God, and at the same time by her own free consent; co-operating, although in dependence upon her divine Son, in the act of redemption; performing therein a part without which the work of Jesus Christ would not be complete; the dispenser, in the Church, of certain graces which, though ultimately owing to the merits of Jesus Christ, are found nevertheless in a certain causal dependence upon her active participation in the redemption of man. She occupies this place in the quality of spiritual mother of the human kind, and as *special representative of her sex in the work of reparation.*"—(*Marialogie dogmatique*, 1850, p. 1, 2.)

But there is a deeper abyss of absurdity and blasphemy to which these worshipers of the Virgin Mary descend. "We assert," says M. Oswald, "that *Mary is co-present in the Eucharist;* this is an inevitable consequence of our *Marianic* theory, and we do not shrink from any of its consequences. If Mary, as Mother of God, took a real part in our redemption, this part, in order that it might not be lost, must have been bequeathed to the Church by its Founder, and must be transmitted in the Eucharist. It is needless to add, that, in accordance with the eucharistic doctrine of the Church, this presence of Mary in the Eucharist is veritable and real, not simply ideal or figurative. *Women receive more in the Eucharist than do men. They receive, in addition to the grace of Jesus Christ, which is common to all, a supplement of Marianic grace!*"—(*Marialogie*, etc., p. 176, foll.)

As a single specimen of the nature of the supplications addressed to the Virgin Mary which are put in the mouths of the multitudes under

to serve for the simple direction of the mind to a devout contemplation of their subjects, is here practiced in a manner that savors of the grossest idolatry. To give a solitary instance: I have spoken of the statue of St. Vincent, the founder of the order, which stands in the Superior's garden, where sometimes we were permitted to work. This figure is held in special estimation. No one passed it without a lowly obeisance, and I have often heard it addressed as a living being. Many of the sisters would approach it timidly, with hands clasped in the attitude of prayer, and, after a profound salutation, exclaim, in beseeching tones, "*Pray for me, father!*"

The old or "professed sisters," whose physical constitution has enabled them to pass through the ordeal of years, are treated with much more leniency, and lead an easier life than the novices. Many of those who are rather advanced in age occupy their own rooms, where they are served by the younger sisters, and are not compelled strictly to attend to all the services. In the community-room they sometimes have "parties," with music and refreshments, to which the priests are invited.* On such occasions, some of the younger sisters are admitted, or allowed a share in the

the spiritual care of the Romish priests, we give the following extract of a prayer which is in use at Rome, and is accompanied by the promise of "an indulgence of one hundred years, granted by the supreme pontiffs Gregory XV. and Clement XII." It begins thus: "O purest and most immaculate ever-Virgin Mary! *Daughter of the Everlasting Father, Mother of the Everlasting Son, Spouse of the Holy Ghost! August and living Temple of the Most Holy Trinity!* Jewel of purity, spotless mirror," etc., etc.

* At Rome they act *comedies* and *tragedies* in the convents. See De Sanctis' letter appended to this work.

delicacies provided, although, for the most part, it is their duty to prepare them. Of occurrences in the community-room I can, however, give no minute particulars from personal observation, as the "seminary sisters" are not allowed to enter that apartment unless summoned to the presence of the Superior, or sent thither with a message; but enough is known outside to excite sorrow and disgust.

CHAPTER XLIV.

NO BIBLE.

It is well known to every one at all conversant with ecclesiastical history that the perusal of the Scriptures by the laity has at all times been discouraged, and on repeated occasions forbidden by the Roman Catholic hierarchy.* When charged with this criminal with-

* This fact, plain and obvious as it is to the reader of history, tells with such power upon the unscriptural character of the Romish system, that the priests can only meet it with an audacious denial. In this country, especially, they do not hesitate to say that the Church of Rome gives full liberty to read the Bible and encourages its use, forbidding only the perusal of a Protestant translation. The means of answering so barefaced a falsehood are not always at hand in a popular discussion, and thus they often succeed in producing the desired impression upon the minds of the uninformed. We shall give here in brief a few statements illustrative of the treatment that the Bible has received at the hands of the supreme pontiffs of that Church, to say nothing of the Bible-burnings and confiscations that occur so frequently in our own day in Roman Catholic countries, where no attempt is made to conceal the enmity of Romanism for the word of God.

The Council of Trent—to go no farther back—declared its anathema against any one who should read the Bible without a license from his bishop or inquisitor, that license to be founded on a certificate from his confessor that he is in no danger of receiving injury from so doing.

Pope Pius VII., in 1816, denounces in a special bull the Bible Society, and expresses himself "shocked" by the circulation of the Scriptures, which he characterizes as a "most crafty device, by which the very foundations of religion are undermined;" a "pestilence," which

holding of God's word from men, it is sometimes alleged, by way of excuse, that in former times the ignorance of the people was an obstacle to the right understanding of the precepts and doctrines of the Bible, and also that the scarcity and high price of copies of the Scriptures prevented their circulation. This apology may be readily admitted with reference to that period of which the assertion is true; but it should be observed that even in the present enlightened age, no encouragement is held out in countries where Romanism predominates for the examination of that holy book,

it behooves him "to remedy and abolish;" "a defilement of the faith, eminently dangerous to souls." He congratulates the primate to whom his letter is addressed on the zeal he had shown "to detect and overthrow the impious machinations of these innovators;" and represents it as an episcopal duty to expose "the wickedness of their nefarious scheme," and openly to publish that "the Bible printed by heretics is to be numbered among other prohibited books, conformably to the rules of the Index; for it is evident from experience that the Holy Scriptures, *when circulated in the vulgar tongue*, have, through the temerity of men, *produced more harm than benefit*."

The same pope issued in 1819 a bull on the subject of the circulation of the Scriptures in the Irish schools. He speaks of this as a "sowing of tares," and that the children are thereby infected with the "*fatal poison of depraved doctrines*;" and exhorts the Irish bishops to endeavor to prevent the wheat from being "choked by the tares."

In 1824, Pope Leo XII. published an encyclical letter, in which he adverts to a certain society, vulgarly called the Bible Society, as spreading itself throughout the whole world, and goes on to term the Protestant Bible the "Gospel of the Devil."

The late Pope Gregory XVI., in his encyclical letter, after referring to the decree of the Council of Trent already mentioned, ratifies that and all similar enactments of the Church in these terms: "Moreover, we confirm and renew the decrees recited above, delivered in former times by apostolic authority, against the *publication, distribution, reading, and possessing of books of the Holy Scriptures translated into the vulgar tongue*."

nor is even the erroneous translation of it which has been sanctioned by the authorities of the Church of Rome freely circulated for popular perusal. But in the United States no such predominancy enables the priesthood to expel the Scriptures from publicity, and here, accordingly, the charge is indignantly denied, and the assertion is exultingly made that the Bible is kept at all the Catholic book-stores, and all Catholics are at liberty to purchase and read it. Without entering upon a discussion of this statement, I will only appeal to Catholics themselves to answer truly whether their priests or confessors are in the habit of recommending the habitual study of the Scriptures to them individually. The fact that no such reference or direction is habitually made by the priesthood to the oracles of God sufficiently proves their indifference, if not their hostility to it.

During the whole period of my connection with the Church of Rome, no such instruction or counsel was given me by my spiritual director; and while a resident at St. Joseph's *I never saw a Bible*, and I had frequent access to the library. My own testimony would certainly go to confirm the general statement, the correctness of which is corroborated by the entire policy of Romanism, to subject the people to the control of the clergy. Apprehensive lest the frequent and unrestrained study of the sacred Scriptures would prove a serious antagonism to their efforts for enslaving the mind, the priests carefully abstain from encouraging their dissemination wherever they do not dare to oppose it openly. Another consideration doubtless acts upon them. Some of the peculiar dogmas of Romanism, such as that of Purgatory and that respecting indulgences, are effectual means of augmenting the revenues of the Church; and these subjects of belief are so flimsily supported even by their own interpretation of Scripture, that they would be rejected if examined by every intelligent student of the holy volume.

The books permitted and recommended for reading at St. Joseph's are the "Lives of the Saints," extracts from the "Roman Martyrology" and the "Conferences." These last are a compilation of rules and regulations to be observed by the Order of Sisters of Charity, as prepared by their founder, St. Vincent. They contain much matter not suitable for edification, nor calculated to promote purity of thought.

CHAPTER XLV.

A DREAM OF FREEDOM.

In a former part of this narrative I have made allusion to the careful prevention of confidential intercourse between members of the community. The regulations enjoining silence, except at a certain hour, are strictly enforced; and even at that period conversation is allowed only on permitted subjects and in the presence of superiors. For two sisters to engage in private interchange of thought would be an offense which, if known, would unavoidably be visited with severe punishment. The want of some sympathizing friend to whom I might unburden my feelings and sufferings, or to whom, in turn, I might afford consolation and support, was bitterly felt. Outward signs of the mental conflict must imperatively be suppressed. When almost overwhelmed with sensations of utter desolation, I was forced to veil, by a powerful effort, my wretchedness. The death-like pallor of the countenance, and often the traces of tears that could not be restrained, would perhaps betray the agony of soul. But I must be calm and collected in manner, and breathe no syllable that might express my misery. Every native impulse of the heart, every prompting of affection, every thought of sympathy and kindness, must be subdued and silenced: such, it is thought, is the duty of all who would render themselves worthy to wear the "holy habit."

Often have I gazed from my window upon the picturesque grounds that environed my prison. How green and beautiful the trees, their slender branches bending in the vesper breeze! The rose of lovely tint, and the many flowers embosomed in the long waving grass—I could not enjoy their sweetness; not even was it lawful for me to inhale at will their delicious perfume, wafted by the breeze that fanned my cheek, once glowing with health and animation, but now marked with the traces of suffering and sorrow.

Ever and anon my listless gaze would wander over the distant landscape. Before me were the mountains, in all their majestic beauty, the western sun, as it set, pouring a flood of golden light upon the dense foliage that covered their summits; and then, as a caged bird dashing against the bars of its prison-house with strong desire to gain its native wild-wood, even so did I yearn to escape from the walls that surrounded me, to roam free and unfettered over those mountain sides, reveling in those sunbeams, or quietly resting in the shade of those towering trees. But I must banish these thoughts—repel the wish to gaze upon and enjoy the beauties of nature. What have I to do with earth? What to me is that world which I have renounced forever? For me the interest of natural life is irrevocably closed, and now, by devoting my existence to the service of God in the holy seclusion of the cloister, I shall purchase heaven! By a life of poverty, suffering, prayer, and penance, win the smile of the holy Virgin and her divine Son! Yes, I will welcome those pains and miseries to save my soul, though they destroy my body. But can not heaven be gained without such a sacrifice? The way is dark and difficult. What now is left me? a lonely heart, a weary life, a disappointed hope. O God! teach my spirit to be resigned to Thy most holy will.

Scenes of other days now pass in rapid review before me. Alas! that memory should add its pangs, recalling years that have forever fled, hours that I would fain forget, moments of thrilling rapture, from whose fond contemplation my vows debar me now.

Scenes of more recent date, with all their blighting woe, come to agonize my heart, yet bleeding with former reflections: a mother's loss, never to be made up, never to be alleviated by the consolations of paternal and sisterly affection; expostulations and gentle warnings disregarded, under the infatuation of a deceived and misguided zeal. Well is it now that little time is allowed for such remembrances. Let me return to the care and weariness of my bondage, and forget the past.

CHAPTER XLVI.

MY ESCAPE.

CONSCIOUS that I was a guarded prisoner at St. Joseph's, I now determined, in secresy if possible, to escape. But could I hope to leave the institution undiscovered during the day? It was impossible, since no one is suffered even to enter or leave a room without express command or obtained permission, and spies are known to be placed in all parts of the building, though individually recognizable as such by none but the Superior.

Considerable time had elapsed since the forming of this resolution without the offering of any special facility to realize the scheme. Finally, I determined to delay no longer, but make an attempt at once. At first I was at a loss what course to decide upon when once I should be outside the walls of the institution. The town of Emmettsburg was but a quarter of a mile distant, and I could easily reach it; but I knew that a large proportion of the inhabitants were Catholics, and that I should run the risk of being discovered and sent back to the community. The "house" of the Lazarists was also located there, between which and St. Joseph's there was constant communication, and the probability of an encounter on the road with some member of the order occurred to my mind. In view of these considerations, I decided that it would be more prudent to proceed to Frederick City. I resolved, accordingly, to seek egress from the building about two hours after midnight, in order that I might catch the stage from Emmettsburg to that place, which passed at about four o'clock in the morning. This resolution was taken on the evening preceding my departure, while sitting at the window of my cell for a few minutes before the ringing of the bell for evening prayers. I had been detained from supper until late, in consequence of having been appointed to take charge of the music-rooms (a duty ordinarily discharged by a vowed sister) while the sisterhood were at their meal, and when I arrived at the refectory nearly every one had left. I took advantage of the opportunity and secured a knife, which I concealed about my person, with the full determination to use it, if my strength should permit, in self-defense, should I be stopped or overtaken on the road; for I was now desperate, and the bare idea of failure filled me with terror.

While seated at the window revolving my plan, as my head rested against the casement, and the chill night air blew in upon me (though for this I cared not, being familiar with suffering and exposure to cold), I was startled from my meditations by the deep tolling of the convent bell calling to prayers. Hastily composing my features, and effacing the traces of tears from my countenance, I rose to obey its summons for the last time, as I fondly hoped. While crossing the corridor on my way to the novitiate, I was accosted by an old sister, who delivered to me an order with which she had been intrusted, requiring that I should sweep out all the music-rooms at an early hour in the morning. I showed her my hand, which I carried in a sling, the thumb having been opened to the bone but a few days before to cure a whitlow, and told her that I should hardly be able to perform the duty. Saying that the order was imperative, she left me, and I proceeded to the chapel, not, it may be presumed, with any purpose of sweeping out the music-rooms the next morning; instead of which, I hoped to be breathing the fresh air of heaven, and exulting in the sense of freedom and deliverance from the horrors of a "living death."

About an hour passed by after the conclusion of the evening devotions, and all the sisters had retired to their cells. Suffering exceedingly from thirst, I resolved, though it was contrary to the rules for a novice to drink after the ringing of the silence-bell, to procure a draught of water, and at the same time to see whether the key of a door leading from a passage across the porch to the infirmary was in the lock. I accomplished my purpose without discovery, but the key had been removed. Returning to my cell, I lay down on my bed to obtain some rest before the appointed hour; but I was too anxious to sleep, and trembled and shivered upon my couch until the cry of the watchman, who has charge of the establishment at night, announced that it was two o'clock. A few minutes after I arose, put on my habit, placing the beads in my pocket, lest they should rattle as I walked along, and then waited for the watchman's cry of "three o'clock." Upon hearing that signal I left my cell, doing so for the first time without making my bed, and groped my way through the darkness down the stairs and along the cloisters, all the while attentively listening to detect any noise. All was silent save the slight sound of my footsteps on the paved floor. Descending a narrow flight of stairs, I proceeded along a dark passage, at the extremity of which there were other steps leading to the chapel. I preferred to attempt my escape in this part of the building for the reason that there was no inclosure immediately outside of it. Having gained the chapel door, I was forced to pause and rest for a few moments to gain composure; for I was trembling violently, and almost suffocated by the impetuous and convulsive throbbings of my heart. There was no time to be lost, however; so, taking courage, I ran across the chapel, and, guided by a faint gleam of moonlight through the crevices, climbed up to a window, opened it, and leaped to the pavement below. I looked around and listened, but no living object was visible, and no sound broke the stillness. The watchman at the building had gone in, but there was another stationed at the gate, whose vigilance I would have to elude. I could not stop, however, to reflect, but fled rapidly down the avenue. When about half way, I heard a slight noise, and approaching nearer, perceived, to my dismay, that the watchman had raised the window of his room, and was leaning from it, as though suspicious of something wrong. My heart sank within me, and for a moment I was literally paralyzed with fear. But I soon succeeded in concealing myself behind a tree, and remained there for some time, anxiously awaiting the withdrawal of the watchman from his post of observation. There was another mode of egress from the grounds, by a path through the grave-yard, where from my station I could see the white crosses gleaming in the moonlight. But this would take me in a direction opposite to that which I intended to follow; and fearing lest I might become confused and lose my way, I resolved to wait where I was.

Another grievous disappointment was in store for me. While at my hiding-place, the stage for Frederick City, in which I had trusted to obtain a seat, passed by, and with it all my sanguine anticipations vanished, and for an instant despair took possession of my faculties. I became partly reassured, however, when I joyfully observed that the watchman, as if satisfied by the passing of the stage, had closed the window and retired. I quickly passed through the gate into the road, feeling that my object was at least half accomplished, the chief obstacle being already surmounted.

I had walked but a short distance in the direction taken by the stage when, approaching a bridge which I was obliged to cross, I saw in the shadow the figure of a man. At this sight my courage again faltered, for I felt assured that, should he prove a Catholic, and suspect from my garb who I was, he would attempt to carry me back by force; but drawing my shawl closely around me, to conceal as much as possible my "habit," I pulled my dark bonnet farther over my face, and grasping the knife as firmly as my wounded hand would allow, I walked boldly past without being accosted. About a mile and a half farther on, hearing the voices of a party of men who were coming toward me, I entered a gate that opened on the road, and knelt behind the inclosure till they had gone by. I was on the point of again proceeding upon my way, after waiting some minutes to make sure that the road was clear, when sounds of fighting and cries of "murder" from a house near by caused me to shrink back in alarm to my hiding-place. There I remained until I heard the Angelus ring at St. Joseph's. I knew then that it was six o'clock; and conscious that I had no time to lose, I re-entered the road and prosecuted my journey with as much speed as my tired limbs could effect.

I had walked a considerable distance, and began to experience great fatigue, when, seeing a woman near a house on the road-side, I ventured to address her, asking "how far it was to Frederick City." "Twenty-two miles," was her answer. I inquired if I could obtain a conveyance thither. Without deigning a reply to my question, she asked me where I came from, and on my telling her "from Emmettsburg," advised me in a peremptory tone to "go back, and start from there." Then turning to a young man who came out of the house, she whispered to him for a few moments, when he immediately started in the direction of the institution.

Convinced from her conduct that the woman was a Catholic, and entertained some suspicion of my being a fugitive from the sisterhood; confident, too, that she had dispatched the young man to give information concerning me, I turned away, and continued my journey. But I was now afraid to proceed on the main road, lest I should be overtaken, and more afraid to leave it, lest I should lose my way. After crossing a creek—Owning's Creek I think it is called—I arrived about nine o'clock at a small village, which a sign-post informed me was Creagerstown. I had walked a distance of ten miles. On inquiring for the principal house of entertainment in the place, I was directed to Stevens's Hotel, the proprietor of which, at that time, with a noble kindness and generous hospitality that acted like a soothing balm upon my wounded spirit, and for which I shall ever be grateful, accorded me the shelter of his house, and assured me of the protection of his arm until the arrival of my father, to whom I instantly wrote, informing him of the circumstances of my escape.

None but those who have felt, after some overwhelming sorrow that threatened to obscure every future prospect, the first cheering rays of hope breaking through the clouds—none but those who, deprived of all sympathy and protection, exposed to evil designs and unscrupulous schemes against their peace and purity, without a glimpse of succor and deliverance, have suddenly been rescued from their perilous condition and restored to safety, can adequately appreciate the exultant joy and happiness that thrilled every nerve of my system when convinced that I had gained shelter and defense among those whose hearts beat in sympathy with my afflictions and my fears. To many noble-hearted citizens of Creagerstown will memory often recur with gratitude for their exertions in behalf of a friendless, and, to them, unknown girl.

As I afterward learned, and at the time conjectured,

the young man sent off by the woman whom I addressed on the road did go to St. Joseph's with the information, but, owing to my disguise, he did not know that I was a member of the community, and told the Superior that a *boarder* had escaped. It was not class-day, but the bell was rung, and the scholars were assembled. None being missed, it was supposed that the messenger had been mistaken. Thus the knowledge of my absence was delayed for a time; and to this delay I am perhaps indebted for the fact that I was not overtaken and forced back.

So soon, however, as my escape became known, persons were sent in search of me in different directions; and my place of refuge was discovered by the overseer of the farm, who had gone to Frederick City, suspecting that I had perhaps sought admission at the convent there, which is a "visitation" convent, and does not stand in very amicable relations with St. Joseph's; but, hearing no tidings of me there, he came to Creagerstown. He requested an interview with me, and stated that the Mother Superior was greatly disturbed at the step I had taken, and promised that if I would return quietly, and without causing an excitement, she would send me home. He added that she was fearful lest, if the circumstances should become known, the institution would be injured. My answer to this plausible message may readily be surmised. After the departure of the overseer, the Superior, being informed where I was, dispatched two "officers" of the community to Creagerstown. On their arrival they endeavored to force their way to my room, but I refused to see them; for the habit of obedience to their

mandates had become so strong, that I actually dreaded the influence of their presence, and trembled at the thought of an interview with those of whom I had so long stood in awe, and to whose wishes and commands submission had become, as it were, a second nature. The landlord of the hotel took part in my anxiety to avoid this meeting. I was locked up in a room on the second story of the house, the window-shutters of which were closed and fastened during the whole time of the sisters' stay. I was in a state of the utmost alarm lest they should reach me. I heard the altercation going on below, and feared that, after all, I should be delivered up. So much had my spirit become subject to the control of these sister-officers of St. Joseph's. But, being unable to obtain access to me, they wrote notes, which were thrust under the door, and a receipt, which I signed, for the articles of my own property which had been brought me. I sent them every thing about my person that they demanded—my "capot," community-book or formulary, etc., etc. I had not felt such alarm at any moment during my escape as during the time that these sisters remained in the house.

CHAPTER XLVII.

AN INCIDENT AFTER ESCAPE.

A SHORT time previous to my departure, one of the boarders had left the academy. She had always appeared much attached to me; and when, on my way home from Creagerstown with my father, we stopped at a hotel in Frederick City, she immediately came upon hearing of our arrival, and, rushing to my arms, embraced me with a cry of delight, "Oh! sister, I am so glad to see you away from that institution!" She did not leave me until we entered the cars for Baltimore. Her congratulations were abundant, and she repeatedly assured me, while we were together in Frederick, that, had she known of my desire to escape, her carriage would have been at my disposal.

After my return home I received a letter from this young lady which I did not answer. Its tenor was such as to satisfy me that already her mind had been biased against me, so little dependence can be placed upon the candid judgment of any one, even a postulant or boarder, who is under the influence of the Superior of St. Joseph's.

It is worthy of notice, however accounted for, that in every case of the flight of a young girl from the walls of a Roman Catholic convent or community, which she may have been induced by plausible but deceitful representations to enter, she is at once regarded as an outcast and denounced as a disgrace to religion by the whole papal society. On this subject the remarks of a recent writer are so pertinent that I can not express myself better than in his words: "Her early associates will upbraid her, her own parents [if they be Roman Catholic] will cast her off, and the papal community in which she lives will avoid her as if infected with leprosy. In *papal countries* she will scarcely be able to get food to keep her from starvation, if they do not rally around her and drive her back to prison, and penance, and punishment.

"Why is this? Is it not very plain that the instructions of the priests to their people are of such a kind that they train them to believe that if a nun escapes, no matter for what cause, she is disobedient to the priest, and will certainly be damned; and though it may appear cruel to treat her so harshly, yet, in the end, if they succeed in compelling her to go back to the convent, the cruelty to the escaped nun will be considered meritorious for their and her salvation?

"To make ample provision for retaining them in these prisons, the priests teach that there is no sin which can be committed while in the convent that will bear comparison with that of leaving off the convent life and being married. Having gotten this idea in the minds of their people of this dreadful sin of escaping from the convent, the people never pretend to imagine for what cause or under what circumstances the individual has escaped.

"Now I will admit that one half, two thirds—nay,

that all the nuns enter willingly, but really ignorant of what is before them. Tell me of what immorality or crime they are guilty when, on finding the convent to be not what they supposed and were taught that it was, they desire to leave, and on finding themselves imprisoned, venture on an escape?"*

There can be little doubt that the consideration of these consequences upon such a step frightens many a novice, and many a professed "*religieuse*" too, from the attempt to liberate herself from the durance in which she is held and the evils to which she is exposed. Whenever the courage of a poor recluse is summoned to so desperate an effort, the entire Catholic community seem actuated by one mind and purpose to denounce and persecute her. The case is prejudged before she can utter a syllable in her own defense. The assertions of those from whose thraldom she has escaped to those to whom she has fled, and whose interest it must be to conceal and misconstrue, are implicitly and blindly believed, while no credit is given to her own declarations. A malignant pleasure seems to be found in holding her up as an object for public scorn, in blasting the character and prospects of an innocent girl, simply because, shuddering and revolting at the fate to which she was doomed, she could not remain a willing or a passive victim. Nay, even some Protestants—to their shame be it spoken—from motives of personal regard, or from interested considerations, do not hesitate to lend their free voices to this combination of priests, superiors, and a bigoted laity,

* *Priests' Prisons for Women,* in Twelve Letters. By Andrew B. Cross. Baltimore, 1854.

in their unpardonable work of malice and uncharitableness.

As a matter of course, I have not escaped such an ordeal. As soon as my departure from St. Joseph's became known, these efforts were commenced, and they have been continued, in various forms, up to the present time. Having in the preceding narrative told, with all candor, the incidents and motives of my entering the institution, my experience while residing there, and the reasons that compelled me to leave it by stealth, I shall now have to narrate a series of injurious and groundless attacks, brought upon me by that step.

CHAPTER XLVIII.

PRIEST O'DONNELL.

THE first onset was made by a meddlesome priest, residing many hundred miles from the locality, who could not resist the tempting opportunity afforded him to display his zeal in behalf of this cherished system of the Romish clergy. The following is a copy of his published letter on the subject:

"Portland, November 25th, 1854.

"MR. EDITOR:

"DEAR SIR,—My attention has been directed this morning to an extract in your paper from a dispatch from Baltimore. It is not my wish to censure you for the paragraph. Probably you had the pleasure to read it for the first time in this morning's edition. I have no other expression for the writer than that of sympathy; for the man who knowingly circulates false rumors to gratify the marvelous appetite is in much need of public sympathy. Such rumors, however, are easily removed in the locality where they originated, but not so abroad.

"The statements are easily made and readily believed; an impression is forthwith made in accordance with the statement, most generally of prejudice and hostility against the calumniated, and there is evidently no manifest desire to suppress the falsehood and circulate the truth. The paper which receives the credit of announcing the singular accident, phenomenon, or marvelous escape, sometimes retracts and makes the *amende honorable*, while other papers, equally responsible to the public, ignore the refutation. I hope, therefore, that my present intention shall not be misconstrued or regarded in an unfriendly spirit, and that the explanation, if satisfactory, will benefit the journals who hold guardianship over Catholics and their doctrine.

"The statement of a young lady nun is radically false. A knowledge of the rules which govern the house of the Sisters of Charity enables me to make this unqualified statement.

"The house of the Sisters of Charity is known as St. Joseph's, near Emmettsburg (not Emmettsbay). There is generally a number of persons demanding admission. In order to secure a reception, they must produce letters from responsible persons, vouching to their good character, etc. They must bring sufficient means to enable them to return home if the society thinks them unfit, either in physical or mental qualifications, to discharge the hard, and, in many cases, repulsive duties of the order. They spend the first two years as postulants, take no vows, and are perfectly free to leave the institution at any moment. There is no necessity for scaling walls, crossing fields, and escaping during the stillness of the night. In a word, any Catholic subject is perfectly free, as far as physical force is concerned, to follow the dictates of her own will.

"The case with scholars is quite different. They are placed under the care of the Sisters of Charity by their parents, to whom the sisters are accountable. The rules of the institution are read by all the scholars, and all who enter must abide by the rules. The young ladies are not permitted to leave the ground or fixed bound, to make visits, to receive or send letters from the institution without examination; in a word, they are constantly under the eye of their teachers. Hence they have no claim on the institution other than an education, an equivalent for their pension. At the end of the school term they can go home, to a friend's, to spend the vacation, or remain and pay their board during the vacation, and are confined to the rules prescribed by the parents.

"It sometimes happens that a young miss is sent by parents to have her removed from a particular circle of society. A romantic, novel-reading girl soon becomes restless under school restriction. A love-engagement or some romantic adventure will urge her to invent means to escape the care and vigilance of her teachers. Her object is soon accomplished; the sisters are in trouble for the truant girl and her disappointed parents; the papers enjoy a holiday on the first intimation of a hairbreadth escape of a nun from a Catholic convent, and the gratified public sleep soundly, well satisfied that, at least in this happy republic, liberty of conscience will be proclaimed by the press, and enthroned in the hearts of the people.

"I hope, Mr. Editor, you will not consider any word of the within personal. I assure you it is not so intended. My aim is not so much to teach in your paper, or in any other, but simply to state facts which are known to me, and seemingly unknown to you and others. J. O'DONNELL."

Any formal reply to this effusion is entirely unnecessary. The reverend writer is evidently a "swift witness," and would, if called upon, perhaps, be willing to swear to any thing to protect the interests of "Mother Church." He pronounces "*the statement of a young lady nun*" to be "*radically false,*" even before she had made a statement, and says he is enabled to do so "from a knowledge of the rules which govern the house of the Sisters of Charity." If such evidence as this were allowed, where would there be found protection for any subject of a system of government and discipline? Does the *existence* of a set of rules always and necessarily imply their *observance*, and especially in a community whose religion inculcates the doctrine that "the end sanctifies the means?" Why, this is the very question at issue. If the regulations, as published, were carried out, there would, of course, be no necessity for an escape. A child can see this as well as the Rev. J. O'Donnell. His letter is unworthy of consideration; but the Mother Superior of St. Joseph's has also published an epistle, which is so ingeniously worded, and carries such an air of truthfulness, that it is well calculated to deceive.

CHAPTER XLIX.

THE MOTHER SUPERIOR'S LETTER.

TO THE EDITOR OF "THE CITIZEN."

"St. Joseph's, near Emmettsburg, December 1st, 1854.

"SIR,—As numerous misrepresentations have appeared in the public prints in relation to Miss Josephine Bunkley's connection with and departure from our institution, I have, from a sense of duty, though with very great reluctance, concluded to communicate to you for publication the following statement of facts, exhibiting the exact truth of the matter.

"About two years ago, Miss Bunkley, of her own accord, came here, and made a spiritual retreat, that is, spent some days in meditation and prayer. She then expressed an ardent desire to become a Sister of Charity—a member of our society. As she was yet young, and a convert to the Catholic faith, she was required to take time for mature consideration, *and was not received.* One year after this she again applied by letter to be admitted as a candidate, and was authorized to come here *on trial.* She accordingly entered the novitiate, as others always do, to try her vocation, perfectly free to leave us at any hour or on any day she might please to select, and with the express and often-repeated assurance given her by us, that she would do wrong to stay with us unless she did so freely, and from the conviction that she was doing the will of God and seeking her own happiness by remaining.

"During the ten months that she was with us she not only appeared happy, but constantly professed to be so, and thus continued to express herself up to the very eve of her departure. Every one who knows any thing of us at all, knows that she had only to say the word, and she could have left us without difficulty and in a becoming manner at any time she pleased. Many novices have left us after trying their vocation here, who can testify how readily and cheerfully they were aided by us in departing. Many who wished to stay have been induced by us to go when we were satisfied that they were not called by Providence to the hardships and sacrifices of a religious life.

"The statement put forth that letters written to Miss Bunkley by her father and others of her family were withheld from her, or returned to the writers, is altogether untrue; they were invariably delivered to her. Her letters to her family or friends were always sent as addressed. On one occasion only, when, after her many professions of her desire to spend her life as a Sister of Charity, she spoke in a letter to her father of spending *six months* at St. Joseph's, I asked her meaning, and she replied that '*she did not wish her father to know of her intention to become a sister, though he suspected it.*' I then told her 'not to deceive her father; that God would not bless her undertaking if she did;' and I advised her to write the letter over again. She did so, and the letter was sent.

I can not now remember whether she took the first letter back, or left it with me to be destroyed. This, I presume, is the incident which has been perverted into a charge against us that we destroyed her letters to her father, written to inform him of her unhappiness at St. Joseph's and desire to leave.

"Miss B.'s extraordinary mode of leaving our house was as unnecessary as it was surprising. She could have left at any hour of the day, and by the front door. There was no occasion to leave at night or through a window; for, though the doors, as of every private dwelling, are locked to keep out intruders, the keys are never removed from them. She had no reason to hide behind a tree, as no one observed her going, and no one would have stopped her even if she had been noticed. I should think it is almost superfluous to add that she was not pursued after her departure became known. Miss B. left here on Thursday morning, the 9th ultimo, before day. On the morning after, I wrote by mail to her father, at Norfolk, informing him of her departure. On the following Saturday, the overseer of our farm went to Creagerstown, and brought back a note from her asking for her trunk, clothes, two watches, and the money which she had on deposit with our treasurer, amounting to $2 62½. No one, in the mean time, had gone after her. No one asked her to come back. It was only on the Monday of the next week that two of our sisters went to Creagerstown, and, without seeing her, delivered the above-named articles and obtained her written acknowledgment of their receipt.

"There are two other inaccuracies, asserted or implied, in the various statements, in this county and elsewhere, in regard to this affair, which I may as well now notice, once and for all.

"It is utterly untrue that Miss B. was in any manner solicited or persuaded to enter our community; on the contrary, she was put off for a year when she applied, and was afterward admitted only on trial at her own earnest solicitation. It is equally untrue that her trunk, clothing, jewelry, etc., were demanded of her when she first entered the institution. They were subject to her order on any day she might choose to leave us. It is also untrue that she ever expressed to me the desire to return home, neither have I heard at any time from any one of our sisters that she ever expressed such a desire to her. It is likewise untrue that she ever, with our knowledge, wrote, or desired to write, to that effect to her father or any one else; and it is the purest fiction that she was ever commanded to take her seat and write to her father or to any other person under our dictation. Every sister and novice, here or elsewhere, attached to our community, is not only free to leave us, but *is urged by us to go* whenever she may think it her duty to do so, and it is well known to the public that, even when the novice becomes a sister, she takes her vows *but for a single year*, and at its close is free to renew them or not, as she may judge proper. Those who have chosen to avail themselves of this alternative have never been impeded or molested in the exercise of their free will, but, on the contrary, pen, ink, and paper to write to their friends, the public coach, and money to pay the fare, are always at the disposal of any one inclined to withdraw. The members of our society are indeed told that, if they desire to be of our number, they must keep our rules, and *in that sense* give up their own *will*, but whoever *wills* to leave is as free as air.

"Miss B.'s clandestine departure may throw a romantic coloring around the matter, but it can in no way reflect discreditably upon this institution, nor make a case contrary to plain facts. I have been informed that Miss B. herself, during her stay in Creagerstown, bore testimony to the truth of more than I have said here respecting her kind treatment and freedom from duress or restriction while she resided at St. Joseph's.

"One word upon the general question. Our sisters have fathers and brothers. We invite them to come and examine if they find their sisters and daughters anxious to leave, or in the least degree unhappy on account of the state of life which they have adopted. Fathers and brothers, relations of every degree, and friends, do come, have always been in the habit of coming. They have free access to their friends who are members of our community. Is it not strange, then, that such a system as has been charged against us could exist for a year or a month? A large number of our community are scattered over the whole United States, are constantly traveling from city to city in public conveyances, and are regularly doing duty as nurses and attendants in the public hospitals and asylums of the country. Can it be believed that they are unable to find means of escape, or of communicating with their friends at home? Moreover, in our school here we have numerous Protestant young ladies who are in daily intercourse with the sisters. These young ladies are constantly visited by their parents and friends, and go home to spend their vacations. They certainly could be made the medium of communication between any sister and her friends, if there were such occasion for it as has been represented by our assailants. The fact that no such instance has ever occurred is sufficient proof that it has never been necessary.

"Finally, it has been stated that sisters have died here 'by inches'—wasting in slow despair. This most charitable assertion is intended to create in the public mind the suspicion or belief that they were the victims of a cruel imprisonment. I have already disposed of this calumny, but I will be excused for adding that it is indeed *most true* that several sisters have died here during the last and preceding years, and it is quite probable that others will follow them. Consumption, slow and rapid, brought on by their arduous labors and nightly watchings at the death-beds of poor men and women, of every clime and of every creed, in the hospitals of the country, has indeed carried off many Sisters of Charity, and will no doubt continue to do its work of death. They go from this their home in the fullness of health, on their missions of mercy, and when they return it is sometimes only to die. If this is matter of reproach, we have no reply to make. If this provokes the taunt of the assailant and feeds the uncharitable, we have only to submit in patience and humility, as far as our weak nature may enable us, in feeble imitation of the example of our divine Master, the Lord Jesus.

"S. M. ETIENNE HALL, M. S. of St. Joseph's."

CHAPTER L.

REPLY TO THE MOTHER SUPERIOR'S LETTER.

THE foregoing letter, of which it was said, on its first appearance, that "the public will discern in this production the mind and Jesuitical craft of the priestly polemic rather than the gushing sentiment of woman's charity," makes a direct issue of veracity between the Mother Superior and myself. As to some of the discrepancies involved in our respective statements, the public must decide on the bare assertion of each; but on the principal question—the right of voluntary departure—to which all the rest are subordinate, I hope to be able to satisfy every unprejudiced mind that this right is a "myth"—a mere abstraction purposed to deceive—a promise to be kept or denied, as may be deemed expedient and politic.

Though, in the preceding pages, I have narrated candidly and fairly the circumstances and impressions connected with my residence at St. Joseph's, I can not, perhaps, reasonably expect a stranger to place greater confidence in my assertions, if unsupported, than in those of the Superior. Hence, before I proceed, let me invite the impartial attention of my readers to what may be styled the "presumptive evidence" of the case.

Let it be remembered that the community of "Sisters of Charity" is one of the most attractive and efficient institutions in the Roman Catholic Church, doing more than any other to engage the interest and approval of those outside of her limits, and make proselytes to her communion. It has already become a very powerful organization. In this country alone, besides the Mother-House, it embraces forty-one "missions," which have their centre at Emmettsburg, but are disseminated over the broad extent of these United States. Under the superintendence of these institutions there are eighteen female orphan asylums, twenty-six schools, and several hospitals, in which six thousand patients are attended in the year. This organization is controlled by the priests; and by its ostentatious charities, and its assumed virtues, and through the instrumentality of its numerous schools, it exerts a vast influence. From their mode of life, the secresy of their endeavors to promote the interests of their Church, and their devotion to the work of education, the Sisters of Charity have not inappropriately been termed the "Female Jesuits." When the importance and power of this community are duly estimated, it will be clearly seen how momentous an object it becomes at all hazards to preserve its reputation unsullied; and when, moreover, it is remembered that the doctrine of "mental reservation" is taught and justified by the Jesuits and other orders in the Papal Church—a doctrine which permits and recommends the utterance of a falsehood to promote the interests of "religion"—the presumption, to say the least, of a strong inducement to enforce obedience by the exercise of a power which lies in the hands of those interested in the accomplishment of that design is plainly made out.*

* The vows taken by the Sisters of Charity are of the same nature with those assumed in the various orders of nuns. The distinction is with regard to the period during which these vows continue binding. In the monastic orders it is for life; in the sisterhood for a stated term; but, as the preceding narrative has shown, the *renewal* of these vows at the expiration of that term is performed while in the institution, and as a matter of course; and the duty of obedience is in force to require the immediate resumption of the obligations just expired. There is no interval of emancipation; so that the difference between this community and that of a "close convent" is simply nominal, or consists in a formal and periodical repetition of the solemn promises made at the outset.

But, apart from this consideration, it will be borne in mind that the *vows* themselves, pledging the individual to poverty, chastity, and obedience, are identically the same, whether taken for a longer or a shorter time. The obligation of a strict, blind, absolute, unhesitating obedience to an arbitrary authority weighs upon the Sister of Charity just as heavily as upon the recluse of a nunnery. And what is the degree of freedom for the exercise of a choice of continued servitude afforded to the inmates of convents in our own day and among our own people? We shall not simply take the attestation of all intelligent observers, who know that bolts, and bars, and gratings, and high walls are the invariable and essential characteristics of those institutions, wherever they exist in our towns and cities; we shall not content ourselves with recalling the numerous, and notorious, and well-authenticated cases of escape, whether attempted or accomplished, from these high walls, and bolted doors, and grated windows of the nunneries of America and England; we shall quote the clear, distinct, unanswerable words of a Roman Catholic author, a saint canonized only a few years since, the founder of a religious order, whose work, entitled The Nun Sanctified, is the text-book of convents—whose entire writings, according to a recent Roman Catholic author, were more than twenty times rigorously discussed by the sacred congregation of rites, which decreed that not one word in them had been found worthy of censure; and we shall quote from an edition published at Dublin in the year 1848, for the use of English nuns and postulants. Hear, then, what St. Alphonsus Liguori says of the "*freedom*" of those under religious vows:

On the other hand, I would ask, in the name of charity and sound reason, can any plausible motive be

"It is true that even in the cloisters there are some . . . . who do not live as religious ought to live. To be a good religious and to be content are one and the same thing. . . . . I have been accustomed to say that a religious in her convent enjoys a foretaste of paradise, OR SUFFERS AN ANTICIPATION OF HELL. To endure the pains of hell is to be separated from God; TO BE FORCED AGAINST THE INCLINATIONS OF NATURE to do the will of others; to be *distrusted, despised, reproved,* AND CHASTISED *by those with whom we live;* TO BE SHUT UP IN A PLACE OF CONFINEMENT FROM WHICH IT IS IMPOSSIBLE TO ESCAPE; in a word, it is to be *in continual torture, without a moment's peace!*"

Elsewhere the language of this saint is, if possible, even more explicit. Under the head of "*What ought a person to do who finds that she has become a nun against her inclination?*" he says—not, as the Mother Superior of St. Joseph's would have us understand, that in such a case the sister may open the door of her convent and go forth—but,

"Perhaps you will tell me you can never have peace, because you find that you have entered religion [*i. e.*, become a nun] to please your parents, and against your own will. I answer thus: If at the time of your profession you had not a vocation, I would not have advised you to make the vows of a religious, but *I would have advised you to suspend your resolution of going back to the world,* and casting yourself into the many dangers of perdition which are found in the world. I now see you placed in the house of God, and made (either voluntarily or unwillingly) the spouse of Jesus Christ. For my part, I can not pity you more than I could pity a person who had been transported (even against his will) from a place infected with pestilence and surrounded by enemies, to a healthful country, to be placed there for life, secure against every foe.

"I add, grant that what you say is true: now that you are professed in a convent, and that it is IMPOSSIBLE FOR YOU TO LEAVE IT, tell me, what do you wish to do? If you have entered religion [*i. e.*, become a nun] against your inclination, you must now remain with cheerfulness. If you abandon yourself to melancholy, you must lead a life of misery, and will expose yourself to great danger of suffering *a hell here* and another hereafter. *You must then make a virtue of necessity;* and if the devil has brought you into religion [*i. e.*, a nunnery] for your destruction, let it be your care to avail yourself of your holy state for your salvation, and to become a saint. Give yourself up to God from the

assigned why I should escape from the institution at a risk of detection and punishment, and travel ten

heart, and I assure you that by so doing you shall become more content than all the princesses and queens of this world. Being asked his opinion regarding a person who had *become a nun against her will*, St. Francis de Sales answered: 'It is true that this child, if she had not been obliged by her parents, would not have left the world; but this is of little importance, provided she knows that the *force* employed by her parents is more useful to her than the permission to follow her own will. For now she can say, If I had not lost such liberty, I should have lost true liberty.' The saint meant to say, that, had she not been compelled by her parents to become a nun, her liberty, which would have induced her to remain in the world, would have robbed her of the true liberty of the children of God, which consists in freedom from the chains and dangers of this world."—P. 26, 549–551.

Here, then, is the Mother Superior of St. Joseph's directly at issue, not only with Liguori, but with the friend of the founder of her own order, the holy Francis de Sales! Perhaps, however, the statements are reconcilable. The Mother Superior is speaking to a Protestant world, outside the walls. To them she says, Don't believe these stories about forced seclusion, and all that; there is perfect liberty here; whoever wills to leave is as free as air. But to the poor prisoners inside she would doubtless agree with the saint in reasoning, *You must make a virtue of necessity;* IT IS IMPOSSIBLE FOR YOU TO LEAVE!

With regard to those members of the sisterhood who, having finished their probation, are sent out into the world on their errands of proselytism in hospitals and private houses, there is no one that questions *their* voluntary adherence to the order whose interests they are serving; nor does any one doubt that there are, in the mother-house itself, a large proportion, if not a majority of members, whose choice it is, from whatever motive, to remain in their position. But will this liberty, granted to some, be alleged in proof that others, who are confessedly under restraint, are also in the exercise of *their* free choice? Does this invalidate the testimony of numerous and unimpeachable witnesses, who, having fled in fear and trembling from oppression and imprisonment, assert and declare what they have both seen and heard for themselves? Let an unprejudiced public decide.

For what purpose, we would ask and reiterate, are such precautions taken against the escape of persons immured in these convents and other religious houses? What signify these tremendous vows, this

miles on an unknown road, exposed to danger and insult, if I enjoyed the privilege of departure at free choice? Until such a rational motive be adduced, is there not a fair presumption, at least, that I have spoken the truth?

surrender of will, these gratings and bars, these prison-like inclosures? If there is freedom, why these semblances of restraint? Why oppose the just demand of a people jealous, for themselves and their daughters, of that sacred right of personal liberty for all guiltless of crime, in the purchase of which their fathers poured out their life's blood? Why refuse to "bring the prisoners out from the prison;" they that are "snared and hid in prison-houses;" that are there "for a prey, and none delivereth; for a spoil, and none saith, Restore?"

As for the facilities enjoyed by parents and relatives in communicating with the inmates of religious institutions, we shall examine this point at large in another chapter.

CHAPTER LI.

OTHER FUGITIVES FROM ST. JOSEPH'S.

THE Mother Superior, in her letter, endeavors to make it appear that no effort was made after my escape to recapture me, and very adroitly suppresses certain facts in order to leave this impression. I shall attempt to show how much truth there is in this statement, and account for the fact that the pursuit was not successful.

I have already said that it was not a "class-day" when I escaped. By this I mean that the teachers or class-sisters were not required to be on duty in the academy upon that day, which was Thursday—a day of recreation for the boarders. I had chosen this day as the most suitable, to avoid an early discovery. If missed at the novitiate in the morning, it would be supposed that I was in the infirmary; and, on the contrary, if missed in the infirmary, it would be presumed that I was in the novitiate. Such, doubtless, was the case; for, as I afterward learned, my absence was not detected until just before night prayers.

Now, on the supposition that the overseer was sent the next morning to the convent at Frederick in search of me—a distance of twenty-two miles—it is evident that he could not well have returned to St. Joseph's, stopping by the way at Creagerstown, before Saturday. On his way through Creagerstown, in going, he inquired if I was at the hotel, and was answered in the negative. On his return, he again stopped to make inquiry, insisting that I must be there, and demanding to see me. The proprietor brought the message to me, and I consented to an interview. This was, I think, on Saturday afternoon; and I should add that the man was intoxicated. Yet the Mother Superior says that "no one, in the mean time, had gone after" me, and again, that "no one asked [me] to come back." It is clear, under these circumstances, that the two sisters who came on the following Monday could not possibly have done so earlier, as they would not have come on Sunday, and were not made aware of my locality until the Saturday evening subsequent to my escape.

It will be seen, from what I have stated elsewhere, that some postulants are sent away from the institution, and this for obvious reasons—the lack of requisites, as wealth or expectation of property, talent above mediocrity, beauty, education, accomplishments, or the possession of some traits of character which render them unfit for the purposes of the community. Of such, and such only, can it be said with truth that they are "*urged to go.*"

The Mother Superior states that "every sister or novice here or elsewhere attached to our community is not only free to leave us, but is urged by us to go whenever she may think it her duty to do so." If this be true, it is scarcely credible that a single inmate, for the sake of mere notoriety, should confront the danger and shame of a stealthy departure rather than make a peaceful and permitted egress from the institution. But the case is not a solitary one. There are a sufficient number of cases to prove, beyond the doubt of the unbiased, that restraint is exercised in the matter.

In the month of June, 1853, a novice who had escaped from St. Joseph's was pursued and caught on the farm of Mr. John Dorsey, four miles south of Emmettsburg, on the main road leading to Frederick City. Her pursuers were two "sisters," who traveled in a carriage. When the poor fugitive recognized them, she left the road and endeavored to escape through a field of wheat; but, leaping from the vehicle, the sisters overtook her, and, seizing her by the arms, led her to the carriage, placed her in it, and drove back to the institution. This much, which can be proved in a court of justice, is all that is known of the occurrence. What was the destiny of this unhappy girl is a mystery probably never to be solved.

The following letter concerning the escape of another novice speaks for itself. The writer is an intelligent Presbyterian clergyman of high character in Emmettsburg. The communication was made to a friend who made inquiry relative to the circumstance.

"Emmettsburg, February 21, 1853.

"DEAR SIR,—The questions you ask with respect to the young lady who eloped from St. Joseph's and came to my house I answer thus:

"She called herself Helen O'Here, O'Here being the name of her mother's present husband. Her true name, she said, was Grier. She was a novice, and had been raised at Albany, New York. If not born in Ireland, she was of Irish extraction. She was at my house for two or three weeks. She left St. Joseph's, *not abjuring the Catholic faith*, but because at the institution she was oppressed with unusual labor, and had, as she said, no time for devotion, the priest often assuring her and her co-operatives that this labor, honestly performed, would be as acceptable as their prayers. She entered as a novice, under the impression that this place was, indeed, the centre of holy influences, and that nowhere else could she serve her Maker with such entire self-consecration; but (as she said) SHE FOUND NOTHING LIKE RELIGION THERE. I asked her but few questions, but she spoke with much freedom, and sometimes, I thought, with intemperate ardor. I heard her assert that 'if continuing to be a "Sister of Charity" would certainly take her to heaven, she would not consent,' so decided was her disgust with what she had seen and passed through.

"She was accompanied on her return to Albany by Mr. J., who resides in the State of Vermont, and who kindly took charge of her. Dr. A. and Mr. D. G. advanced the necessary funds, the amount of which was shortly returned.

* * * * * *

"She never said she was not a Catholic, and she is at this time with her mother in Albany.

"Very possibly, all these statements she may, under certain influences, say are false.

"R. S. GRIER.

"Rev. G. W. A."

The reader will note the peculiar features of the case here stated. Helen O'Here was evidently brought up in the Roman Catholic Church, and was averse to divulge the true reasons for her escape. The causes alleged by her are not sufficient to account for the strong and decided expressions of disgust and aversion uttered by her in reference to the institution.

I might confidently rest my case here, the chief assertion of the Mother Superior having been clearly disproved—that, namely, of the entire liberty of all the inmates of the institution to depart at pleasure. Little reliance can be placed upon the assertions connected with such an utter distortion of facts ; but I desire to notice a few additional passages in the letter, and shall consider them in as brief a manner as possible.

CHAPTER LII.

REPLY CONTINUED.

"DURING the ten months that she was with us, she not only appeared happy, but constantly professed to be so, and thus continued to express herself up to the very eve of her departure."

The motives that compelled me to conceal my discontent and sorrow while a member of the community I have already stated. The slightest murmur of dissatisfaction or complaint was sure to be visited with punishment. This I had learned by experience as well as observation, and hence my silence, my dissimulation, if any choose to call it so. The situation was a trying one, and the views and feelings peculiar to it should not be harshly judged by one who has never been placed in the same position of distress and apprehension. One thought alone might influence to such a concealment, and that is the fear of being transferred at any time to a distant and strange locality, when all hope of relief would be given up. With this anxiety weighing upon her mind, and the superadded dread of present punishment, who can blame a timid and unprotected woman for dissembling her true state of mind?

With respect to the account given of my letter to

my friends, it will be perceived that the only material difference between that and my own statement lies in the *motive* alleged. The *fact* that a letter was written by me to my father, announcing my intention to spend *only six months* at the institution—that it was read by the Superior and disapproved of, and that the writing of another letter was procured, is admitted; but this fact is distorted by the extraordinary assertion that I wished to *deceive my father.* Is this to be believed? Why should I wish to practice this deception. Far from it. I was chiefly anxious to confess my error, to tell him of my sad disappointment, to acquaint him with my change of views.

But if, as the Superior states, letters from members of the community are always sent as addressed, and "pen, ink, and paper to write to their friends are always at the disposal of any one inclined to withdraw," *how came it that she read this letter of mine? Why was it not forwarded without examination?*

I might thus continue to examine, seriatim, the several statements composing this ingenious document, but I can not think this necessary. At all events, having, in the preceding pages, told my unvarnished story, I can do no more than reiterate. Let me only add, that this "freedom to depart at will" is a mere fiction for the uninitiated. It is well known who can be trusted and who must be watched. Suppose, however, that such a rule exists, to the effect that all who wish to do so are at liberty to depart. It may be doubted whether many would leave the institution even openly and by daylight, without means, friends, or a knowledge of the locality, and throw themselves upon strangers, with the certainty, too, that their character would be assailed. But suppose that one should summon the resolution to make the attempt. Pretexts and means would most unquestionably be found speedily enough to detain her. Those, on the other hand, *who have no desire to leave*, would, if asked, promptly reply that "they could go home if they chose." *But let them grow discontented and try it!* They would find it a promise made only to the ear.

CHAPTER LIII.

ANONYMOUS ATTACKS.

IN addition to the letters which I have thus noticed, there have been made various allegations and insinuations of a baser kind. Some of these are ridiculous, involving my mental sanity, etc.; others, more malignant, accusing me of willful falsehood and deception. Those who know me can decide upon these charges. Vulgar and threatening letters, from sources unknown, have also reached me, the contents of which were of a nature to provoke only contempt and disgust. That the public may judge of these effusions, I subjoin copies of two, written, evidently, in a disguised hand, and by the same person, whom I suppose to be a priest, whose signature, however, can not be made out. Both are post-marked Baltimore, one bearing date January 23d, and the other March 16th, but the inside contains neither place nor date.

"MISS BUNKLEY,—It is announced in the 'Frederick Examiner,' and copied into the Baltimore papers of this morning, that you are engaged in writing a work for publication regarding your disgraceful conduct at St. Joseph's, Emmettsburg.

"As it appears to be your intention to gain a little

notoriety, your situation is any thing but an (*un*)*enviable* one. The notorious Maria Monk, who published, a few years since, 'Awful Disclosures,' and was backed by a host of idle vagabonds—Protestant preachers (who are now, we learn, engaged in the same dirty work with you at Norfolk), was confined in the New York City Prison, where she had been sent as a common vagabond, thief, and open prostitute, and died there. The public, having been humbugged so often by such lying tales, will not soon again encourage any similar work. Do you understand that!!! And you may inform the Protestant preachers, who are now gulling you, that their efforts will be all in vain. Come, now, no lies; give us the truth, and give us the names and residences of the editors all over the Union that have made offers unprecedented for a narrative of your life. Ha! you are caught in your own trap, eh! Oh shame! shame!! shame!!! When your work appears, I will give you and your fellow co-laborers such a basting through the public press as will make you shed almost tears of blood, as I know something about you. So look out! publish the work, now, if you dare. Send this to the editor of that vile sheet, the *Frederick Examiner*. Your very obedient servant."

So much for No. 1, whose threatened excoriation and denunciation of the "Protestant preachers," the "Frederick Examiner," and my humble self, judging from the above classic and scathing epistle, are doubtless tremblingly anticipated by all the objects of the writer's wrath. No. 2 is still more refined, delectable, and overwhelming.

"MISS BUNKLEY,—I inclose you a letter, published in last Saturday's 'Catholic Mirror,' for your information, and in order that you may know what a very pretty notoriety you may have obtained throughout the land—another 'Maria Monk'—a new authoress of 'Awful Developments'—'Two Years in a Convent.' How much money have you received from the many and numerous letters you have received from editors and publishers in every part of the Union!!! Bah! when you do utter falsehoods, you know how to utter a good one. Bah! you common ass! all you want is that animal's long ears, his tail, and hoofs, to make a complete ass of yourself. You put out a work!! That you are unable to do. The miserable wretches of preachers who have been with you may indeed publish a second edition of 'Maria Monk,' who died in New York City Prison in September, 1839, where she had been confined as a common prostitute, a common drunkard, and a common thief. Why did not those preachers fly to her aid, to rescue her from so vile an end? This is the miserable end of all who attack the Church founded and established by Jesus Christ, and, as He says, 'the gates of hell shall never prevail.' Oh! when your death-bed scene comes, how will your tune be altered. 'You shall call upon me,' says our Lord, 'and you shall not find me, and you shall die in your sins.' I have been waiting a long time now for your work; come, come, let the public have it. But I can assure you, I stand ready to put the dissecting-knife over it in a manner you little dream of—so now beware! Yours, etc."

Accompanying this precious effusion was a document from the *Catholic Mirror*, purporting to be a letter from a personage who signs himself "J. J. E. N.," and speaking of my escape from St. Joseph's. It contains little else than a repetition of what the Mother Superior had said before. The initials appended to this article I recognized as those of a Catholic priest, named Norman, who has an elderly sister at the institution, and whose visits, of course, are eagerly welcomed. I recollect perfectly the circumstances of a visit made by him during my stay at St. Joseph's, and the pains taken to render it agreeable. The article, however, contains no intimation that its author was a *priest*—one of a class whose interests and purposes are well subserved by lavishing praises on these institutions, these "priests' prisons for women," as they have been not inaptly styled by an eloquent and fearless writer.

CHAPTER LIV.

THE AUTHOR'S DESIGN.

THE public mind has begun to appreciate, with some degree of correctness, the evil influence of monastic establishments, and those of a kindred character. It has, at least, commenced to perceive the anomaly of such a system of personal restraint and forced obedience in a land of free institutions and liberal principles. Jesuitism, in its worst phase, is now the conservative power of the Roman Catholic Church, compelled, in self-preservation, a second time to appeal to the order of Loyola for aid and defense. The United States teem with these intriguing priests, as well as with their confederates, the "Jesuits of the short robe," or lay Jesuits, among whom even women are numbered. Convents and religious communities, such as those of the "Sisters of Charity" and the "Sisters of Mercy," are among their chief instrumentalities to promote the ends of the papacy. The most strenuous efforts are made, in every variety of mode, to augment the numbers and swell the resources of these institutions, and hence the alacrity and energy with which so many protectors rush to their vindication when it is threatened to reveal the truth concerning them. Nor is it always the case that exertions to secure fresh victims are confined to the use of persuasion and advice, but physical assistance can be tendered to convey those whom circumstances might prevent from following the desired course to the place of confinement. There is a married lady residing in the vicinity of St. Joseph's who has been known to take young girls, in the absence of their parents, without the consent of their natural protectors, and despite their known wishes, and remove them to that institution and to the convent in Frederick. I have in my possession the names of the parties, and can, if necessary, give proof of the occurrences.

If, by my simple narration of facts, I shall succeed in communicating a salutary caution to enthusiastic and innocent girls, who, by devout and blissful pictures of a "religious" state, artfully presented to their minds, may have been led to entertain the thought of becoming members of a convent, or an institution of similar nature, I shall have reached my utmost aim. For such I entertain the warmest sympathy, and the kindest appreciation of their motives and desires. But I would, God helping me, preserve them, if it be possible, from suffering, sorrow, and, it may be, moral death. He who reads the heart knows the purity of my intention and the truth of my declarations.

CHAPTER LV.

INTERVIEWS WITH MY CONFESSOR.

I HAVE only, in conclusion, to relate one of the attempts made to bring me back within the possession of my enemies, and into the pale of the Church of Rome. To do this understandingly, reference must be made to the period of my entrance upon convent life.

When on my way to St. Joseph's, to enter as a postulant at that institution, I wrote to my confessor, the Rev. ——, of Norfolk, and acquainted him with the determination at which I had arrived, contrary, however, to his own advice. My letter was mailed at a small town between Baltimore and Emmettsburg. I do not know that he ever received it. As I have elsewhere stated, I saw him at the institution. He was not of the Order of Lazarists, and had often recommended me not to go to St. Joseph's.

Some months, however, subsequent to my entrance, his sister was placed there as a boarder. It was not long before her health began to fail. I frequently saw her in tears, and at times, when passing her, endeavored to learn the cause of her distress. I noticed that she was not treated with kindness by the community, and on one occasion, when meeting her in the passage to the infirmary, whither she had been sent, she told me of her unhappiness, of her desire to return, and how she wished her brother might know how miserable she was. Saying this, she burst into tears. A few weeks passed, and I missed her from the academy entirely. I learned that she had been again sent to the infirmary.

One day, passing by the library, I saw some one sitting just behind the door, and, conjecturing that it might be this young lady, I entered the room. I was struck with her pale and emaciated appearance; and she, too, remarked how altered I was. She thought I must be unhappy, and said I should have taken her brother's advice not to enter the institution. I dared not, however, confide my real feelings to her. I had often heard unkind remarks made respecting this young person by the directress and others of the academy.

Her brother, hearing of her ill health, came to St. Joseph's. I saw him, but had no opportunity of conversing with him without risk of being reported. After his departure she grew worse, and was sent to the Baltimore infirmary. The directors and officers of the community were much displeased because her brother had not taken her away when he came, and I overheard one of them say that it was a piece of imposition, etc.

This priest visited me twice at my father's house, the first time shortly after my escape. This call was quite unexpected to me. I was seated, in company with a young lady, in the parlor, at the piano, when the Rev. —— was announced. I was both surprised and alarmed. He entered, and, advancing toward me, extended his hand, remarking, "I am happy to see you at home, Josephine." I answered hastily, "Are you *really* glad to see me at home?" "I am," he repeated. I told him that I regretted he had thought it necessary to call, as my father would be much displeased to meet him or hear of his visit. He then stated his object, which was to induce me to go to the church to *confession* and to *attend mass.* I told him it was impossible; that I would never again enter that Church; and, indeed, that there was a report in circulation to the effect that if I should attempt to enter it, I would be put out for scandalizing it. He begged me to fear nothing of the sort; and assured me that if any person should dare to touch me for such a purpose, he would announce his displeasure from the altar. He left, urging me to come to church, insisting that he could not go without my promise, and assuring me that he would still continue to regard me as a member of his flock.

In the course of this conversation I told him of the treatment his sister had received at the institution, and that I thought it would be well to send for her at the Baltimore infirmary, as I knew she would be happier away from it.

On his second visit, two or three weeks after this interview, I was alone. He remained half an hour. He told me that he had come, thinking I was in trouble in consequence of the Lady Superior's letter. He had read it that very day, and considered it quite uncalled for; he was sorry it had been written. As I had made no charges against the institution publicly, there could be no occasion for writing and publishing that document. He again urged me to come to confession and to attend mass. I answered that I had no wish to do so, but that, even if I desired it, my father would never permit me to enter his door again. He was aware, I said, how strong had been his opposition from the outset, and now it would be much stronger than ever. I expressed the fear that my father would be greatly displeased should he come home and find him there.

During these remarks, when I refused to attend mass, assigning, among other reasons, that my father would not consent to my doing so, he exclaimed, "Come, then—come with me *now;* I will protect you; I have a home for you; come with me!" It was in the evening, just before twilight. I trembled with agitation; my former attachments and predilections for the Roman Catholic Church rushed upon me with such force that I feared for my own steadfastness and my safety. I did not reply for some time: a conflict raged within my breast; but an earnest desire to do my duty toward God and my conscience prevailed. I hesitated, and reflected for a few moments, until my composure was regained and my former determination resumed. I then said, faintly, "I can not—I can not." He rose from his seat, leaned against the mantle, and seemed overwhelmed with disappointment. He repeated, "I can not leave without your promise to return to the Church." I told him that could never be, and desired that he would not come again. Then, laying his hand upon my arm, he said, "Josephine, have I lost you? Josephine, have I lost you? Have I lost a lamb from my fold? Am I no more to be your confessor?" As I made no reply, he continued, "I am at least your friend, as I have ever been; and when you are alone in the world, I will be your friend, no matter what may happen. Josephine, mark these words: Don't utter a syllable of what I have said to you, either to a Catholic or to a Protestant." He finally made me promise that I would reflect upon all that he had said, and write him a letter; and assured me that, should I request it, he would not come again. As he was going toward the door, he turned to me, saying, "How can I leave you without your promise to come back to the Church?" Then, reluctantly bidding me good evening, he withdrew.

I went to my room in a state of excitement impossible to describe, and that evening penned a letter with a view to prevent another visit, being greatly intimidated by what had passed. Indeed, I feared that, had he come again, I should have been lost.

In this letter, the details of which I can not now accurately recall, I think I intimated to him that I retained yet some attachment for the Roman Catholic Church, and hoped once more, at some future time, to kneel before the altar where I had passed so many hours in silent but ecstatic contemplation. This letter produced the desired effect. He did not call again.

The first visit of the priest soon became known in the neighborhood, and a report was circulated, as I believe by himself, that I had sent my sister for him. This was untrue; I had no wish to see him, nor to be urged to enter the Church again, although there yet lingered in my mind something of those sentiments which had been assiduously cultivated for years by priestly influence, and had not been completely dissipated even by those circumstances so calculated to remove them through which I had just passed.

Other attempts have been made to allure me back, and repeated threats have been made to take me back by force, but of these I shall not speak more fully. In my own mind there remains no doubt of a deliberate purpose to injure me, as well as to throw discredit upon my testimony with regard to the institution of St. Josephs.

CONCLUSION.

BY THE EDITOR.

I. INSPECTION OF CONVENTS.

IN the year 1852, a movement was commenced in Great Britain for the purpose of petitioning the legislative body of that country to provide in some manner for the placing of convents, and other institutions of similar character, under legal inspection and control. This object will be more fully gathered from the following document, circulated in England, and signed by many thousand women, for presentation to Parliament:

"Your petitioners are deeply sensible of the blessings of civil and religious liberty enjoyed by the people of this country; but they regret to observe that from one class of their fellow-subjects these blessings are in a great measure withheld, in consequence of the existence of the conventual system—a system altogether opposed to the pure and benevolent character of the Gospel, and under which young and inexperienced females are immured in nunneries; denied the privilege of free intercourse with their relatives and friends; deprived of the profitable and wholesome discipline of social life, and exposed to concealed dangers; from which unnatural restraint, if they should repent of vows taken in ignorance or rashness, escape is almost impossible. Your petitioners therefore entreat your honorable House to pass such a measure as may effectually open these establishments to regular inspection, so that no person may be received into, or detained in, or dismissed from them without the knowledge of the proper authorities."

It is not a little remarkable that a proposition of this nature should have excited among the Roman Catholics of Great Britain, under the instigation, doubtless, of their priests, a storm of opposition and abuse. Those who are conscious of the integrity of their motives and the rectitude of their course do not ordinarily shrink from an examination of either. It might reasonably be imagined that a system so continually lauded to the skies as the perfection of purity and sanctity on earth, could well afford to court the scrutiny of the public. Deeds of light do not require the darkness or the shade. An effort, however, to open the nunneries of England to a legal inspection, for the prevention of possible oppression or restraint, instead of being hailed as a measure which would infallibly add lustre to the virtues and attractions of those establishments, was denounced with every epithet of indignation and horror. It was characterized as "the grossest of insults;" "cowardly and wanton;" "a most unmanly attempt to deprive these sisters of a security which even the meanest slaves have insured to them."

It is difficult to see how the appointment of such a committee of inspection, constituted as was proposed, of an equal number of Roman Catholics and Protestants, could be regarded by intelligent laymen as in itself so dreadful, and worthy of reprobation. But, on the other hand, it is more easy to perceive the *motive* which may have actuated the priesthood of Rome in making every imaginable effort to defeat the project.

The proposed measure involved no infringement of the privilege of assuming religious vows, or living in religious communities. "If," as an able writer has well said, "ladies choose to dress themselves in a monastic fashion—black, white, and gray—with rosaries and crucifixes, it may all seem to us extremely silly, but we have no right to interfere, and any interference would be an infringement of their civil and religious rights. If ladies choose to live in lonely houses, with ladies like themselves, and altogether secluded from men, it may be a self-inflicted penance, very foolish in our eyes, but we have no right to interfere. . . . . But if it be found that young girls of sixteen years of age are entrapped into these establishments before they are capable of forming a judgment upon the importance of such a step; if young persons are allured into these establishments with the view of obtaining power over every right and property to which they may afterward become entitled, and then are not permitted to leave them when they desire to depart from them; and when they change their religious opinions, and desire to withdraw, are not permitted to withdraw; then, I say, we are justified in interfering, not, indeed, interfering against ladies, but interfering in order that those ladies may enjoy the free exercise of their civil and religious liberties. And in asking that nunneries be subjected to visitation on the part either of her majesty's justices of the peace, or on the part of Royal Commissioners appointed for the occasion, all we ask is that there may be secured to every person in these establishments free ingress and free egress; in other words, *that they shall enjoy, in their full extent, their civil liberty and their religious freedom.*"

II. UNWILLING NUNS.

But would Protestant readers know by what strong arguments and illustrations the opponents of this proposed examination vindicate the restraint of the convent? Let them hear the language of "The Catholic Institute" of Great Britain, in a pamphlet issued on this subject.

"Under our free government, are we not ourselves living in perpetual restraint? Is not our liberty curtailed and limited by many prohibitions and laws? *Are not our soldiers bound by an irrevocable engagement as soon as they are enlisted, by which single act—almost always done from want, or in a frolic, or in a state of intoxication*—are they not subject to a discipline a thousand times more severe than that of the most rigid religious orders? Are they not, in truth, merely passive instruments in the hands of their commanding officers? Are not their diet, their sleep, their dress, even their motions, under continual restrictions? Willing or unwilling, are they not doomed to go wherever they are sent, even to the extremities of the world, and to the most unwholesome climates, to fight the battles of their country, with scarcely a hope of seeing their friends again in their native land? Is not marriage among us subject to restrictive laws? When contracted as the law directs, is it not indissoluble? And is not the unfortunate young person who has been sacrificed to the avarice and ambition of her unnatural parents, or has been the melancholy victim of her own blindness, condemned to pass her days beneath the yoke which she can never more shake off? To bring the question nearer home—by the sole fact of our being born in England, are we not deprived of what appears to be an essential part of liberty, the liberty of disposing of ourselves as we think best, and of choosing the climate and the form of government which we judge to be the most conducive to our happiness? From the single fact, in which we never concurred in the beginning, nor which we ever subsequently approved of, have we not contracted with our native country an engagement so irrevocable that it can never be dissolved by any act of our own?"*

We need add nothing to this line of argument. Monastic imprisonment is justifiable, in the view of its own advocates, by the same pretext as the enlistment of soldiers under a drunken oath, or the miserable bondage of a wife "sacrificed to the avarice and ambition of unnatural parents." The condition of the nun is and ought to be as hopeless, as wretched, as desperate as these.

There are, then, *unwilling nuns;* this is acknowledged, as indeed it were useless to deny it; and their confinement, in opposition to their own choice and desire, is justified. Nay, as we have seen, this unwillingness is considered something so frequent and so much to be expected, that, in the books furnished and approved for the special edification of the sisters, there

* "Nuns and Monastic Institutes," a tract "published under the superintendence of the Catholic Institute of Great Britain."

are express exhortations addressed to persons in this predicament. We have already cited some of these passages. The great Saint Alphonsus Liguori pleads very tenderly with these poor wretches of nuns who are imprisoned against their will. He urges them to "MAKE A VIRTUE OF NECESSITY." "Grant," he adds, condescending to argue with the unfortunate defenseless one, "grant that what you state is true; now that you are professed in a convent, and that it is IMPOSSIBLE FOR YOU TO LEAVE IT, tell me, what do you wish to do? If you have entered religion against your inclination, you must now remain with cheerfulness. If you abandon yourself to melancholy, you must lead a life of misery, and will expose yourself to great danger of suffering *a hell here* and another hereafter. *You must, then, make a virtue of necessity.*"*

Well may an eloquent writer exclaim, "To what paltry shifts and quibbles will not Roman Catholic writers resort to disguise the cruelty of this practice! Nuns are described as superhuman beings, as angels on earth, without a thought or wish beyond the walls of their convents. The effects of habit, of religious fear, of decorum, which prevented many of the French nuns from casting off the veil at a period when the Revolutionary storm had struck awe into every breast, are construed into a proof of the unvariableness of purpose which follows the religious profession. Are nuns, indeed, so invariably happy? *Why, then, are they insulted by their spiritual rulers by keeping them*

* The True Spouse of Jesus Christ, or, the Nun Sanctified by the Virtues of her State. Translated from the Italian by a Catholic Clergyman. 8vo. Dublin: Duffy, 1848, p. 551.

under the very guards and precautions which magistrates employ to secure external good behavior among the female inmates of prisons and penitentiaries? Would the nuns continue during their lives under the same privations were they at liberty to resume the laical state? *Why, then, are they bound fast with awful vows?* Why are they not allowed to offer up, day by day, the free-will offering of their souls and bodies?

"The reluctant nuns, you say, are *few*. Vain, unfeeling sophistry! First prove that vows are recommended on divine authority; that Christ has authorized the use of force and compulsion to ratify them when they are made, and then you may stop your ears against the complaints of *a few sufferers*. But can millions of submissive, or even willing recluses, *atone for the despair of those few?* You reckon in indefinite numbers those that in France did not avail themselves of the Revolutionary laws. You should rather inquire how many who, before the Revolution, appeared perfectly contented in their cloistral slavery, overcame their religious fear, and fled to the arms of a husband as soon as they could do it with impunity. *Two hundred and ten nuns were secularized in Spain* during the short-lived reign of the Cortes. Were these helpless beings happy in their former durance? What an appalling number of less fortunate victims might not be made out by averaging in the same proportion the millions of females who, since the establishment of convents, have surrendered their liberty into the hands of Rome!"*

* Blanco White's "Practical and Internal Evidence against Catho-

III. COERCION THE LAW OF THE CONVENT.

To satisfy himself that restraint is contemplated by the monastic system, let the reader turn for a moment to the ritual for the assumption of the veil in convents, and examine the tenor of the curse there pronounced.

"By the authority of Almighty God and his holy apostles Peter and Paul, we solemnly forbid, under pain of anathema, that any one draw away these present virgins, or holy nuns, from the divine service to which they have devoted themselves under the banner of chastity; or that any one purloin their goods, or hinder their possessing them unmolested; but if any one shall dare to attempt such a thing, let him be accursed at home and abroad; accursed in the city and in the field; accursed in waking and sleeping; accursed in eating and drinking; accursed in walking and sitting; cursed in his flesh and his bones; and from the sole of his foot to the crown of his head let him have no soundness. Come upon him the malediction which, by Moses in the Law, the Lord hath laid on the sons of iniquity. Be his name blotted out from the book of the living, and not be written with the righteous. His portion and inheritance be with Cain the fratricide, with Dathan and Abiram, with Ananias and Sapphira, with Simon the sorcerer, and with

licism." 1826, p. 138. Of this writer, who had been a Roman Catholic priest for many years, Dr. Newman, the distinguished pervert from Oxford, says, while dissenting strongly from Mr. White's opinions, "I have the fullest confidence in his word when he witnesses to facts, and facts which he knew." He describes him as a person "whose honor you may depend on;" "a man you can trust."—*Lectures on the Present Condition of Catholics in England.* London, 1851.

Judas the traitor, and with those who have said to God, 'Depart from us, we desire not the knowledge of thy ways.' Let him perish in the day of judgment, and let everlasting fire devour him, with the devil and his angels, unless he make restitution and come to amendment. *Fiat. Fiat.* So be it. So be it."

This is not the voice of the Christian minister, gently encouraging a devout soul to engage upon a course of willing obedience, to be spontaneously and joyfully persevered in unto the end. It imposes on the conscience an awful weight from the outset. It is designed to remain a fearful monument of that one act by which, in the truthful language of the Roman Catholic tract we have already quoted, the poor nun is "bound," like the miserable recruit, "by an irrevocable engagement."

And if, in subsequent years, at the thought of friends, and family, and home; tired of the dull, weary monotony of the cloister, or, it may be, sick at heart of the priestcraft, the superstition, the vice, which may be secretly practiced within the convent walls; or, perhaps, having changed her religious sentiments, she wishes for the free light of the Gospel of Christ, yet, the moment she thinks of these things, the awful malediction, as a ghastly spectre, rises before her,

"Let her perish in the day of judgment, and let everlasting fire devour her, with the devil and his angels."

Or if her father, in after years, desires to bring back his long-lost daughter to his bosom; or if her mother should sigh over the dangers which she has learned are rife within the cloisters; or if her brother, brave and generous, makes an effort to secure the freedom of his sister, then the vision of the prelate stands before him, with crosier and mitre, and proclaims the sentence,

"Let him perish in the day of judgment, and let everlasting fire devour him, with the devil and his angels."

Nay, were the chief justice of our commonwealth to issue the writ of *habeas corpus* to bring this young recluse into court before him, or were a committee of inspection appointed by our judiciary to visit the establishment, and invite the prisoner, if such be her choice, to go forth free, the sentence falls upon their heads,

"Let them perish in the day of judgment, and let everlasting fire devour them, with the devil and his angels."*

But while the Church, in this imposing service, lays upon *the mind* of her captive, and on the minds of those who might be induced to procure her freedom, the most forcible restraint that fear and terror can create, it is no less evident that the practical measures taken for the continuance of this captivity are equally strong to confine and imprison the body. The Council of Trent enjoins all bishops to enforce the close confinement of nuns by every means, and even to engage the assistance of the secular arm for that purpose; entreats all princes to protect the inclosure of the convents; and threatens with instant excommunication all civil magistrates who withhold their aid when the

* Reverend M. H. Seymour.

bishops call for it. "Let no professed nun," say the fathers of the Council of Trent, "come out of her monastery under any pretext whatever, not even for a moment." "If any of the regulars [men and women under perpetual vows] pretend that fear or force compelled them to enter the cloister, or that the profession took place before the appointed age, let them not be heard, except within five years of their profession. But if they put off the frock of their own accord, no allegation of such should be heard, but, *being compelled to return to the convent*, THEY MUST BE PUNISHED AS APOSTATES, being, in the mean time, deprived of all the privileges of their order."

Such is the law of the Church of Rome concerning all who have fled from the walls of religious houses. It applies fully to every one of those who, in our own day and in our own land, have succeeded in making their escape; and if the institutions and the public opinion of this country allowed it, that law would be seen to be publicly carried out to the letter among us, as undoubtedly it has been secretly within the precincts of those establishments which, in the midst of our boasted freedom, constitute small despotisms of the deepest oppression.

In view, therefore, of the fact that by the very testimony of the Roman Catholic Church herself, in her popular publications, in her public rites, and in her authorized standards of doctrine and discipline, an actual restraint is and must be imposed upon the inmates of monastic establishments; and in view of the conceded fact that there are some, if not many, who are thus unwillingly confined, we urge the enactment of some provision to extend the territory of our American freedom over these institutions; to apply the precious principles of liberty of thought, speech, and person to these unhappy beings; to proclaim to the reluctant though submissive bondwoman of the convent, if there be but one such in our land, "There is no law to keep you here; you are free to stay or to go forth; make your choice without fear of man; remain, if so you will, but be assured that you need do so no longer than your own free purpose shall last."

A few farther considerations will be noticed, however, before we reach the full examination of this point.

IV. FACILITIES OF COMMUNICATION.

It has been urged that a sufficient method of redress for the occasional instances of unwillingness that we have here referred to, is provided by the system, in the free access of parents and relatives to communication with the nun. Such is the argument of the Mother Superior of St. Joseph's in her letter respecting the author of this narrative. Such is the favorite strain of all who attempt to set aside the proofs of oppression and restraint furnished by numerous witnesses. Our nuns and sisters, they say, have fathers and mothers, brothers and friends, who may at any time visit them freely, and can surely be relied upon to ascertain the true state of their feelings, and to procure their departure should they themselves desire to leave.

What, then, is the fact respecting this facility of intercourse? What opportunities have the members of the convent or the sisterhood to acquaint their friends with their views and wishes? Every one knows how it is. The interview, when allowed at all, takes place at an iron grating, where the nun stands like a prisoner behind bars, which present an impassable barrier. These interviews generally, if not invariably, take place in the presence of a third person—a nun appointed for the purpose. The sister, taught, as we shall see, to regard these interviews as dangerous to her spiritual safety, and carefully instructed to avoid all demonstrations of attachment to her former state, and desire to return to the world, and required to express an entire contentment and satisfaction with the "religious" life, can not be supposed to exercise a reasonable choice in the matter, or to make known her interior sentiments under this fourfold restraint of spiritual fear, mechanical obedience, the consciousness of being watched, and an actual prevention of free converse by means of the iron barriers that separate her from her friends. But remember that the nun is bound to be in a condition of abject submission to her Superior's will; that this is the very essence of that sanctity to which she is taught to aspire, an entire sacrifice of moral independence. The idea that with such discipline and such habits, to say nothing of the dread of penance, whether it consist in flogging,* solita-

* Under the less harsh name of *discipline* or *flagellation.* "This is a species of mortification," says St. Alphonsus Liguori, who died only seventy years ago, "strongly recommended by Francis de Sales, and universally adopted in religious communities of both sexes. All the modern saints, without a single exception, have continually practiced this sort of penance. It is related of St. Lewis of Gonzaga that he often scourged himself unto blood three times in the day; and at the point of death, not having sufficient strength to use the lash, he besought the provincial to have him disciplined from head to foot. *Surely, then, it would not be too much for you to take the discipline once in*

ry confinement, or irksome duties, as a determent from infraction of the commands given her, is simply absurd.

"What progress," asks St. Alphonsus Liguori, "can be expected from the religious who wishes to have her relations near the convent; who, if she do not see them, is constantly sending letters and messages to request a visit from them; and who, if they yield not to her entreaties, is disturbed, and complains by frequent letters of their absence and neglect? It is impossible for a nun of this description ever to obtain a close union with God. 'Whoever,' says St. Gregory, 'wishes to be truly united to the Father of all, must be separated from relations.'"

"The nun who leaves her relations in effect and *in affection*, shall obtain eternal beatitude in heaven and a hundred-fold on earth; she will leave a few, and shall find many sisters in religion; she will abandon a father and a mother, and in return shall have God for her Father, and Mary for her mother.

"Hence, convinced that detachment from kindred is highly pleasing to God, the saints have sought to be *wholly removed* from their relatives. 'For my part,' says St. Teresa, 'I can not conceive what consolation a nun can find in her relatives. By attachment to them she displeases God, and, without being able to enjoy their amusements, she shares in all their troubles.'

"How applicable to you, O blessed sister! is this reflection of the saint! . . . . . Oh! what an excess of folly to imagine that you can not be happy without

the day, or at least three or four times in the week!"—*The True Spouse of Christ*, etc., p. 181.

frequently seeing your friends! Ah! *if you keep aloof from them,* what torrents of consolation and happiness would your spouse, Jesus, infuse into your soul! St. Mary Magdalene de Pazzi used to say that *an abhorrence of the grates* should be the principal fruit of the communion of religious. And as an evil spirit once said to the venerable sister, Mary Villain, there is certainly no place where the devil does so much injury to religious as in the parlor.* Hence St. Mary Magdalene de Pazzi would not even pass through it; and such was her hatred of it that she could not even bear to hear it mentioned. Whenever she was obliged to go to the parlor, she would begin to weep, and say to her novices, 'My dear children, pray to God for me, for I am called to the grate.'

"But you will say, 'What am I to do? Am I never to see my friends? When they visit me, must I send them away, and refuse to go to the grate?' I do not require so much from you; but *if you refused to see them, would you do wrong*—would you do what would be inconvenient, or what is never done by religious?"

But another injunction is given by the same teacher in reference to intercourse with relations at the grate, and we have reason to believe that the rule is dwelt upon with much urgency in the instruction of nuns: "Be careful not to make known to externs the internal concerns of the convent, *and particularly what may tend to the discredit of the Superior or the sisters.*"

"Ah!" continues the saint, "what rapid progress

* *Parlatorium*, the room where the grate is.

in divine love does the religious make who resolves NEVER to go to the grate. When you, O blessed sister! go to the parlor, be careful at least to conduct yourself like a religious. In your intercourse with seculars, you should not only guard with great care against *all affectionate expressions*, but should also be very grave and reserved in the parlor. St. Mary Magdalene de Pazzi wished her nuns to be as uncultivated as the wild deer—these are her very words. And the venerable sister Hyacinth Marescotti used to say, 'The courtesy of nuns consists in being discourteous, by cutting short all discourses in the parlor.' "*

So much for the reliance to be placed upon the facilities of intercourse between the "religious" and her relations as a means of redress or escape from restraint. The author of the present narrative has stated how she herself was directed and compelled to mislead her friends as to her true sentiments, and to disguise from them all dissatisfaction with her position at the institution.

V. DESPOTISM OF THE CONVENT.

There is another consideration, bearing, as we believe, with no slight force upon the propriety of legislative action with reference to convents and other establishments of like order. We refer to the extent of power irresponsibly lodged in the hands of the superiors of those institutions, and wielded by them with absolute sway over the moral and physical condition of individuals completely abstracted from domestic and legal protection.

* "The True Spouse," etc., p. 361–366.

In these United States—for it is of them alone that we at present speak—all women of sound mind born free, who have reached the age of discretion, and have not forfeited by crime their civil rights, are supposed to live under the shelter of laws, and to possess privileges of personal self-control. Besides the guardianship of natural protectors—their fathers, husbands, and brothers, who are generally those most interested in their well-being—they can at any time invoke the interference of justice, and claim its covenanted defense. Surrounded by relatives, neighbors, and friends, to whom they can instantly appeal against even the possible abuse of authority at home, they are seldom exposed to restraint, hardship, or maltreatment for any continued period. Whatever the obligations of domestic regard, it is not understood that these involve the relinquishment of personal will within reasonable and lawful bounds. This fact, however, is not of universal application; for while, as a rule, such freedom exists and is guaranteed by law to all American women, there is an exception most significant and remarkable. We have in the United States a considerable number of institutions, containing many hundreds of females, who are under absolute and despotic control. These establishments are conducted by persons exercising an assumed authority not committed to them by the civil power, but lying beyond its cognizance, dispensing with its sanction, and acknowledging no accountability to its courts. They come not under the head of asylums, penitentiaries, or prisons. For those there are particular provisions in our codes; they are open to official inspection and governed by official appointment, but such is not the case here. The subjects of this discipline, though not culprits or criminals, are adjudged to close seclusion and loss of natural immunities; like them, they are immured for life or for a stated term, within buildings surrounded by high walls, beyond which they can not proceed without permission; like them, they are under control of superiors, who govern all their actions, though undesignated and unrecognized for such purpose by the state. They are not looked upon as apprentices or persons held to service according to any known law of the land, yet they are bound by solemn vows and obligations to absolute obedience and abandonment of choice and volition, without hesitancy or reflection. For all the benefit they derive from the liberal institutions of our country, they might as well be situated under the despotisms of the Old World, or in a condition of avowed bondage.

There is, then, it can scarcely be denied, some ground for the inquiry, What are these establishments, that they should exist among us outside of all civil jurisdiction? What are these nunneries and religious houses, that the daughters of freemen should be pent up within them like outcasts from society and convicts of justice, yet unknown as such to the judges of our courts and the legislators of our states? What is there so mysterious within those precincts that there the domain of freedom does not extend, that there the light of publicity can not enter, that from thence the voice of appeal to justice can not be heard? What are these nunneries? Are they institutions recognized and authorized for the public good by the government of our land? Why, then, are they closed to an inspection that may insure against maladministration? why is not their condition reported to the public for approval or censure? Or are they establishments of a strictly private character, such as our schools and associations of benevolence? Then wherefore should they arrogate to themselves over adults of sound mind, guiltless of crime, a control of will and action utterly incompatible with the enjoyment of civil freedom?

Until, as we apprehend will not soon be the case, there shall be enacted by our Legislatures some special provision for the existence of institutions where persons of free birth, good fame, and mental sanity may lawfully be confined, restricted in their personal freedom, and subjected to absolute government of will or physical coercion, however they may have been persuaded to consent at the outset to such a course of discipline—until, we say, some such law shall be added to our codes, the monastic system will continue to be as it is now, *illegal*. There is at present nothing in our laws to warrant that system. There is nothing that gives to any individual, whether priest or layman, the privilege of exacting the bounden service of an American woman under vow of absolute obedience. There is nothing there that entitles any person, whether Abbot or Lady Superior, to deprive women of liberty and restrain them from exit. There is nothing that provides even for such a voluntary act of disfranchisement as would be involved in the complete sacrifice of will required by the rules of the convent. That system is not only opposed to the spirit of republican freedom, it is unknown to our civil polity, and clearly hostile to every principle of justice and right that belongs to our age.

It can not even be urged for the system of monastic discipline that it should find countenance in a country where domestic servitude is recognized and made legal. It may not be compared for a moment with that institution. There is no part of our land where laws do not exist for the security of the slave in the enjoyment of life and good treatment. There is no state of this Union where the complete exercise of control over life, health, and virtue is vested in a single individual so absolutely and without the shadow of responsibility as in the case of the superiors of convents.

The advocates of these religious penitentiaries tell us, for the quieting of all apprehension in the matter, that the objects of this discipline are most pure and commendable, that their regulations are such as every one would approve, that the sanctity of its design insures the excellence of the system. Such is the argument of Mother Etienne, the Superior of St. Joseph's, and a curious one it is. If such a line of defense could be set up in all such cases, there would be few criminals found worthy of sentence. Grant that the regulations of a society may be admirable in all respects: does that fact secure their perfect execution? Does it do away with the necessity for any check upon abuse and injustice under the system so wisely drawn up on paper? Where is the judge of its actual agreement with these avowed regulations? Where is the court of appeal for any complaint? What opportunity of redress for particular grievances? The bishop or the Pope, doubtless; and whenever, thanks to the secret workings of Jesuits, clerical and lay, our people shall be prepared to establish the canon law of Rome in this country, then it will be time to acknowledge the sufficiency of such a plea.

VI. INSTANCES OF ESCAPE.

Where absolute and arbitrary power resides in any fallible being, the chances of its abuse are unquestionably great. Where restraint is imposed upon the freedom of a considerable number of persons, it is quite probable that some, however willing at the outset to submit, may finally become weary of their bondage, and desire release. We have already adduced repeated acknowledgments from Roman Catholic authorities to the effect that there are cases of reluctant and constrained submission. We have only now to instance some few out of a great number of such, where this oppression has been felt to exceed endurance, and the desperate victim of the cloister has been driven to insanity, or to the hazards of an attempt at escape.

A single fact of this nature might, to an impartial judgment, prove the existence of those evils which we have been delineating. But these occurrences have been frequent and notorious. How many similar attempts may have been thwarted and concealed from public knowledge by the vigilance of those interested in their suppression, we can only estimate from the frequency of such as have proved successful.

On the 18th of August, 1839, a nun by the name of Olivia Neal, formerly of Charles county, Maryland, but who had been for nineteen years a prisoner, under the appellation of "Sister Isabella," at the Carmelite nunnery in Aisquith Street, Baltimore, succeeded in escaping from that institution. After being repulsed by several families, she was received and protected by a worthy citizen living a few doors from the convent. Efforts were immediately made by the confessor of the convent and others to have access to the fugitive and convey her back. The rumor of this fact having spread in the city, an immense crowd gathered around the house, and signified their determination to prevent the abduction. The mayor and other gentlemen having come to the spot, she was taken to a place of safety.

This nun stated to all who questioned her that she had entered the convent at a very early age; that she *had long desired to escape;* that on one occasion before she had gotten out, and was met and carried back by the priest. She demanded, in a most earnest and touching manner, the protection of the people.

The assertion was at once made by the authorities of the convent that Olivia Neal, or "Sister Isabella," was out of her right mind. This plea is invariably set up in similar cases. A physician was induced to state that she was a "perfect maniac;" and five others united in the conflicting statement that she was a "*monomaniac*," or at least afflicted with a "*general feebleness of intellect.*" Hundreds, however, of the most respectable citizens of Baltimore concurred in declaring that Miss Neal gave every indication of sanity, correct judgment, and resolute will.

The Reverend Robert J. Breckinridge, D.D., a distinguished and most estimable clergyman of the Presbyterian Church, was at that time a resident of Baltimore, and was requested to have an interview with this escaped nun. He thus relates it: "As we entered the room, he [a friend] said to her, 'This is Mr. B.,' naming us. Her reply went to our heart. She extended her hands toward us, and, repeating our name, said, almost convulsively, 'I claim your protection!' We told her we had come to her for no other purpose.

"A rapid conversation, in which several took part, immediately ensued, from which we learned, in substance, that her name was Olivia Neal, originally from Charles county, Maryland, but now called 'Sister Isabella;' that she had been put into the convent very young, and been in it nineteen years; that she had been *long anxiously trying* to get out, and had once succeeded in making her escape into the street, when she was met and *forcibly carried back*, and subjected to severe penances; that, having again escaped, her anxious desire was for present protection—a desire she repeatedly expressed; that, however, she wished all to understand that she did not desire to change her religion, but *only her condition as a nun;* that she did not wish any violence offered either to the nuns or priests on her account, against whom, indeed, she was not disposed to make any accusations; that she felt agitated, and unfit for any extended conversation on the subject of her past trials, and asked only for security, repose, and tranquillity, till she could collect her faculties and decide on her future line of conduct, which was the more necessary, she said, *as they had told her that her mind was weak;* and that, having no friends in whom she could confide, she was obliged to throw herself on the public for protection.

"Much more was said, which we do not think it worth while to repeat at present; but, as a sample of the general style of conversation, we will detail one item more minutely. She was asked if a nun had not escaped some months ago. 'Yes; it was I,' was her reply. 'How happens it that you were back again?' 'I was met by a gentleman immediately after getting out, and carried back.' 'Who was that gentleman?' No answer. 'Was it priest Gildea?' 'Yes, sir.' 'What was done to you when you were carried back?' 'There are penances to undergo; I was subjected to these.' 'Did they whip you?' No answer, but a mournful smile. 'Did they imprison you?' 'I have said I endured the usual penance.' She was not pressed farther on this painful subject, being evidently unwilling to speak fully of it."*

The sequel to this sad story of oppression and suffering exhibits the triumph of Romish intrigue over the natural and legal rights of a feeble woman. A distant relative was found who was willing to serve the purposes of priestly craft. He came to Baltimore, obtained *ex parte* certificates contradictory of each other, insufficient in law or reason, none of which were sworn to, and no cross examination permitted; on which certificates he took his kinswoman and placed her precisely where she had most earnestly desired never to go again—under the power of the nuns and priests.† Nothing more has been heard of her for

* Papism in the United States. By Robert J. Breckinridge, D.D., p. 235–245.

† Papism, etc., p. 265.

years. Miss Bunkley, in the preceding narrative, mentions having seen in the asylum at Mount Hope a person who, as she had reason to believe, was the unhappy "Sister Isabella."

The author of this volume has also specified several instances of attempted escape from the institution of St. Joseph at Emmettsburg. That of Helen Grier is authenticated by unimpeachable witnesses.

Facts like the following have frequently met the eyes of our readers in the public journals:

"On the night of the 18th of April, 1842, as a patrol was going along the narrow street which runs by the side of the convent of the Bon Pasteur, in the town of Ouest, in France, he found a girl lying on the pavement, and screaming from the injury she had received by a fall in attempting to escape from the convent through one of the upper windows by means of a sheet. On being taken to the hospital, it was found that her leg was broken. When able to speak, she said that, on account of a trifling disagreement with some of the nuns, she was put into solitary confinement, and allowed only bread and water. Driven to despair, she had contrived to force away the planks by which the window was blinded, and attempted, in the manner described, to reach the ground."*

"We have before us," says the writer upon whose authority we have stated the above, "an octavo volume of four hundred pages, entitled 'Sœur Marie, Benedictine,' published at Caen in 1846, written by an eminent French advocate, M. Léon Tillard.

"Mademoiselle de Monnier, whose name 'in relig-

* Nuns and Nunneries, p. 216.

ion' was Sœur Marie Joseph, entered a Benedictine convent at Bayeux at the age of twenty-one, in 1823, and, by her superior education and talents, she became of great use to the convent. The other sisters were ignorant and illiterate, and the new postulant was at once placed in charge of the school. Under her care it greatly throve, and the number of pupils rapidly increased. At length she assumed the veil. Several changes took place in the convent, a new Lady Abbess came, and poor Sœur Marie became the object of a long-continued persecution, beginning with things so small as hardly to be perceptible, but which, like the dropping of water on the stone, wore upon the mind of the wretched victim. She was removed from the school, some nuns having joined the establishment who were better educated than those originally there, and, after some time, *no one was allowed to speak to her.* This was continued year after year. At last matters came to a crisis; the Superior provoked Sister Marie, drew her into an altercation, and then declaring that she was *mad,* had her seized by the gardener and others, and locked up in a small cell. The physician of the convent was sent for, and, without having seen the victim, signed a certificate declaring her to be mad. In the dead of the night she was roused from her cell, carried off in a carriage to the Bon Sauveur at Bayeux, and there placed among the insane on the strength of this certificate. The physician of this new asylum, however, soon found that she was perfectly sane, and at length dismissed her at her own earnest entreaty. But where was she to go? She returned to her old convent, but there they would not receive her. She appealed to priests and bishops, to nuns and abbesses, but every door was closed against her except the mad-house of the Bon Sauveur. M. Tillard generously took up her cause, and endeavored to obtain justice for her. But all in vain. Worn out, harassed, and persecuted, poor Sœur Marie at length became duly qualified for the Bon Sauveur. Her mind failed her, and she is now within its walls, a harmless lunatic!"*

In these facts, strikingly analogous to those connected with the case of the unhappy Olivia Neal, we see more manifestly the design of the tyrannical and merciless autocrat of the convent, working by incessant annoyances the mental ruin of the object of her hatred, until at length, successful in destroying the power of thought and will, her victim is reduced to the living death of a maniac.

VII. LETTER FROM DR. DE SANCTIS.

We have now to present some extracts from a letter addressed to the editor of this work by the distinguished and excellent Dr. De Sanctis, who occupied for many years the post of curate of the church of the Maddalena at Rome, was "qualificator" of the Inquisition, censor of the Theological Academy in the Roman University, and filled other prominent offices of trust in the service of the Church of Rome. He was in this capacity commissioned by the Cardinal Vicar to preach and hear confessions in the convents of that city; and during ten years and more, passed scarcely a day in which he did not exercise these func-

* Nuns and Nunneries, p. 219–223.

tions at some one or more of those institutions. Written by one so competent to speak from personal observation upon the subject of monasticism, and so worthy of trust as an able and faithful minister of the Gospel since his conversion from Roman Catholic error, we are sure that these statements will command the attention of our readers.

THE CONVENT A PRISON OF DELUSIONS.

"The convents of Rome may be designated as prisons—horrible prisons of religious delusion. This statement will require some explanation. A young girl at Rome, who is to any degree interested in religion, if she receives her education at a convent, must absolutely remain there forever, as I shall hereafter explain; or, if not so educated, must necessarily enter a convent in the end. The Roman Catholic priest knows nothing of conjugal love in its holy and chaste character, and for this very reason he hates it, he detests it, often with the utmost sincerity and perfect good faith. The declamations of the priests, whether from the pulpit or the confessional, against this love, are of a nature to make one shudder. These men are truly to be pitied: ignorant as they are of the pure, the legitimate affection of the married state, and knowing only of a sensual and bestial passion, they have reason to declaim against such love. The young girl who blindly follows the path of piety, blindly believes the priest; for want of experience, she can not distinguish the innocent from the guilty affection; and when she feels the first impulses of that love which would lead her to become a wife and a mother, she confesses to the priest as a grave offense those sentiments which pertain to the normal state in which God has framed her being. And the confessor, most generally from ignorance, and with honest persuasion, augments this uneasiness, declaring that this impulse is a temptation of the devil in order to eradicate the love of Christ. He intimates that there is no better method of overcoming such temptation than to fly from a world which is but a troubled sea, and to withdraw into the haven of security, to wit, the convent. And here he commences to adduce before the kindled imagination of his charge all those mystic incidents, examples, histories, and revelations, of which the legendary literature of asceticism is full, thus inflaming the mind of the young penitent, and convincing her that there is no harbor of safety for her soul other than the state of a recluse. All that she sees in the world without becomes to her an object of aversion. The persons most endeared by natural affection—father, mother, brothers—become odious, and she longs for the moment when she may inclose herself within those sacred walls, where alone she now hopes to find peace and salvation. The world is represented to her as a wild and corrupt stream, flowing with impetuous current before her, while the convent, overlooking it, offers the only secure retreat. Her father, her brother, her sisters are being carried away by the river; for her there is safety only there. The dream lasts a while after she has entered, and then it disappears; the abode of peace is transformed into a perpetual prison, where a life pays for the religious delusion of a day.

"Many young girls are drawn to the convents in

this manner, but there are others, and perhaps these constitute a majority, who are attracted in a different way. Many, to whom nature has denied those external graces and charms which captivate the regard of men, finding themselves neglected, and conscious of an irresistible need of loving some object, seek to be loved, as they say, by our Lord Jesus Christ. 'The heart of Jesus' is the chosen devotion of such. It is after this fashion that the 'heart of Jesus' is represented at Rome. Our Lord is depicted as a young man of marvelous beauty, who, with a heart shining with love, seen transparent in his breast, invites with the most winning look. The young girl who has not met with a response in the regard of men, enthusiastically begins to cherish an affection for this picture and object. The priests know well how to encourage such a tendency; they place in her hands the lives of St. Teresa and other visionaries, who relate their intercourse with a heavenly spouse, and already she hopes that a like experience will be hers. Another need that she feels is that of making some human heart the depository of her thoughts and emotions, and for want of a lover she chooses as a confidant her confessor. With him she spends whole hours of every day in secret colloquies, and, supposing the confessor to be a saint, according to the Romish idea, the unavoidable result of all this is that she will go into a convent. The dream after a while is scattered, and there remains the sad reality of a perpetual prison as the fruit of a religious delusion.

"There is a third class of young persons, who, being educated from childhood in the nunnery, remain there, and become nuns without knowing why, and give up with alacrity a world which they have never seen. By what arts and wiles they are drawn into this course I shall relate elsewhere, when I come to speak of the education given in convents.

MORALITY OF THE CONVENTS IN ROME.

"Such is, for the most part, the method by which the convents of Rome are peopled. I must now say a few words respecting the morality of those institutions.

"That there have occurred some flagrant abuses of this nature, and more especially in convents where the education of the young is prosecuted, can not be denied. Two fearful examples have taken place within my own recollection, the general publicity of which created a painful excitement. The one occurred at the Convent of 'San Dionisio alle quattro Fontane,' an establishment of nuns affiliated with the Jesuits, in which the confessor pursued a most infamous course in relation to a large number of young persons under the care of that institution. The other case was that of the 'Conservatorio della Divina Providenza,' where the confessor seduced no fewer than sixteen of the most beautiful persons educated in that convent. * * * * As a general thing, however, the convent (so far as Rome is concerned) is neither, on the one hand, a terrestrial paradise inhabited by angels, nor, on the other hand, is it generally a place of open and shameless crime.

"An event of no unfrequent occurrence in the convent is the 'spiritual assistance' of the sick. When a nun is dangerously ill, the confessor, director, or another priest spends the night at the institution. Often it will happen that, in a case of sickness, fifteen or sixteen successive nights are thus spent. This has happened more than once to myself. In the convent there are generally two well-furnished rooms for such a contingency: the one is a small parlor, conveniently arranged, where the confessor eats; the other a bed-room, where, also, nothing is omitted for his comfort. The supper of the reverend father confessor is no ordinary one; it consists of all the niceties of food that are to be procured. While the holy man is at his meal, several nuns will be standing around him, urging him to eat this and drink that. Supper over, the father goes to see the patient, sprinkles her with holy water, and then retires to his bed. The doors are left open, in order that he may readily be called should the invalid grow worse. I can not say that all precautions are taken in such cases, nor that disorders fail to occur, and that with sufficient frequency. I can only state matters as I know them to exist.

"And here I may incidentally mention a fact that will surprise the good Christian people of America, although at Rome it appears quite natural. In Carnival,* the inmates of all the convents are permitted the masquerade. The monks who act as confessors send their habits to their respective nuns, who put them on, and enact a thousand ridiculous scenes. Any one can understand the indecency, and, to speak more clearly, the

* A period of five or six days preceding Lent, during which, in Roman Catholic countries, every species of merriment and buffoonery is tolerated.

immorality of such procedures; but this is nothing: on the contrary, it seems so natural that a nun who should fail to join in these amusements would be regarded as over-scrupulous even by her confessor himself. In convents devoted to education, there are, besides these, theatrical performances, and comedies are recited. To these representations are admitted the confessors, priests, monks, and the relatives of the nuns and pupils. On such occasions you would see some one of these young girls ornamented with mustaches, declaiming the part of an officer, and dressed in uniform, while another would take the character of a lover, etc., etc. In convents where superior sanctity is affected, profanations still greater are committed. There are given dramatic entertainments called sacred, and these are nothing less than Scripture facts set forth in comedy. There you would see a young girl assuming the part of Moses, another that of Aaron, thus turning into ridicule those holy characters, and casting contempt upon the word of God itself. I once saw at one of these places a young person who represented an angel, while another filled the rôle of the devil. Between them they concocted a dialogue so ludicrous that every body was exploding with laughter.

HEALTH IN THE CONVENTS OF ROME.

"In order to make what I have to say respecting these institutions more clear, let me divide them into two classes: the one consisting of those where the inmates have no other occupation besides prayer, the other in which they are employed in giving instruction to the young.

"With regard to the former class, we must again distinguish those convents where the rigor of discipline is carried to such an excess of fanaticism as to tread under foot the most sacred laws of nature; and here I do not speak of individual excesses of fanaticism, but of abuses belonging to the community itself, approved and sanctioned by the Superiors of the institution.

"There is at Rome, in the 'Regione de' Monti,' in a spot almost unknown to the world, a convent entitled that of the '*Vive Sepolte*' ('*buried alive*');* and the miserable inmates are really in the condition expressed by their name. Once admitted within those walls, it may be said of them,

"'Leave hope behind, all ye who enter here.'

"They are indeed *buried alive*. They come to confession, but a double grating, the one at a considerable distance from the other, an iron plate punctured with small holes between the confessor and the penitent, through which the voice can scarcely pass, and a black cloth fastened upon this plate to intercept even the rays of light—such is the mode in which the confession takes place. When these nuns commune, they present themselves at a small window, about half the size of the countenance; and there, with a thick woolen cloth over the face, suffering only the tongue to be seen, they receive the element from the hand of the priest. In case of sickness, they are led into a room called the infirmary, and there the physician prescribes for his patient through an aperture in the wall. If he wishes to feel the pulse or draw blood, the arm

* More properly, "*Religiose Francescane dette 'Vive Sepolte.'*"

of the invalid must be extended to him through the aperture.

The physician of this convent related to me these facts as I was visiting the institution, and stated that many of the nuns had died in consequence of these impediments to a proper medical attendance. He told me that on one occasion, indignant at this suicidal course, he went to Cardinal Patrizi, the patron of this convent, who replied to his complaint that there was no need of interference, these persons being, not suicides, but *victims of holy modesty.*

"When the nun enters this establishment, she is, I have said, '*buried alive.*' She must henceforth know nothing of her relatives. Once in the year it is allowed that relatives of the first degree present themselves at the monastery, and speak in the hearing of the recluse; they may not, however, see the countenance of their daughter or sister. When a near relative of a nun dies, the Mother Superior, on the evening after that event, says at prayers, 'My sisters, let us pray for the soul of the father, or mother, or brother of one of our number, who died yesterday or to-day;' and it is not permitted that any one know who it is that has died: hence each imagines that it may be her own father, mother, or brother; and in this uncertainty she is left, in order that she may, with more fervor, from day to day, pray for the deceased. Such is the abuse that fanaticism makes of religion! But things of this sort are not generally known or believed, and for this reason I state and affirm the facts. If you should publish them, do so with my name, as I am willing to be responsible for them.

"When a youth, I resided in the neighborhood of this convent, and I remember that one day the Pope, Leo XII., made an unexpected visit to the institution. It excited much curiosity in the quarter to know the occasion of this visit, which was as follows: A woman had an only daughter who had taken the veil in that convent. Left a widow, she came often to the institution, and with a mother's tears besought that she might be allowed, if not to see, at least to hear the voice of her daughter. What request more just and more sacred from a mother? But what is there of sacredness and justice that fanaticism does not corrupt? The daughter sent word by the confessor to her mother that if she did not cease to importune her, she would refuse to speak to her even on the day when she would be allowed to do so. That day at length arrived; the widowed mother was the first to present herself at the door of the convent, and she was told that she could not see her daughter. In despair, she asked Why? No answer. Was she sick? No reply. Was she dead? Not a word. The miserable mother conjectured that her daughter was dead. She ran to the Superiors to obtain at least the privilege of seeing her corpse, but their hearts were of iron. She went to the Pope: a mother's tears touched the breast of Leo XII., and he promised her that on the following morning he would be at the convent and ascertain the fact. He did so, as I have said, unexpectedly to all. Those doors, which were accustomed to open only for the admittance of a fresh victim, opened that day to the head of the Church of Rome. Seeing the wretched mother who was the occasion of this visit, he called her to him, and ordered her to follow him into the nunnery. The daughter, who, by an excess of barbarous fanaticism, thought to please Heaven by a violation of the holiest laws of nature, concealed herself upon hearing that her mother had entered the convent. The Pope called together in a hall the entire sisterhood, and commanded them to lift the veils from their faces. The mother's heart throbbed with vehemence; she looked anxiously from face to face once and again, but her daughter was not there. She believed now that she was dead, and, with a piercing cry, fell down in a swoon. While she was reviving, the Pope peremptorily asked the Mother Superior whether the daughter was dead or alive. She replied, at length, that she was yet living, but having vowed to God that she would eradicate every carnal affection from her breast, she was unwilling even to see her mother again. It was not until the Pope ordered her appearance, in virtue of the obedience due to him, and upon pain of mortal sin, that the nun came forth. This outrage upon human nature, which might have resulted in parricide, is denominated in the vocabulary of monasticism '*virtue in heroic degree.*'

"Besides the convent of the '*Vive Sepolte,*' there are at Rome other institutions of a similar cast; for example, that of the Capuchin nuns of San Urbano, those of Monte Cavallo, the Teresians of San Giuseppe a Capo le case, those of San Eligio in Trastevere, and so forth. Numbers of these poor wretches every year commit suicide through a false spirit of penitence. They go without necessary food; they wear haircloth when nature demands restoratives; they refuse themselves remedies which would arrest disease, and this from a false modesty which forbids the communicating of their ailments to the physician. Many have I known to die of such procedure. You will call these nuns poor victims of delusion; the world will call them mad; but, in the dictionary of the convent, they are termed '*holy martyrs of sacred modesty.*'

"I will not relate to you all the minutiæ of the convent life; it would take a volume instead of a letter to do so. Imagine what must be an establishment where fifty or sixty women live, as it were, in a prison—women brought together without knowledge of one another, gnawing the curb of an imprisonment which they affect to make appear voluntary, and which they seek to persuade themselves is such—and you will perceive what must be the nature of their life. * * * * Suicide by means of the rope or poison is not a very frequent occurrence in nunneries at Rome, but a species of suicide little known to the world is most frequent there: I mean that which proceeds from imprudent penances, the injurious repression of innocent affections, the persistent effort to contradict and thwart nature in every possible mode, the refusal, from false modesty, to make known, for medical advice, whatever maladies may occur—these and other reasons suffice to account for the fact that a very considerable proportion of nuns perish in youth, and so many others drag through years an existence of continued ailments and infirmities. * * *

THE NUNS AND THEIR CONFESSORS.

"There are other convents of 'contemplative life'—such is the appellation given to those where the principal occupation is or ought to be prayer—in which matters proceed quite differently from the 'Vive Sepolte.' At such institutions you would see, from early in the morning till evening, a string of priests and monks going and coming; these are the *confessors* of the nuns. To enable you to understand this more clearly, let me say that for each convent there is a confessor, so called. This confessor is a priest, appointed by the bishop and supported by the nunnery, who must always be at the convent for the 'spiritual direction' of its inmates. He is the pastor of the community, and all ought, according to rule, to confess to him. But it is not the practice of nuns to confess to the ordinary confessor. Each one has her own in particular, and some have two or three; but these particular confessors can not be called by that name; they are termed 'directors.' Each 'director,' as he reaches the institution, is received by his nun, who, if it be in the morning, regales him with a cup of excellent chocolate, or, after dinner, with refreshments, of which sweetmeats always form a part. While this holy director is eating, his nun converses with him; ordinarily the interview lasts about half an hour; then they go and shut themselves up in a confessional, where they remain at least an hour. This occurs at least twice a week, and often every day. The conversation is commonly any thing but religious; it is apt to consist chiefly of small-talk and scandal. * * *

EDUCATION AT CONVENTS.

"I have promised to speak of those convents which are devoted to education and instruction. Nearly all the nunneries contain some young persons who are in process of education, and are supported there by their relatives for this purpose; but there are convents which have for their principal scope the instruction of youth. For these institutions the description I have given of the others will, in general, answer to the truth; but it must be added that the young persons receiving their education at the convent do not know all that takes place in the establishment. They live in a particular portion of it, separate from the greater part of the nuns, whom they see only in the choir and at the refectory. They are under the charge of a nun who superintends their education.

"But wherein does this education consist? *Culture of intellect* they can not derive from the reading of ascetic books, legendaries, lives of the saints, and particularly from those works which speak of the felicities of the monastic life and the horrors of the world. In their tender minds this is the cardinal idea inculcated, that outside of the cloister it is almost impossible to find salvation. All books save those that speak of these things are absolutely prohibited. Hence geography, history, and all other branches of useful and necessary knowledge are completely banished from these places as worldly studies.

"*The culture of the heart* is shockingly profaned. Ignoring the life of the family, they learn to detest it. With the pretext that every human relation is profane, they alienate themselves, under the garb of sanctity, from parental love. They love none but those whom they believe to stand in the place of God—the confessor foremost of all, and then the mother mistress. Should one of these young persons leave the convent and marry (I relate what I have known in many cases), broils and strifes arise in the domestic circle. She refuses to obey her husband until the confessor has instructed her in matrimonial duties, and has commanded her to obey. Is this always innocence? I answer, *No.*

"For a young girl educated in a convent to be a good wife and a good mother is a thing most rare. At Rome it is a common saying, 'Do you want a faithless woman? Marry a girl brought up at a nunnery.' This rule has its exceptions, but be assured they are exceptions; fifteen years of experience at the confessional have taught me this. Such a person can not be a good mother, because, not educated in the family, she knows nothing of domestic life. She can not be a good housekeeper, because the superintendence of a household is something to her quite new. Few are the husbands who have not speedy cause to repent of marrying a young girl just out of the convent. With regard to work, the nuns teach only how to embroider church cloths.

"There is some difference, however, in the case of those convents which are destined more particularly for the education of the young. Of this nature there are at Rome the nunnery of 'Torre di Specchi,' for the high aristocracy; that of the 'Sacred Heart,' embracing all classes of persons; and that of the 'Ursulines,' for the middle class. * * * At the 'Sacred Heart,' the instruction given is certainly better than at other convents; but let us examine its character. Geography is taught; it may, however, be denominated geography applied to Jesuitism. Respecting every country and kingdom described, it is explained whether there be Jesuits in it, how much good they have done if there, how much evil has resulted if they have been driven away. History is taught; with the sole design, however, of convincing that Popery and Jesuitism are the only source of all good, and that where these have not been found, every crime and horror has thriven. Thus the young mind is so thoroughly imbued with prejudice, that it shudders at the bare mention of Henry the Eighth, Cromwell, or Washington. * * * The religious instruction consists of weak superstitions. She who can best adorn the image of her favorite saint, whom she changes every month, is the most devout.

NATURAL AFFECTIONS DESTROYED.

"That, however, which constitutes the chief object of instruction, and wherein the nuns wonderfully succeed, is the eradication of filial love and respect, to be supplanted by a blind obedience to the priests. And thus it is that they proceed. Two principal motives are brought into play for this purpose—pride and religion. They begin by exalting the freedom of the individual. They say that it is a gift of God, and we must not suffer it to be taken away. A doctrine most true; but listen to the application. The parents of the young girl propose to her, for instance, a match, it may be most desirable. The young girl has been taught to look upon this proposal as an attempt upon her individual liberty, and she accordingly declines. Her parents endeavor to persuade her; they urge that they do not wish to compel her assent, but only recommend what seems for the best. She, however, has learned from the nuns a quantity of stories about young people who have been rendered miserable by acceding to the will of their parents, and she persists in her refusal. The parents then are obliged to go to the *confessor*, and obtain of him that he will persuade the young girl. The confessor gathers information respecting the person in question, and if the match suit the Jesuits, the young girl will be persuaded, otherwise her disinclination will increase. Say what you will of the father and mother being her best friends, the most deserving of confidence—domestic life has become extinguished in the convent; for its inmate there is no father but the confessor, no mother but the 'mistress mother.'

"But, beside this motive of self-will, that of religion is brought in to set aside the parental right. This seems incredible; it is nevertheless a fact. The favorite principle that constitutes the theme of the exhortations of the 'mistress mother' is the explanation —I should say, rather, the infamous perversion, of a passage in the Gospel, 'He that loveth father or mother more than me, is not worthy of me.' From this text they inculcate upon these youthful minds that when they feel themselves inspired to do or not to do any thing, they are not to listen to their parents, who may command or counsel them against that inspira-

O 2

tion, otherwise they would love father or mother more than Jesus Christ, and render themselves unworthy of him. Then, to assure themselves of such inspiration, there is but one method—to consult the confessor. The confessor, being consulted, replies that first of all it is requisite to spend some time in prayer; he therefore prescribes a '*novena*' [nine days' devotion] to the 'Sacred Heart,' or to some favorite saint; meanwhile he ascertains the facts of the case. If the result of this inquiry be favorable, and the young girl feels herself inspired to say *No*, then he shows her that the inspiration is a temptation which must be withstood. If his decision be negative, then the opinion of the confessor, harmonizing with the *no* of the young girl, proves it to be a real inspiration from God. The whole family may go to ruin, it matters not, because 'he that loveth father or mother more than me, is not worthy of me.'

"With such principles as these, a young person educated at a convent becomes a blind instrument in the hands of the Jesuits. Imagine how good a daughter, wife, and mother she will prove.

"I have thus given you, dear sir, a rapid sketch of the nunneries of Rome. I can assure you that I have stated only what I have seen and known from close observation, to the truth of which I pledge myself. Believe me your devoted servant and brother in Jesus Christ,

L. De Sanctis, D.D.,

"Minister of the Holy Gospel.

"London, *Sept. 20th*, 1855."

VIII. REFORMATION OF CONVENTS.

If the testimony of individual witnesses, well authenticated, be yet deemed insufficient in proof of the abuses incidental to monasticism, we have only to conclude with a brief review of the legislation that has been found necessary, at almost every period of ecclesiastical history, for the redress of evils that have become too flagrant to be concealed.

Whether by individuals high in office in the Church of Rome, or through the interference of civil rulers, there have been attempted numerous reforms of the monastic orders and checks upon the excessive corruption into which the ascetic system has always shown an inherent proneness to run.

History tells us that in the Middle Ages luxury and vice grew to such a pitch that new rules were at various epochs introduced, for the express purpose of restoring a discipline which had given way to every imaginable irregularity. With this view, the monastery of Clugny, in Burgundy, was founded in 910, and a considerable number of monasteries in Spain, Italy, and Germany were reformed on the same model, while other institutions were based upon new schemes and stricter regulations. These, in turn, acquiring by their special repute for sanctity fresh influence and wealth, became proud and luxurious, and demanded, by their mutual dissensions and jealousies, the frequent interposition of successive popes. When the sixteenth century dawned, the condition of these orders, for the most part, was not less debased than in the darkest age preceding. The enormities developed by the light of the Reformation in connection with the monasteries of Germany, Scotland, and Italy, disgusted all enlightened men with the entire system, and amply justified its abolishment in Protestant countries.

It was not in these alone, however, that the urgency of reform in the monastic organizations became obvious with the spread of intelligence and cultivation throughout the countries of Europe. Statesmen of Roman Catholic governments became convinced that insufferable injuries to the welfare of nations were necessarily connected with the unrepressed growth of the so-called "religious" orders. The effect of this system upon the increase of population, by the encouragement held out to celibacy; upon general industry, by the unproductive idleness of those who thus lived on the earnings of others; upon the general thrift and wealth, by their incessant grasping at the estates of the rich; and upon public morals, by the crimes notoriously committed within their walls—all this was apparent to the Roman Catholic legislators of the eighteenth century. In 1781, the houses of some monastic orders were wholly abolished by Joseph II. of Austria; and those which he suffered to remain were limited to a certain number of inmates, and cut off from all communication with any foreign authority.* In 1790, the abolition of all religious orders was decreed in France, and the example was soon followed by the

* To the disgrace of modern civilization, a *concordat* has just been effected [in the autumn of 1855] between Austria and the Pope, by which the restoration of all these monastic establishments is authorized, and the control of education committed to the hands of the Jesuits.

majority of the Roman Catholic states of Europe. In our own day, the republics of South America have followed in this career of reform; and still later, Sardinia and Spain have enacted laws for the suppression of monasteries. In the former kingdom there were nearly four hundred of these haunts of idleness, containing some forty thousand monks and nuns, and holding *more than one half of the real estate of the realm, exempt from taxation!* The perseverance of the government in effecting this reform has brought upon it the impotent threat of excommunication from the Pope. In Spain, the Cortes have passed, by large majorities, a bill for the sale of a considerable amount of ecclesiastical property.

We have room only to signalize, in passing, some of the developments of vice and crime made in the course of these various attempts to redress a system of innate corruption and propensity to perpetual deterioration. To go back no farther than 1489, in the reign of Henry VII. of England, a bull was issued by Pope Innocent VIII. for the "reformation of monasteries." In this decree the pontiff states that he has heard with deep displeasure that many monasteries in England have relapsed from their rules, and that many of their inmates, having put away from themselves the fear of God, and given themselves up to a reprobate mind, lead a lascivious and too dissolute life. The facts by which this declaration is corroborated in the history of English monasteries and nunneries are too revolting for reproduction in our pages. The enormous vices that led to the visitation and suppression of these establishments in the succeeding reign of

Henry VIII. are well known. With regard to Germany and France in the preceding period, repeated bulls of popes and decrees of councils have stereotyped the evidence of the fact of a total and general depravation of morals in the conventual houses of men and women throughout those countries.

As late as the close of the past century, an Italian prelate, Scipione de Ricci, bishop of Pistoja and Prato, undertook the reform of certain flagrant disorders existing in his own diocese. For years this excellent man labored to accomplish the work of expurgation. The irregularities of life which he has depicted in his memoirs as of common occurrence among the Dominican nuns of Tuscany are positively frightful. Crimes unexampled and unheard of were rife within those secret inclosures. The access and intercourse of the monks of the corresponding order was attended with every variety of immoral behavior. But these evils were not of a day's growth. As far back as 1642, petitions were on record, addressed to the then Grand Duke, and signed by the representatives of the people of Pistoja, asking for a prompt remedy of the outrages upon decency and religion notoriously committed at these institutions. These repeated records, says Ricci, "showed that the spiritual ruin was beyond description, arising from the familiarity which existed between the monks and the nuns, and from *the facility of ingress to the convents which the monks enjoyed.** They ate and drank with those who were their

* The reader may for himself compare these statements, and those of Dr. De Sanctis to the same effect, with the intimations contained in Chapter XXVIII. of the preceding narrative. Reason and reflection,

favorites and the most devoted to them, remaining with them *tête-à-tête* in some cell, and even sleeping

however involuntarily, can not but pause at this singular adaptation and correspondence of male and female orders in the monastic scheme. The shop-keepers at Rome have for sale a "panorama" of the various fraternities existing in that city. In these colored prints there will be seen, on opposite pages, in their correlative garb, the "Olivetani" Monks and "Olivetane" Nuns; the "Agostiniani" and the "Penitenti di S. Agostino;" the "Domenicani" and the "Monache di S. Domenico;" the "Carmelitani" and the "Carmelitane;" the Capuchins, Carthusians, Franciscans, Trinitarians, etc., etc., male and female, each confronting the other in good fellowship and loving recognition, like lawful man and wife in decent Christian wedlock. It is a general arrangement of Romanism, and apparently not without some significance and propriety, to establish in contiguous positions the male and female institutions of those particular orders, who observe the same "rule," and derive their sanction from the same founder. Thus we have the institutions of the Lazarists and Sisters of Charity both at Emmettsburg, Maryland. The brethren are the confessors of the sisterhood. They have the same official head, and are regulated by the same system. "*The Superior-General of the Congregation of the Mission, or Lazarists, is* ex officio *Superior-General of the Daughters of Charity; and hence their direction is confided, when practicable, to a clergyman who is a Lazarist.*" These words are not an inference of our own, but the statement of the Rev. Charles I. White, D.D., in his "Life of Mrs. Seton, Foundress and first Superior of the Sisters or Daughters of Charity in the United States of America," published by Dunigan & Brother, New York, 1853; page 464, *note*. Now all this would be well enough, and perfectly unexceptionable and praiseworthy, if it had but the sanction of God's ordinance instituted expressly for the consecrating of this sort of relationship and mutuality of rule and life. Then it would be legal—then it would be holy; for "marriage is honorable *in all, but*"—"God will judge."

Nor let it be said that we are conjecturing where there is neither fact nor probability to support. Of the *facts*, as already in some small part specified, and elsewhere accessible in detail, the reader is competent to judge. Of the PROBABILITIES, hear the acknowledgments of the distinguished Roman Catholic historian, Dr. Lingard:

"This scheme of monastic polity," says he, "singular as it may now appear, was once adopted in most Catholic countries. Its origin may

in the convent, in a room, indeed, set apart, but still within the cloisters." Addressing a cardinal, Ricci says farther: "In writing to the Pope, I would not enter into infamous details which would horrify you. Yet what have not these wretched Dominican monks been guilty of? Provincials, priors, all alike, instead of remedying the disorders committed by the confessors, have either allowed or else themselves committed the same iniquities."

It must be added that all Ricci's efforts to reform the convents of Tuscany were vain. Upheld by his enlightened sovereign, he was thwarted by all around him; and when that prince was called from the ducal

be ascribed to the severity with which the founders of religious orders have always prohibited every species of unnecessary intercourse between their female disciples and persons of the other sex. *To prevent it entirely was impracticable.* The functions of the sacred ministers had always been the exclusive privilege of the men, and they alone were able to support the fatigues of husbandry and conduct the *extensive estates* which many convents had received from the piety of their benefactors. But it was conceived that the difficulty *might be diminished, if it could not be removed;* and, with this view, some monastic legislators devised the plan of establishing *double monasteries.* In the *vicinity* of the edifice destined to receive the virgins who had dedicated their chastity to God, was erected a building for the residence of a society of monks or canons, whose duty it was to officiate at the altars and superintend the external economy of the community. The mortified and religious life, to which they had bound themselves by the most solemn engagements, was *supposed to render them superior to* TEMPTATION; and, to remove even the suspicion of evil, they were strictly forbidden to enter the inclosure of the women except on particular occasions, with the permission of the Superior, and in the presence of witnesses. But the Abbess retained the supreme control over the monks as well as the nuns: their Prior depended on her choice, and was bound to regulate his conduct by her instructions."—*Anglo-Saxon Church*, vol. i., p. 173.

throne of Tuscany to the imperial throne of Austria, Ricci was left helpless among his enemies. He was forced to abdicate his see, and, after enduring much persecution and imprisonment, he ended by abjectly humbling himself before the Pope, and signing a full recantation drawn up for him at Rome.*

One addition to this painful recital, and we close. In our own times, within a year past, a revelation of monastic enormities such as must sicken the very heart, has been laid open to the world. We have before us "The Petition of Ubaldus Borzinsky, of the Order of the Brothers of Mercy, to Pope Pius IX." It has just been made public. The monastery to which Ubaldus Borzinsky belongs is at Prague, in Bohemia. In thirty-seven distinct and full specifications, Borzinsky exposes a catalogue of crimes of the deepest dye, committed to his knowledge and that of the other monks in various monasteries of the Brothers of Mercy in Austria. The petition commences as follows:

"Holy Father,—As nothing we undertake can prove successful without the assistance of the Most High, I therefore earnestly implore the Holy Spirit to communicate his enlightening influence and gracious aid in the matter I now lay before you, which also involves an humble request.

"The task I have proposed to myself is far from being a pleasant one, as it only exhibits painful events, and is calculated to awaken very distressing feelings

* *Nuns and Nunneries;* Sketches compiled entirely from Romish authorities. London, 1852. Pages 242–273.

in the mind of your Holiness. But it is necessary, in order that I may have peace in my own mind, through the favor and grace of your Holiness, that I should bring both to your consideration. I have also thought of the maxim, '*De' grandi e de' morti, parla bene o taci* [Of the great and of the dead, speak good or else be silent]; but mindful, Holy Father, that truth should not be concealed when we would appeal to so august and holy a tribunal as yours, I commence under the help of the Most High."

Borzinsky then proceeds to narrate the gross immoralities of Vitus Hreschich, Prior of the Brothers of Mercy in the monastery of Presburg, in Hungary, and also those of the Prior Sanctus Martens. The former of these became provincial of the order, and then sold his priorship to the highest bidder. He was succeeded in 1853 by Odilo Rayth, a man of notorious dissoluteness. Next follow statements of the seductions, adulteries, and more monstrous and unnatural offenses of priors and brothers, in a large number of houses connected with the order in Hungary, Bohemia, Moravia, and at Vienna itself. Much of this statement is unfit for translation. We quote only the concluding item of this shameful account.

"XXXVII. Paschal Fiala was for twenty years provincial of the order, and acted as his predecessor did and as his successors have done, in selling the priorates and higher offices of the convents. * * * This Paschal Fiala kept two ladies in Vienna, the one Madame von Ledwinka, and the other Madame von Sebald, which many of the older brothers yet well remember. These females divided the greater part of the sale of priorates and other conventual offices between themselves. They lodged in the city of Vienna, in apartments consisting of four or five rooms, the rent of which was 500 or 600 florins per annum. They kept two or three servant-maids; and all this expense was defrayed from the property of the sick poor. Most of the priors obtain wagon-loads of farm produce, such as butcher's meat, butter, fowls, corn, eggs, dried fruits, and *eimers* of the most exquisite wines for their own tables, the property of the poor. If any right-minded brother of the order, whose heart bled when he saw that the sick poor on this account were badly attended to, and necessarily deprived of part of their allowance, dared to make any remark regarding the injustice of these proceedings, that man was at once marked for persecution and oppression to the very utmost. * * *

"Help me, therefore, most Holy Father," concludes Borzinsky, "if this my most humble petition should ever reach your hands. In my soul I look on the matter I have represented—and I could bring much more before your Holiness—with deep affliction, even now in my prison-house. Help me out of the order altogether, most Holy Father, and I will pray for you all my life long. I shall end my life very unhappily unless you may exert your great power to deliver me from the order of which I am a member.

"Your Holiness orders that our convents be visited, that better conduct may prevail in future. The old forgotten statutes of the order are to be restored to their power, and to be punctually observed. Your intentions, most Holy Father, are the best; but here, however, there will be no improvement; for even those who observe not the new rules, nevertheless promise to do all which you, most Holy Father, would have them to observe. * * *

"I most respectfully kiss your Holiness's apostolic feet, and beg you graciously to regard the petition, which I, with child-like and profound veneration, present to the notice of your Holiness.

"(Signed), UBALDUS BORZINSKY,
"*In the monastery of the Brothers of Mercy at Prague.*

"Prague, October, 1854."

How long, we ask, after a perusal of this startling document, will it be before scenes like these shall be acted in our own land? Romanism is advancing with rapid strides among us. A throng of priest-ruled emigrants presses upon our shores. The institutions of Jesuitism, which the old governments and nations of Europe, even the most absolute and the most thorough papal, have felt to be an intolerable burden upon their prosperity, are already obtruded on our young and vigorous state. Swarms of foreign priests and nuns are settling down upon our soil, and seducing to their prison-houses the daughters of our people. What may be already occurring in those secret places we do not know, nor can we foretell how soon a shuddering public may hear the voice of exposure, in recitals like those just echoed from distant Austria. Rome dreads nothing so much as exposure. Crime may be borne with so long as it can be hushed; but "*scandal*"—the disgrace and shame of notorious guilt—is the calamity of all others to be foreclosed. In view of such a policy, we can only prognosticate results from the experience of the past. Shall we heed the voice of warning that comes to us from thence, or shall we hasten to add to the record another example of ruin, spiritual and temporal, from the overspreading blight of priestcraft and monasticism?

In the name of humanity, we call for the imposition of legal limits to the arbitrary rule of the convent. We ask that liberty be proclaimed to the captives of a severe and cruel system. These institutions, existing already among us, but in glaring opposition to the fundamental theories and principles of a republic; these institutions, that are but so many organizations of despotism transplanted to our soil—we ask that liberty of conscience and rights of self-control be extended to their unhappy inmates; so that, though there be but one among all those victims of delusion that is unwillingly detained, she may be sent forth to enjoy the common privileges of the land. We ask that it be made by law impossible for a system of peonage—a system that involves the total surrender of personal will, whether for life or for a stated term to be formally renewed—an act as yet unlegalized—a system of moral suicide and civil death—to continue in force among us. We invoke the concurrence of all, whether Protestants or Catholics, who hold dear the hereditary rights of freemen, in petitioning our Legislatures for the passage of some provision whereby the doors of closed convents and all other institutions where vows of absolute obedience are taken, shall be opened at stated periods for the admittance of commissioners, appointed by our legislators or judges, who shall personally inquire of every individual whether she be there of her own choice or by compulsion. The prosecution of this just demand is the scope of our desires in sending forth this book. Without the sanction of so worthy a purpose, the labor of its preparation would be but ill repaid in satisfying popular inquiry, however natural and proper. That these pages may arouse some who read them to vigilance and effort against the plots of which they reveal a part, is the sincere prayer of the writer.

NOTE.

THE following description of the institution at Emmettsburg is taken from the "Life of Mrs. Seton," by the Reverend Charles I. White, D.D.,* which professes to give an authentic sketch of the sisterhood from its foundation. It will be read, we think, with interest.

"Although two spacious edifices had been erected to meet the wants of St. Joseph's sisterhood and academy, the increasing prosperity of the institution rendered it necessary to provide additional room. For this purpose, a large building, fifty-seven by sixty-nine feet, and three stories high, was commenced in 1841, connecting with the eastern extremity of the academy, and running at right angles with it in a southern direction. It is surmounted with a cupola and belvidere, which command one of the most extensive and delightful prospects that can greet the eye. Having mentioned the different buildings appropriated to scholastic purposes, we shall briefly state the particular uses of each. The main edifice is distributed into rooms for recitation, the cabinet of natural sciences, the library, dormitories, etc., and in the lowest story are the important arrangements of the culinary depart-

* Published by Dunigan & Brother. New York, 1853.

ment. Another building in the rear contains the refectory, infirmary, bathing establishment, and a large hall for drawing, painting, and embroidery. The last-mentioned edifice has three grand divisions: a study-room, a hall for public exhibitions, and one for the exercises of vocal and instrumental music.

"A few years after its erection, in 1844, another extensive structure was undertaken for the exclusive accommodation of the sisters and novices, and was completed in little more than twelve months, having been occupied in September, 1845. It stands east and west, connecting the academy and the chapel, with lateral projections to the south, inclosing on three sides a court-yard seventy feet by forty in extent. The new residence of the sisters is two hundred and thirty-two feet in developed length, and forty in width, with two stories and a roomy attic, and is constructed of brick and cut stone, colored of a light slate or gray. It is after the conventual style of the fourteenth and fifteenth centuries, with embattled parapets; high-pitched roof, with dormers, surmounted by a belfry thirty feet high; the windows of the second story square, with transom forming a cross; the lower windows mullioned with hood-moulds; the lateral walls broken by buttresses; and with porches to the first and second stories, running along the north wall. The building is truly Catholic in its external appearance. . . . . The interior parts of the edifice are well adapted to their sacred uses. The lower and second stories are severally fourteen feet in height. On the first is a cloister, running around the entire court-yard and communicating with the chapel, and also the public rooms for the use of the community, among them the Superior's apartment and chapter-room. The other stories are occupied as dormitories, and for the infirmary, refectory, and other purposes."—P. 455–7.

The chapel of the institution, consecrated in 1841, is thus described: "This beautiful church fronts the western extremity of the academy, at a distance of about seventy feet. The style of its architecture is Tuscan. It is a spacious building, one hundred and twelve feet long, and ninety-one wide, with a lofty steeple, and embracing at the rear end two wings, one of which serves as a vestry-room, the other for the orphans and strangers who wish to attend the divine service. The body of the church is reserved for the sisters and the young ladies of the academy. The façade is very appropriately set off with a finely-sculptured statue of St. Joseph, and bears a Latin inscription, which states that the edifice, erected at the expense of the Daughters of Charity, was dedicated by them to the glory of God in honor of their chief patron. As you enter the front door, on the left, is a recess, containing an altar commemorative of the seven dolors of the Virgin Mother, which are exhibited by a well-executed group in composition. This group was presented to the chapel by a pious nobleman of France, to obtain a share in the rich blessings which God so readily grants to his cherished spouses. In the recess, on the right, is an altar sacred to St. Philomena, which the piety of former pupils has raised and decorated with costly gifts. . . . . In the spacious chancel of the church rises a marble altar, of the purest white, and of matchless elegance; and. elevated high above it, in the niche of a canopy constructed of the same rich material as the altar, stands a well-sculptured image of the blessed Virgin, with the child Jesus in her arms. Above the tabernacle, on either side, is seen a cherub in the posture of profound awe and adoration before the holy of holies. The interior of the chapel contains, moreover, several paintings of merit." —P. 450–1. "The bell which hangs in the steeple of St. Joseph's church is one of the many articles of this description which were brought to this country from Spain during the ascendency of Espartero."—Note, p. 519.

THE END.

BUNGENER'S COUNCIL OF TRENT.

History of the Council of Trent. From the French of L. F. Bungener, Author of "The Priest and the Huguenot." Edited, from the Second English Edition, by John M'Clintock, D.D. 12mo, Muslin, $1 00.

Most persons know that the Council of Trent was a product of the Reformation, but comparatively few, we suspect, know much about its history. Those who wish to know (and it is a matter worth knowing) will find ample means of information in this volume. * * * He (the author) is clear in statement, subtle and consecutive in his logic, and steers as far from dullness as from sourness.—*Perthshire Advertiser.*

It is all that a history should be—perspicuous in language, discriminating in detail, dignified and philosophical in manner, candid and faithful in the narration of facts, and bears evident traces of extensive reading and enlarged information. —*Caledonian Meecury.*

This history is invaluable.—*Christian Advocate.*

Characterized by clearness, truthfulness, and vigor in the narrative, acuteness and terseness in the reasoning, and a spirit of Christian fidelity and charity.—*Watchman.*

The work before us is undoubtedly one of the very best that has appeared on the subject. The writer has abundant materials, and has used them with fidelity, impartiality, and talent. His brilliant style radiates in every department of the work.—*Philadelphia Evening Bulletin.*

A work of permanent interest, which should be well understood by the ministry of our church and country.—*Christian Observer.*

It is adapted for popular reading; while, as a true portraiture of men and things in the Council, it is invaluable to the theologian.—*Christian Intelligencer.*

MEXICO AND ITS RELIGION;

Or, Incidents of Travel in that Country during Parts of the Years 1851–52–53–54, with Historical Notices of Events connected with Places Visited. By Robert A. Wilson. Wiih Illustrations. 12mo, Muslin, $1 00.

This is a record of recent travel in various parts of Mexico, including full statistical details, historical reminiscences and legends, and descriptions of society, manners, and scenery. A large portion is devoted to the influence of the Catholic Church, and relates many piquant narratives in illustration of the subject. The author writes in a lively, graphic, and, sometimes, humorous style. He gives a great deal of valuable information, and his travels can not fail to find numerous readers and prove a most popular volume.

SEYMOUR'S JESUITS.

Mornings among the Jesuits at Rome. Being Notes of Conversations held with certain Jesuits on the Subject of Religion in the City of Rome. By Rev. M. Hobart Seymour, M.A. 12mo, Muslin, 75 cents.

INEZ,

A Tale of the Alamo. 12mo, Muslin, 75 cents.

We have to recommend the book to pious parents and guardians as written under the influence of the strictest Protestant principles; and to introduce it to young ladies in general, as containing some very nice "love," seasoned pleasantly with just enough fighting to make the whole story agreeable.—*Leader.*

When the Texans threw off the Mexican yoke and entered into our National Confederacy, no portion of her people felt the change more keenly than her Romish priesthood, and especially the Jesuits. Their counter and insidious duties of social and domestic life is the moral of this story. The lady who wrote it has studied the Romish argument, and has managed it with effect. It is not a book of the "Maria Monk" stamp; it is a successful refutation and exposure, in popular form, of some of the worst points of the Romish system.—*Church Review.*

A most inviting story, the interest of which is sustained throughout its narrative of stirring events and deep passions.—*Mobile Register.*

The descriptions of scenes of carnage, and the alarms and excitements of war are graphic, while the polemics are not so spun out as to be tedious. The portraiture of the Jesuit padre is any thing but flattering to the Catholic priesthood, while her dissertations upon the doctrines, traditions, practices, and superstitious follies of the Holy Mother Church prove her to be no respecter of its claims to infallibility, and no admirer of the disciples of Loyola.—*Constitutionalist and Republic, Ga.*

We have read this work with the liveliest pleasure, and we venture to assert, that no one can take it up without going through with it.—*Richmond Whig.*

LE CURÉ MANQUÉ;

Or, Social and Religious Customs in France. By EUGÈNE DE COURCILLON. 12mo, Muslin, 75 cents.

The autobiography of a young French peasant who was trained for the Church. Its specific purpose is to give an account of the social and rural life and superstitions of the peasants of Normandy, and to show the relations existing between them and their priests. The author also describes, in a very interesting manner, the routine and customs of the French ecclesiastical seminaries.

"Le Curé Manqué is a curious work, for its pictures of French peasant manners, its account of village priests, and its quiet but bitter satire on the selfishness of the Romanist country clergy, and the ignorance in which they leave their flocks. The filling up of the story shows remarkable skill, for the easy natural way in which it carries out the authors intention of exhibiting "social and religious customs" in provincial France.—*London Spectator.*

The strange state of society, with its French and Papal habits which it portrays, will set new facts before the mind of even-traveled readers.—*Presbyterian Banner.*

Le Curé Manqué (the Unfinished Priest) is a title which very accurately conveys an idea of what the book is. It lets the public behind the scenes in a remarkable manner, and is one of the most readable books of the season.—*N.Y. Daily Times.*

A most agreeable and entertaining narrative, opening to most American readers novel, strange, and (many of them) charming scenes. Though the Church may be a loser (which is doubtful, however), the world has certainly been a gainer by his apostacy from his sacred calling.—*Savannah Journal.*

The exposition of the Romish ceremonials, and of the subjecture of the masses of the French people to priestcraft are peculiarly interesting. We quote, "How a mass may be said for a pig, and refused for a Protestant."—*N. Y. Commercial Advertiser.*

WOMAN S RECORD;

Or, Sketches of all Distinguished Women from the Creation to the Present Time. Arranged in Four Eras. With Selections from Female Writers of each Era. By Mrs. Sarah Josepha Hale. Illustrated with 230 engraved Portraits. Second Edition, revised and enlarged. Royal 8vo, Muslin, $3 50; Sheep, $4 00; Half Calf, $4 25.

"Many years have been devoted to the preparation of this comprehensive work, which contains complete and accurate sketches of the most distinguished women in all ages, and, in extent and thoroughness, far surpasses every previous biographical collection with a similar aim. Mrs. Hale has ransacked the treasures of history for information in regard to the eminent women whom it commemorates; few, if any, important names are omitted in her volumes, while the living celebrities of the day are portrayed with justness and delicacy. The picture of woman's life, as it has been developed from the times of the earliest traditions to the present date, is here displayed in vivid and impressive colors, and with a living sympathy which could only flow from a feminine pen. A judicious selection from the writings of women who have obtained distinction in the walks of literature is presented, affording an opportunity for comparing the noblest productions of the female mind, and embracing many exquisite gems of fancy and feeling. The biographies are illustrated by a series of highly-finished engravings, which form a gallery of portraits of curious interest to the amateur, as well as of great historical value.

This massive volume furnishes an historical portrait gallery, in which each age of this world had its appropriate representatives. Mrs. Hale has succeeded admirably in her biographical sketches.—*Philadelphia Presbyterian.*

"Woman's Record" is, indeed, a noble study and noble history. The sketches are all carefully and even elegantly written.—*Philadelphia Evening Bulletin.*

What lady, who takes a pride in her sex, would not desire to have this volume on her centre-table? and what husband, lover, or brother would leave such a wish ungratified.—*Washington Republic.*

This superb monument of Mrs. Hale's indefatigable devotion to her sex is illustrated by 230 portraits, engraved in that style of excellence that has deservedly placed *Lossing* at the head of his profession.—*Philadelphia Saturday Courier.*

We are pleased with the plan of the "Record," and with the manner in which that plan is carried into execution. The book is a valuable and permanent contribution to literature.—*New Orleans Baptist Chronicle.*

This work merits the warmest commendation.—*Sun.*

This is a large and beautiful book, and covers the ground marked out by the title more fully and satisfactorily than any other work extant. It is a most valuable work.—*Southern Ladies' Companion.*

Here we have placed before us a book that would do credit to any author or compiler that ever lived, and, to the astonishment of some, produced by the head, heart, and hand of a woman.—*N. Y. Daily Times.*

This is a very curious and very interesting work—a Biographical Dictionary of all Distinguished Females—a work, we believe, quite unique in the history of literature. We have only to say that the work will be found both instructive, amusing, and generally impartial.—*London Ladies' Messenger.*

The comprehensiveness of the work renders it a valuable addition to the library. —*London Ladies' Companion.*

A Female Biographical Dictionary, which this volume really is, will often be consulted as an authority; and the great extent of Mrs. Hale's information as to the distinguished women of modern times, supplies us with a number of facts which we knew not where to procure elsewhere. It is clearly and simply written. —*London Gardian.*

LOSSING'S PICTORIAL FIELD-BOOK

Of the Revolution; or, Illustrations, by Pen and Pencil, of the History, Biography, Scenery, Relics, and Traditions of the War for Independence. 2 vols. Royal 8vo, Muslin, $8 00; Sheep, $9 00; Half Calf, $10 00; Full Morocco, $15 00.

A new and carefully revised edition of this magnificent work is just completed in two imperial octavo volumes of equal size, containing 1500 pages and 1100 engravings. As the plan, scope, and beauty of the work were originally developed, eminent literary men, and the leading presses of the United States and Great Britain, pronounced it one of the most valuable historical productions ever issued.

The preparation of this work occupied the author more than four years, during which he traveled nearly ten thousand miles in order to visit the prominent scenes of revolutionary history, gather up local traditions, and explore records and histories. In the use of his pencil he was governed by the determination to withhold nothing of importance or interest. Being himself both artist and writer, he has been able to combine the materials he had collected in both departments into a work possessing perfect unity of purpose and execution.

The object of the author in arranging his plan was to reproduce the history of the American Revolution in such an attractive manner, as to entice the youth of his country to read the wonderful story, study its philosophy and teachings, and to become familiar with the founders of our Republic and the value of their labors. In this he has been eminently successful; for the young read the pages of the "Field-Book" with the same avidity as those of a romance; while the abundant stores of information, and the careful manner in which it has been arranged and set forth, render it no less attractive to the general reader and the ripe scholar of more mature years.

Explanatory notes are profusely given upon every page in the volume, and also a brief biographical sketch of every man distinguished in the events of the Revolution, the history of whose life is known.

A Supplement of forty pages contains a history of the *Naval Operations of the Revolution*; of the *Diplomacy*; of the *Confederation* and *Federal Constitution*; the *Prisons* and *Prison Ships of New York*; *Lives of the Signers of the Declaration of Independence*, and other matters of curious interest to the historical student.

A new and very elaborate analytical index has been prepared, to which we call special attention. It embraces eighty-five closely printed pages, and possesses rare value for every student of our revolutionary history. It is in itself a complete synopsis of the history and biography of that period, and will be found exceedingly useful for reference by every reader.

As a whole, the work contains all the essential facts of the early history of our Republic, which are scattered through scores of volumes often inaccessible to the great mass of readers. The illustrations make the whole subject of the American Revolution so clear to the reader that, on rising from its perusal, he feels thoroughly acquainted, not only with the history, but with every important locality made memorable by the events of the war for Independence, and it forms a complete Guide-Book to the tourist seeking for fields consecrated by patriotism, which lie scattered over our broad land. Nothing has been spared to make it complete, reliable, and eminently useful to all classes of citizens. Upward of THIRTY-FIVE THOUSAND DOLLARS were expended in the publication of the first edition. The exquisite wood-cuts, engraved under the immediate supervision of the author, from his own drawings, in the highest style of the art, required the greatest care in printing. To this end the efforts of the publishers have been directed, and we take great pleasure in presenting these volumes as the best specimen of typography ever issued from the American press.

The publication of the work having been commenced in numbers before its preparation was completed, the volumes of the first edition were made quite unequal in size. That defect has been remedied, and the work is now presented in two volumes of equal size, containing about 780 pages each.

HARPER'S NEW MONTHLY MAGAZINE.

EACH Number of the Magazine will contain 144 octavo pages, in double columns, each year thus comprising nearly two thousand pages of the choicest Miscellaneous Literature of the day. Every number will contain numerous Pictorial Illustrations, accurate Plates of the Fashions, a copious Chronicle of Current Events, and impartial Notices of the important Books of the Month. The Volumes commence with the Numbers for JUNE and DECEMBER; but Subscriptions may commence with any number.

TERMS.—The Magazine may be obtained of Booksellers, Periodical Agents, or from the Publishers, at THREE DOLLARS a year, or TWENTY-FIVE CENTS a Number. The Semi-Annual Volumes, as completed, neatly bound in Cloth, are sold at Two Dollars each, and Muslin Covers are furnished to those who wish to have their back Numbers uniformly bound, at Twenty-five Cents each. Eleven Volumes are now ready, bound.

The Publishers will supply Specimen Numbers gratuitously to Agents and Postmasters, and will make liberal arrangements with them for circulating the Magazine. They will also supply Clubs, of two persons at Five Dollars a year, or five persons at Ten Dollars. Clergymen supplied at Two Dollars a year. Numbers from the commencement can now be supplied.

The Magazine weighs over seven and not over eight ounces. The Postage upon each Number, *which must be paid quarterly in advance*, is THREE CENTS.

The Publishers would give notice that that they have no Agents for whose contracts they are responsible. Those ordering the Magazine from Agents or Dealers must look to them for the supply of the Work.

Each month it gladdens us and our household, to say nothing of the neighbors who enjoy it with us. Twenty-five cents buys it—the cheapest, richest, and most lasting luxury for the money that we know. Three dollars secures it for one year: and what three dollars ever went so far? Put the same amount in clothes, eating, drinking, furniture, and how much of a substantial thing is obtained? If ideas, facts, and sentiments, have a monetary value—above all, if the humor that refreshes, the pleasantries that bring a gentle smile, and brighten the passage of a truth to your brain, and the happy combination of the real and the imaginative, without which no one can live a life above the animal, are to be put in the scale opposite to dollars and cents, then you may be certain, that if Harper were three or four times as dear, it would amply repay its price. It is a Magazine proper, with the idea and purpose of a Magazine—not a book, not a scientific periodical, nor yet a supplier of light gossip and chatty anecdotes—but a Magazine that takes every form of interesting, dignified, and attractive literature in its grasp.—*Southern Times.*

Its success was rapid, and has continued till the monthly issue has reached the unprecedented number of 150,000. The volumes bound constitute of themselves a library of miscellaneous reading, such as can not be found in the same compass in any other publication that has come under our notice. The contents of the Magazine are as "various as the mind of man." In the immense amount of matter which it contains, it would be strange, indeed, if there was not *something* to gratify every taste. The articles illustrating the natural history and resources of our country are enough to entitle the Magazine to a place in every family where there are children to be taught to love their native land. The Editor's Table presents every month an elaborately prepared essay on some topic intimately connected with our politics, our morals, or our patriotism, while the Easy Chair and the Drawer of the same responsible personage—doubtless a *plural unit*—display gems of wit, humor, and fancy, in any quantity to suit the temper of any reader. —*Boston Courier.*

Mexico and its Religion;

Or, Incidents of Travel in that Country during Parts of the Years 1851–52–53–54, with Historical Notices of Events connected with Places Visited. By ROBERT A. WILSON. With Illustrations. 12mo, Muslin, $1 00.

Parisian Sights

and French Principles, seen through American Spectacles. By JAMES JACKSON JARVES. Second Series. With Illustrations. 12mo, Muslin, $1 00.

Italian Sights.

and Papal Principles, seen through American Spectacles. By JAMES JACKSON JARVES. With Illustrations. 12mo, Muslin, $1 00.

Art-Hints.

Architecture, Sculpture, and Painting. By JAMES JACKSON JARVES. 12mo, Muslin, $1 25.

Christian Theism:

The Testimony of Reason and Revelation to the Existence of the Supreme Being. By ROBERT ANCHOR THOMPSON, M.A. (The First Burnett Prize of $9000 was awarded to this Treatise.) 12mo, Muslin, $1 25.

A Child's History of the United States.

By JOHN BONNER. 2 vols. 16mo, Muslin, $1 00. (Uniform with Dickens's "Child's History of England.)

Lily.

A Novel. By the Author of "The Busy Moments of an Idle Woman." 12mo, Muslin, $1 00.

James's Old Dominion.

The Old Dominion; or, the Southampton Massacre. By G. P. R. JAMES, Esq. 8vo, Paper, 50 cents.

Miss Bunkley's Book.

The Testimony of an Escaped Novice from the Sisterhood of St. Joseph, Emmettsburg, Maryland, the Mother-House of the Sisters of Charity in the United States. By JOSEPHINE M. BUNKLEY. 12mo, Muslin, $1 00.

Learning to Talk;

Or, Entertaining and Instructive Lessons in the Use of Language. By JACOB ABBOTT. Illustrated with 170 Engravings. Small 4to, Muslin, 50 cents.

A LIST OF NEW BOOKS,

PUBLISHED BY

HARPER & BROTHERS.

Squier's Central America.

Notes on Central America; particularly the States of Honduras and San Salvador: their Geography, Topography, Climate, Population, Resources, Productions, &c., &c., and the proposed Interoceanic Railway. By E. G. SQUIER, formerly Chargé d'Affaires of the United States to the Republics of Central America. With Original Maps and Illustrations. 8vo, Muslin, $2 00.

Napoleon at St. Helena;

Or, Interesting Anecdotes and Remarkable Conversations of the Emperor during the Five and a Half Years of his Captivity. Collected from the Memorials of Las Casas, O'Meara, Montholon, Antommarchi, and others. By JOHN S. C. ABBOTT. With Illustrations. 8vo, Muslin, $2 50.

Helps's Spanish Conquest.

The Spanish Conquest in America, and its Relation to the History of Slavery, and to the Government of Colonies. By ARTHUR HELPS. Large 12mo, Muslin. (*In press.*)

Loomis's Arithmetic.

A Treatise on Arithmetic, Theoretical and Practical. By ELIAS LOOMIS, LL.D. 12mo, Sheep.

Barton's Grammar.

An Outline of the General Principles of Grammar. With a Brief Exposition of the Chief Idiomatic Peculiarities of the English Language. To which Questions have been added. Edited and Enlarged by the Rev. J. GRAEFF BARTON, A.M., Professor of the English Language and Literature in the New York Free Academy. 16mo, Muslin, 37½ cents.

Ewbank's Brazil.

Life in Brazil; or, a Journal of a Visit to the Land of the Cocoa and the Palm. With an Appendix, containing Illustrations of Ancient South American Arts, in Recently Discovered Implements and Products of Domestic Industry, and Works in Stone, Pottery, Gold, Silver, Bronze, &c. By THOMAS EWBANK. With over 100 Illustrations. 8vo, Muslin, $2 00.

www.ingramcontent.com/pod-product-compliance
Lightning Source LLC
LaVergne TN
LVHW010205110826
845151LV00002B/611

9781425535452